NOT DROWNING BUT WAVING

Peter Thornthwaite

HEDDON PUBLISHING

First published in Great Britain 2025 by Heddon Publishing

www.heddonpublishing.com

Copyright © Peter Thornthwaite 2025

A catalogue record for this book is available from the British Library

Paperback ISBN 978-1-913166-96-0
Ebook ISBN 978-1-913166-97-7

All rights reserved. No part of this publication may be reproduced, stored in a retrieval system or transmitted in any form or by any means, electric, mechanical, photocopying, recording or otherwise, without the prior permission of the publisher.

This is a biographical work based on true history with real historical characters. Includes appendices for data, maps and images.

The right of Peter Thornthwaite to be identified as the author of this work has been asserted by him/her in accordance with the Copyright, Designs and Patents Act 1988.

Cover Design: Catherine Clarke Design
www.catherineclarkedesign.co.uk

For my mother,
who didn't want to be remembered.

Peter Thornthwaite was born in Oxford in 1951 when postwar rationing was still in place, though he didn't notice it at the time. Outwardly there was nothing remarkable about his life before he moved to Brighton (Sussex University) in 1970. His further education included a year (1972-73) at a renowned college for women – Smith College in Massachusetts – where Sylvia Plath had been a student two decades earlier, and postgraduate studies at McGill University, Montreal, where Leonard Cohen once studied.

Mr Thornthwaite went on not to complete a PhD in American Literature, though it had provided a temporary sense of direction. There then followed years of changing addresses, relationships and jobs. But slowly, sporadically, and largely unbeknown to himself, a project was taking shape concerning his lost mother and her first family, the lost Lewinsohns of Breslau: a story waiting to be written.

In January 2021, after thirty years of social work, and having run out of excuses to postpone the project any longer, he retired and began the translating, researching and writing of *Remember Who You Used to Be*. This coincided with the second Covid-19 lockdown. The aim was to complete the project in a year, thus timing the ending with the fiftieth anniversary of his mother's suicide, 2 January 1972.

When that investigation of his mother's life before he had known her and his own half-hidden heritage came to an end, it was meant to mark his first and last words on the subject. After giving her far more unwanted attention than when she was alive, he was happy to live with her absence until his own came. But this second time around she was disinclined to lie down and die. It was then that Mr Thornthwaite realised two things: that, having brought her back to life, he missed her – he was used to having her around and was loath to let her leave again – and that the finished account of her life, despite being drawn from her own diaries and family letters, had missed something vital. She was still there for the finding, but this time an entirely different approach was called for. This book, *Not Drowning but Waving*, is the result of that second, deeper search.

NOT DROWNING BUT WAVING

FOREWORD

It is easier to say what this is not than what it is. It is not a memoir or a family history, and it is not a follow-on from *Remember Who You Used to Be*, the previous book about my mother Gerda and her German-Jewish family – before, during and after the Second World War – in the sense of adding vital new information or uncovering surprising new evidence. It is not a book I intended or wished to write, but for some reason unknown to me when I set out on a return journey, I felt compelled to do so.

On reflection, the completion of a long if vaguely conceived project had left me with an acute sense of its incompleteness and it was only when I perceived the shape it had assumed that it seemed the wrong shape and not what I had in mind. Then there was the question of my mother. She too had gone wrong somewhere. Just how wrong, I realised after bringing her back to life. As for arriving at some sort of resolution, that wasn't anticipated so wasn't missed when it never came. But I had at least expected to get her right and conclude that, yes, this is her for better or for worse. After relying on personal diaries, old family correspondence, and various love letters to tell the story, how could I have missed something important? If such primary and contemporary sources of information couldn't get me there, there was really nowhere else to go.

Obviously, a different approach was required to reach her; that much I realised as I began this second book straight after finishing the first. As I reflected on what this approach might be, words such as *imaginative*, *intuitive*, *speculative* and *conjectural* sprang to mind. By comparison, the first book was factual, evidence-based, insofar as it uncovered fragmentary evidence of Gerda's life and the lives of her displaced and dispersed family in personal records from the German 1930s to the English 1960s. Mostly, I let them narrate their own stories, and if my mother hadn't left such copious paper evidence behind for me to find and appropriate as my rightful inheritance, their stories would be untold and forgotten, subsumed into the vast absence from which I salvaged them three years ago. Much to her dismay, no doubt (had she been here to see it), she and her first family were brought out into the open.

Having opted for oblivion and nothingness, it was the last thing she wanted, and possibly for that reason my mother never fully emerged for me in that first book about her, despite telling her own story in her own inimitable way. Perhaps because I was less sure where I was going with this further attempt to reach her and ventured so often into conjecture, her presence is more palpable, and I have even sensed her guiding and directing me as I tap away at the keyboard, towards a different, a truer view of Gerda. In that sense, my long-dead mother is the co-author of this present book and must take some responsibility for it.

It is not always enough to revisit the dear departed; it

is sometimes necessary to re-revisit them – especially if, like Gerda, they withhold their secrets. Apparently, she hoped that suicide would secure hers. No such hope, mother dear. Hers had the opposite effect, attracting me as a queen draws a drone. It wasn't that I needed to settle the question of her suicide once and for all, though I admit it intrigued me and that another return visit allowed me to look into it. What drew me back to her, irresistibly, was the suspicion that she was still somewhere out there for the finding and this time wanted to be found.

It wasn't until I first read the diaries and came across some late entries concerning me that I realised the extent of our previous estrangement. Indeed, it did occur to me as I resumed what might turn out to be yet another thankless task that all I was really doing was trying to work through our difficulties and differences and find some peace at last. Nothing could be further from the truth.

Whereas finishing the first book exposed an underlying sense of frustration and failure, which I admitted to myself if not to others, this second time around I have finally got somewhere. In the Foreword to *Remember Who You Used to Be*, I wrote: 'So, Gerda – like it or not – this book is for you.' In retrospect, that was disingenuous, for it did her no favours. This present book really is for my mother, and if she could only overcome her former disapproval of my efforts to restore her to something like life, she might at last appreciate what I have done for her and how much she meant – and means – to me.

I began by describing what this book is not. What it is remained unclear until more recently, and I suppose I had to write it before I could see where it was taking me. Quite simply, it is a different view of someone I thought I knew well enough after pinning her down with her own diarised words. I didn't know her, of course. Words like *uncertain*, *exploratory*, *questing* and *questioning* would better describe this further effort to get up close and personal. My first attempt to fix her in print was bound to be one-sided because I took her at her own low self-estimation. The evidence of my mother's diaries is so much evidence against her, and there is enough negative commentary, too, in the family correspondence to confirm her sense of deficiency. Then there was my own take on her during the last years. These viewpoints combined to give a more negative impression of her life than was warranted, though she had a dark enough history for the story to fit.

The title of this book tells me that this time I had something else in mind for my mother. *Not Drowning but Waving*. I was on the look-out for the affirmative, the positive, and if you look long enough for something, in my experience you find it. Actually, her 'story' is full of positives. Yes, it ended in suicide, but that too can be seen as a positive choice, and if it hadn't been for that memorable ending, I wouldn't have dedicated the last three years of my life to working out how she got there.

A warning: this book contains some unpleasant content concerning Nazi luminaries such as Josef Mengele, the notorious 'doctor' of Auschwitz, and Hans Frank, Governor-General of occupied Poland, who oversaw the murder of millions. Gerda escaped Germany on 23 May 1939, before the official policy of the Third Reich towards

Jews changed from emigration to extermination, so such men played no direct part in her life. But while again browsing through her history, I reinvestigated that large brown suitcase packed with newspaper cuttings from around the time of the trial of Adolf Eichmann (1961), who on 20 January 1942 had attended the Wannsee Conference and helped plan (and afterwards implement) the 'Final Solution to the Jewish Question'.

As the 1960s approached and then suddenly happened, my mother looked through national and local newspapers for the Holocaust headlines and articles which the efforts of Nazi hunters and the seizure and subsequent trial of Eichmann had restored to the world's attention and hers. She had painstakingly cut them out and put them away for the future. Evidently they meant a lot to her, and in my continuing search for my mother I could not avoid giving such men more of my belated attention too. They help define the almost unimaginable enormity of what she had escaped. The place of the Holocaust in her own history merited further consideration.

Gerda was born in Breslau in 1921, a teenager during the first six years of the Third Reich, so the Holocaust and its aftermath featured in her life, though she lived in London during the first years of the war and in Oxford after 1945. Inevitably, I have traced through her history the shadow of the persecution and diaspora she and her family went through. Hers is the history of a Jewish woman who got out just in time and survived to live another life, but who could never forget who and what she was. She escaped the coming Holocaust in 1939, but it came back to claim her twenty-one years later. For Gerda, there was no escaping the past. Yet she was always more than merely a victim of it. It has taken this second book about my mother to uncover her complexities.

She had no time for history. At least that is the impression given by her diaries. Even during the prewar years of persecution, there is no mention of wider external events, though that could have been deliberate self-censoring from fear that her diaries might end up in the wrong hands and be turned against her. As I recall, though, from the outset she appeared largely uninterested in the wider world. That big suitcase of newspaper cuttings from 1959-61 suggested otherwise, but she kept such things to herself. To all outward appearances, the only history ever to reach my mother concerned Israel in the context of conflict and war.

In spring 1938, Gerda considered emigrating to Palestine. Once raised as a possibility, it never came up again in her diary. While writing this foreword, I briefly wondered about her view of current deaths in Palestine: the war in Gaza intensifying with Israeli tanks in Rafah, twenty-one Palestinians reported killed in the latest strikes (as I write) and Al Jazeera reporting of the 'latest mass killing of displaced civilians'. I wondered what my mother would have made of this. No doubt, the global spikes in antisemitism would have caught her attention and confirmed her view that history repeats itself and it is always the Jews that are to blame. As for accusations of genocide and the International Criminal Court seeking warrants for the arrest of key Israeli as well as Hamas leaders, would she have seen this as history once again turning against the Jews? Would she have sided with a right-wing Israeli government as civilian deaths rose? I don't know. But I do know this: for my mother, Jews could only ever be the victims of genocide. That the State of Israel could be deemed the perpetrator would have been inconceivable to her, a shocking reversal of history.

She survived the Holocaust but the Holocaust survived in her and never let her go or see the world from another viewpoint. She too was once a displaced civilian deprived of family and home and country and human rights, so might have even identified with the Palestinians, but not to the extent of criticising, let alone condemning, Israeli actions. Also, as I write this, following the recent surprise announcement of an early general election in the UK, 'illegal' immigration is a key issue for the nation – 'stopping the boats' and the Rwanda deportation scheme equalling in media prominence others such as the rising cost of living and the future of the NHS. What, I wonder, would my mother have thought of that, given her own experience of emigration and refugee status in 1939?

The foreword to *Remember Who You Used to Be* suggested that she was 'not at home' in her life, though by Christmas 1971 she had lived in England for over thirty years and had an English family. As a Jew and refugee, Gerda could never forget who she 'used to be' – who she still was – and lived in fear of being found out. A year on from that first and (as I then supposed) final account of her life, I don't question my earlier view but have since reframed her. She was always other than I thought. I don't claim to have got her right yet, and of course she isn't around to approve or reject this latest version of herself, but then who could disagree with being seen more positively? Gerda escaped persecution, not just for a better future but for any kind of future. Though modest in her aspirations, she expected a lot from life, and I'm glad for her sake as well as mine that she made the most of it – not always, perhaps, but at decisive moments. This present book is my attempt to make more of her than she was disposed, in the darker days to come, to make of herself.

So this is not a sequel; a follow-up to the first. Factually, it has little to add, though there are a few revelations missing from the earlier account. Writing it so soon afterwards risked repeating myself, and though careful editing has excised much repetition, no doubt some remains. Indeed, it was unavoidable as the diaries and letters remained key points of reference. Returning to them was not so much repetition as reinterpretation, for on a second or third reading I found different implications and meanings, and realised she needed revising. It is only by going back to the same places that you see them differently.

Though I have edited out more conspicuous repetitions, I make no apology for those that remain. Decisive events in Gerda's life – leaving the Third Reich and her dual German-Jewish life on 23 May 1939, and (a final departure) getting away from her second family almost thirty-three years later one December night in 1971 – keep drawing me back for further questioning. With her diaries to hand, I can turn back her years and return to the key transitional moments to check if I had missed something important. By now (6 June 2024, which happens to be the 80th anniversary of D-Day), after more than two years of reading and rereading her diaries, words and phrases from the later ones especially are on continuous automatic replay at the back of my mind:

Peter Thornthwaite

It's up to Kismet now.
Get a lot of money soon.
Don't over-eat.
Greed = Downfall.
Might get in trouble.
Definitely pack it in while the going is good.
Break with things.
Be strong.
Resist temptation.
Know when to stop and the time is NOW.
I am getting too much junk.
Enough of everything.
I am getting bulked out with clothes.
Remember moths!

The things that played on her mind constantly now play on a spool in mine. This was hardly anticipated when I first delved into her diaries on 2 January 2021 after a half-century hiatus. That I would end up internalising her unresolved difficulties and daily angst and make them my own was almost inconceivable, in view of such marked differences of outlook and life experiences. We saw the world from opposite ends, my mother and I. And yet here I am, mouthing her word for word. Those familiar phrases of hers are here to stay, part of my DNA, and it seems I have become my mother in going over the same ground with no awareness of repeating myself. Like mother like son, with a vengeance.

But it also occurs to me that she was looking for a new direction, a way through her life, and though she didn't quite manage it, it was now my turn to try on her behalf.

She was probably no more prone to repeat herself than anybody else, but with her three decades of diaries at my disposal, the evidence is all here. It was one of her more endearing idiosyncrasies that she never seemed to mind writing exactly the same things in page after diary page and year after diary year. She was always 'going to pack in jumble sales for one year at least' and 'start afresh again really and truly today'. It was always 'up to Kismet'. The favourite words and phrases of her last decade (the 1960s) – *No more*, *Never again*, *Resist temptation*, *Willpower*, *Sacrifice* – were powerful incantations, capitalised and reinforced with three and even four exclamation-marks. Yet they apparently achieved nothing more than a transient sense of purpose. Did she believe she could make something happen – some big and longed-for change in her life – by writing it down and repeating it often enough? That was my working assumption during the first two years of trawling through all her diaries. Intractable problems, unresolved dilemmas, resolutions and 'rules' recur as if, with sufficient repetition, things must turn out differently and a new Gerda break through the old. There is no indication that she ever wearied of this, other than writing no more diaries after 1969, but I can see she was looking for a breakthrough, a way out of an enclosing life. *Break with things*, she repeated. *Break with circumstances before they have broken you.*

So, if I was following my mother's example and going over the same things repeatedly, it was in the hope of a breakthrough. 'I am making a new start, I am starting afresh again,' she wrote. Me too. Having gone over everything since 2 January 2021, gleaned what I could from the extant records, by 2 January 2023 I was ready to start afresh with this second book about her, make a new start. And this time I really was doing it for her.

Peter Thornthwaite

Though this renewed search for a mother has some obvious connection with the first (they share the same subject), it could hardly be more different in its approach. It could be considered a companion-piece to the first, yet more often than not they disagree. *Not Drowning but Waving* questions the earlier narrative and reaches different conclusions, and this time around I rely less on the diaries and old correspondence. Perhaps I exaggerate the differences between two books about the same woman to rationalise and justify going over the same ground. The later account also complements the first, so I recommend reading both as linked rather than standalone accounts of the woman who was also my mother for a while. I do so not to encourage sales of books likely to remain largely unknown, but because there was much more to my mother than I realised. She was Gerda long before I met her. It seemed to me when I first looked into her life that they had parted company, but I was wrong.

CHAPTER ONE:

'THE FIGHT WITH DESTINY'

In January 2021, I started reading my mother's diaries. She killed herself in 1971 so she was unaffected by my intrusion, and there were things I needed to find out. Though I had occasionally been tempted to dip into them during the half-century since her suicide, something had always held me back, as though an unofficial secrets act kept the diaries, letters, etc safe from unauthorised entry for a specified period. By 2021, it seemed that time limit had expired. It had taken me fifty years to get round to it, and she was fifty when she died, which suggested an auspicious synchronicity.

Since by then she had no say in the matter, she gave up her secrets despite Rule No. 10: *Keep it all to yourself.* (Gerda's diary, December 1967).

Among the many 'secrets' revealed as I read her diaries from the last (1969) to the first (1937), the following spring to mind:

- Her father, Elkan Lewinsohn ('Tatta', she called him), got out of Germany in October 1941; just in time, since mass deportations were imminent.

In fact, Elkan's younger sister (Gerda's 'Tante Bertha') was caught up in one such deportation the following month, transported to Kovno (Kaunas) in Lithuania and killed, although there is no evidence that Gerda was aware of this, then or later.

- Joe, a Jewish German refugee from Berlin, whom she met on the *SS President Harding* after it left Hamburg on 24 May 1939, was for six months 'the Big Love' of her life before turning into a 'stinking arsehole' and disappearing out of it.
- Tatta died in Quito of cancer of the intestines three months after reaching Ecuador.
- The diamonds Gerda smuggled out of Germany and later hid inside her gas mask (as she told us), did not 'go missing' when an ARP (Air Raid Precaution) warden came while she was out and replaced the mask, taking the old one away. She didn't 'lose' the diamonds, she sold them because she 'needed the money'.
- In January 1960, with 'the world starting to hate the Jews all over again', she remembered her past 'wickedness' to her father and Aunt Bertha.
- She followed the 1961 trial of Adolf Eichmann. As a key Nazi, who had been hiding out in Argentina (where Gerda's missing brother Kurt also lived), his trial evidently absorbed my mother, who filled a large suitcase with newspaper cuttings about it, together with other Holocaust 'stories' freshly headlined fifteen years or so after the death camps were 'liberated'

in 1945. If she also noticed that the date of the Wannsee Conference (where Eichmann helped plan the 'Final Solution', also referenced in one of the newspaper articles) coincided with Tatta's arrival in Ecuador in January 1942 to join his son Gunther, I don't know.

- Gerda followed the career of Colin Jordan, a belated British version of Hitler, born in Birmingham and elected 'World Fuhrer' in August 1962.
- She loved jumble sales, but felt 'degraded' by them, complaining she was 'bulked out with worn and shabby clothes' only good enough for 'the ragman', and felt weighed down by 'loads of junk' (diary entries, various, 1960s).

Under cover of her diaries (1960s) she admits she was 'going to pieces' and 'out of my mind'.

My mother's threats to kill herself were more than just threats. (Strictly speaking, this was not a 'secret' hidden from us, as she was open about her occasional suicidal thoughts. The 'secret', if there was one, was that she really meant to do it when things got too much for her.)

Secrets are intrinsically interesting, especially those belonging to a mother who kept most of her life a secret. At last I was finding out who she really was and where she came from and how she got from there to us. No disrespect to my father, who was from Sunderland, but Gerda's history intrigued me more than his because it was 'European'; with 'Brexit' still in mind, my preference (notwithstanding my inherited dislike of Germany) was for European rather than British roots. That I was researching family history rather than merely nosing into other people's diaries and letters justified it as a long-awaited retirement project. It lent it legitimacy, since I was only doing what many others do as the end approaches: looking to an expanding past to compensate for a diminishing future; looking for family in foreign places.

Though she wouldn't thank me for it, I was doing it for her, too. This was her chance to make up for the suicide. The least she could do was open herself up and let me get to know her posthumously.

Fortunately (having discarded nothing but her life), she retained more written evidence of a previous existence than is usually available to those in search of antecedents. Gerda came from a time when people still wrote letters, and she was an inveterate if erratic diarist. The suitcases, in which she had conveniently and with unwitting foresight packed herself away for posterity, had one last journey to make: travelling in time to 2021 and to me. That is putting it rather fancifully. Actually, the diaries and letters were no 'inheritance', as she never meant or expected anyone to read them, let alone write a book about her life and history based on personal records. Intended or not, they proved the best inheritance. Those primary sources gave me a close-up and personal view of history as it was actually experienced against a backdrop of world war, Holocaust and diaspora. I couldn't have asked for more to fill my housebound days during the first year of retirement and second national Covid-19 lockdown. There, in those five suitcases, family history intersected with History.

In 1939, emigration remained the official if obstructed

route to a 'Judenfrei' Reich. Loathing Jews, the Nazis were in a quandary: impatient for them to leave but determined to make it difficult for them to do so. Gerda had left it late, with both brothers gone and *Kristallnacht* still a recent memory.

Kurt, the eldest, had been the first to leave, joining the exodus of Jews from the Reich in 1933 when Hitler became Chancellor. He sought exile in Switzerland then France where (as he wryly wrote to Gerda (17 November 1935): 'idealistic Kurt', a trained lawyer, was earning his living 'feeding pigs'. In the first of the two prewar letters he sent his little sister (as he always saw her), he remembered Gerda as 'the little girl who played with trains' and feared he had 'lost sight of her'.

That letter, from nearly ninety years ago, is in front of me now on the old oak desk in my attic study in this small town in Shropshire and as I reread it for the umpteenth time, I notice that he thanked her 'very much' for her 'lovely letter from the mountains'. It had not previously occurred to me that my mother was not only a lifelong diarist but a writer of 'lovely letters'. Writing to Kurt 'from the mountains' (Austrian Alps?) in 1935, when she was only fourteen, Gerda was of the right age to write 'lovely' letters to an absent big brother and to love being praised for them. The few photographs I have of Gerda from around that time are also from the mountains. Holidaying with the rest of the family, she can be seen with skis or toboggan or ice-skates. The fashionable fourteen-year-old, with her jauntily tilted black beret, baggy Turkish trousers, and long black coat with wide, pointed lapels, took time to write to her pig-feeding brother in France. Turning back to his letter, I see that in

November 1935 he seemed in a darker place than his sister, despite the Nuremberg Race Laws of September 1935, with Hitler's Germany now two years behind him and four more years of it ahead for his sister, for he felt 'completely isolated' in rural France and had only 'the frightening uncertainty of tomorrow' as a future.

It apparently took Kurt a further four years to write to his not-so-little sister. He makes no mention of the gap and possibly they corresponded more often and the intervening letters are lost. Dated 21 May 1939, from Buenos Aires, Kurt's letter arrived too late for Gerda to read it in Germany and was presumably forwarded to her in London by her father, and here it is next to the black laptop on my desk, ready for further inspection.

As before, Kurt thanks his sister for her 'lovely letter'. Though I have only limited prewar correspondence to go on, it is likely that, as the more distant of the two brothers, Kurt made a point of complimenting Gerda on her 'lovely' letters as it helped close the widening gap between them. Though an obvious endearment, his compliment makes me uncomfortable, and I wonder if it had the same effect on Gerda when it reached her, for nowhere does he acknowledge in his letter her predicament in Nazi Germany. Kurt went on to praise his sister's 'understanding and subtle taste', the 'wonderful person' she had become – 'practical and sober-minded' but still 'idealistic' – yet he seemed oddly incurious about the darker realities of her situation. By 21 May, he presumably knew that their brother, Gunther, had left for the US the previous November aboard the *SS New York*, having timed his departure with uncanny prescience to miss by six days the nationwide pogrom known as

Kristallnacht – the 'Night of Broken Glass'. Gerda was the last of the siblings to go. After all, she was still his 'little sister', and Kurt must have worried terribly about her. It is all very well extolling her 'lovely letter' and the other lovely things about her as she turned from girl to woman, but they were unlikely to keep the Nazi noose from tightening around her lovely throat. There is no reference to her circumstances, and the remainder of his letter largely concerned his difficult relationship with their father, whom he described as 'selfish' and 'thirsty for power', though he also admitted to being 'a bad son' and to Tatta being in a 'bad position'.

In May 1939 Kurt would have been well aware that his sister was in a bad position, too. Reading between the lines of his letter, I wonder if his praise for her practical yet idealistic outlook indirectly alluded to the difficulties she confronted. Far from overwhelming Gerda, adverse circumstances had brought out a new strength of character and purpose commensurate with the risk. I now think Kurt intentionally encouraged rather than commiserated with her. In this new light, I re-examined his first letter from exile, specifically its reference to his sense of utter isolation at the time with only the 'frightening uncertainty of tomorrow' before him. By the date of his second letter, Gerda was also familiar with 'frightening uncertainty'. Doubtless aware of this, Kurt avoided the subject out of consideration for his sister and almost certainly to strengthen her resolve. When he wrote from Buenos Aires, Kurt couldn't have known that she had succeeded. Gerda's delighted diary entry – 'To my surprise I have got the Permit! I have also got the Visa' – is dated 20 May, the day before Kurt wrote to her from his new life in Argentina. Familiar as she was with 'frightening uncertainty', Gerda had reached the other side of it.

Gerda's escape from Nazi Germany was really the start of the story for me when I first looked into it in January 2021. Though it began and ended with her, my 'research' was shaping up as a family history project rather than a more questionable search for a long-dead mother with whom I had (like Kurt with his father) unfinished business. If anyone wondered what I was getting up to every day in my attic study, I truthfully reported that it was 'research' into my mother's German-Jewish family via diaries and correspondence going back to the Third Reich. This explanation had the merit of marginalising her as incidental to a broader investigation. I was researching my European antecedents and regarded my mother's old diaries as helpful historical documents. The project did not merely concern her, and as for Gerda's postwar 'English' family, they were of slight interest to me and still less to anyone else. As such, the project needed a suitable title. Titles determine the direction of travel and define the story; I wanted to know where I was going, and this is how I put it to myself three years ago:

By January 2021, when the writing commenced, I had a working title: Looking For Lewinsohn. I liked the sound of it – at once personal and impersonal. Other Holocaust-related memoirs had similar titles and were also looking for lost connections. There was something moving and melancholy about it too, because some families just can't be found.

Having set off in that direction, I found all that could be found with least effort. Her father, Elkan Lewinsohn, *Inhaber der Firma* (owner of the company) Schonfeld, was a well-established Breslau businessman, a man of property and wealth and of good standing in the community, until reduced to 'a Jew'. He was my mother's 'Tatta'. Her mother died when Gerda was six and is absent from the diaries and letters as though she never existed, except when Gunther had forgotten the date of their mother's death[1]. Of Tante (Aunt) Bertha, Elkan's younger sister, nothing survives except three letters to her niece in 'faraway London', asking for help to get out of Germany. Aunt Bertha brought Tatta his morning coffee after Gerda left, and was there in 1941: as Gunther noted, 'Aunt Bertha is still assisting father as usual' (letter dated 28 June 1941). There is no specific reference to what then happened to her. She finally surfaced (eighty years later) in internet searches for Lewinsohns as: Bertha Lewinsohn, deported from Breslau 25 November 1941 to Kovno (Kaunas) and killed on 29 November.

Of course, that could have been another Jewish woman of the same name. In the 1960s, Aunt Bertha was remembered by my mother (who, lacking access to the internet, can be forgiven for this) as 'a poor relation clinging on and being a damned nuisance'. Gunther, also ignorant of his aunt's fate, though assuming she had 'perished', could be just as dismissive. As far as Aunt Bertha is concerned, that was it – all there was to find except an internet epitaph possibly concerning another woman.[2]

---

[1] In his letter of 25 December 1964, he wrote 'The date of her death is unknown to me'. He hoped that Gerda might fill in the blank, but there is no evidence that she did.

[2] I have since confirmed her identity, having connected the date and place of birth (8/12, 1888, Hirtakol, Kowno) with those of the aunt deported and murdered almost 53 years later. Although the archive

Kurt, who after his second letter to Gerda in May 1939 also vanished, bobbed up one last time, in Buenos Aires in 1963, before sinking several months later. According to his widow, Elena, as he neared death Kurt was so prematurely aged as to be mistaken in hospital for her 'sick FATHER'.

Then there was Gunther, who alone tried to keep the dispersed family together. When his temporary US visa expired in 1940, Gunther found a life in Ecuador. From there he maintained contact with Tatta and Gerda; sometimes losing sight of her, 5725 miles and a world war away, but always finding her again. He remained my mother's lasting and last connection with the family.

Gunther was the easiest to track down through the war years and after, leaving a trail of letters behind him like breadcrumbs in a forest. In the secrecy of her later diaries, my mother called him a 'bully', hoping he would never visit as he promised; hoping too that he would leave her all his money when he died.

The Lewinsohns had hidden stories to tell: stories as lost as themselves and unlikely to be told – not by me, anyway, and I am the only one still interested. There was nothing more to find, no unread evidence of their lives, and for all the plenitude of paper my mother kept as proof of a previous existence, it never amounted to much of a history, and a disconnected one at that. I had done as much as possible with a limited resource. Questions remain as to how her father managed; how he coped with

---

records (Das Bundesarchive. Lewinsohn Bertha) refer to Fort X1 at Kowno (Kaunas) as the end point of her last journey, it was more likely the 9th Fort, the place of mass execution for Jews.

the 'daily persecutions from the Gestapo' – after waving goodbye to Gerda from Hamburg's docks. From the few letters he sent in the months following her departure, he evidently felt 'abandoned'. His anxiety about his 'child' was 'limitless' and he cried 'many tears'. Those letters (June to December 1939) were my last sightings of him in Hitler's new Fatherland. Apart from how it ended, the story of what happened next for Tatta is missing from Gerda's suitcases, and I can only guess how he got by without his beloved daughter and everything else integral to his status. His daughter was the last in a long series of losses, and I see from his letters how much it affected him, yet his alternately appealing and demanding letters from Breslau unfortunately estranged her further as he desperately reached out to the girl who was no longer there. The last of them (18 December 1939) wasn't to her but to a Frau Salomon (apparently a family friend in London), whom he thanked 'most cordially' for giving him news about his daughter. He would be 'very pleased', he wrote, if Frau Salomon could keep him informed

That last letter opened up for me, if not for the daughter it concerned, the enormity of his loss; rereading it, I notice something that should have been obvious before. Presumably he stopped writing to Gerda, fearful of alienating her altogether; instead, he appealed to a more compassionate go-between. Yet here it is with the other letters from that period in one of her old brown suitcases. The only possible explanation is that Frau Salomon showed or forwarded it to her; perhaps she waited until Tatta died to share a father's letter with his daughter. In her role as advocate for a lost and anguished father, Frau Salomon could not reunite them, but she might still do some good. As the gracious woman to whom Tatta appealed because appealing to his daughter only made matters worse, she possibly played a significant part in the family story, yet this is the last we see of her. Perhaps she visited the errant daughter in London and after a long and illuminating conversation Gerda reflected on her own attitude towards her father and suffered a change of heart. Momentous things happen off the page as well as on it. Whatever Gerda felt for her father at the time, or later, his poignant letter to Frau Salomon followed her to the end of her life and travelled as far as me.

With only the extant letters and diary entries to go on, all this is mostly guesswork. After leaving Germany, Gerda rarely referred to Tatta in her London diary. From other primary sources (such as the German photographs from 1927 to 1933, especially the beach scenes in which she and her towering father seem inseparable), I can see that Tatta, with his totemic face and physical bulk a bulwark against history, was once a massive and immovable presence in her life, like no other before or since. All that changed when she left, as one undated diary entry revealed: 'I hate Tatta. There isn't a trace of sympathy, let alone love. I wouldn't like ever to have him in England.'

After the 'I hate Tatta' entry, he almost disappeared from the record, though surfacing occasionally in Gunther's letters, as on 2 July 1939, when he is described as 'desperated and of broken heart'. If by adding that final 'd' to 'desperate', for deliberate emphasis (rather than as a grammatical error), Gunther purposely brought Tatta's situation closer to home for Gerda, I don't know, but no doubt she appreciated her brother's intermittent updates. Gunther found out all he could about their father's situation from Jewish refugees still leaving Breslau. Gerda, meanwhile, eighteen years old and making the most of an as yet un-bombed London, was busy with 'movies, theatre, dance, etc' and her first 'Big Love'. A dutiful brother, Gunther reminded her of their father's desperate situation in a not quite 'Judenfrei' Reich, and that was some reassurance that he was not forgotten.

Gunther provided my only glimpse (from a distant family perspective) of what life was like in Hitler's Germany for a Jewish father left behind, and that was pretty much all I had to go on when my investigations began and I found myself looking for Tatta nearly eight decades after his death. Gunther informed Gerda how much it was costing him to get their father out of the Reich, but otherwise Tatta was nowhere to be seen during the first two years of the war. The exact date of his departure is also missing from the records, though I wouldn't have expected Gerda to know, since Gunther was the one to look into such things. I assumed that Tatta left for Ecuador via Cuba around October 1941. There is no reference to it in Gunther's letter of 10 October 1941, which possibly impressed Gerda with its close-up of her distant brother 'sitting very lonesome in the nice Russian Boris-Bar' in Quito where he played his 'clever music' to 'multitudes on Saturday and Sunday'. But as only a fragment of that letter remains, Tatta might well have been in the missing section. That the father reached Quito I know from his final letter to his daughter (20 January 1942), and I also know from Gunther's letter of

30 April 1942 that 'father is dead' from 'a tumour of horrendous evolution'.[3] It took Tatta three months to die after escaping a worse fate in Germany, and a further two years for Gerda to acknowledge it.

I mention this now not to be critical of her or suggest she was unaffected by the news, which I'm sure was not the case, but to show how much of her family history remains forever hidden and how vanishingly small the information available turned out to be against my initial expectations. The brief outline above is as much of Tatta's story as can be gathered from the limited evidence available. In later years Gunther remembered their father and the 'huge fortune' lost to the family. Gerda would also remember him, though for reasons more to do with her own sense of guilt and sin than Nazi Germany's. Tatta lived on for both, one way or another, but by 2023 I had exhausted the suitcases and myself in the search for hard evidence.

So much for a 'family history'. If the spine of a

---

[3] It is curious how vital information can hide in plain sight. In his letter of 30 April, 1942, informing Gerda of Tatta's death, he also gives details of their father's journey from Breslau to Quito: 'Father embarked on the end of October 1941 and arrived in Barcelona'. Gunther then refers to the 'food on board the steamer, *Isla de Tenerife*, as 'awful' and to Tatta getting dysentery and losing much weight. 'Completely exhausted he landed in hospital of Cuba. Nevertheless, his trip to Ecuador was going on by means of airplane via Colombia.' Although I have often reread this letter, I either skimmed this crucial part of it or forgot it until glancing at it recently. The date of Tatta's departure from Nazi Germany – end of October 1941 – is interesting. This seems very late in the day to have got out, considering the memorandum of 26 July 1941 by the Breslau Chief of Police that Jews would be removed from their homes and deported. If Tatta left end of October, his younger sister – Gerda's Aunt Bertha – was deported from Breslau barely a month later.

chronological narrative connected the separate stories, that was almost entirely down to Gunther. He was the only one not to have died or disappeared before he could leave a legacy of letters. That Gerda's letters date from at least 1935 I know only through Kurt's reference late that year to her 'lovely letter' from the mountains. Unfortunately, all the 'lovely' letters she wrote during three tumultuous decades have no place in the oeuvre because she sent them and they disappeared into the ether. They are a lost resource and I can only mourn their passing and wonder what they might have shown. As for her diaries, she herself disappears from them for days, weeks, months – even years – at a time, and as I assembled the scattered parts of the family 'story', I realised that Gunther's letters are often the only connection – not just between brother and sister but between the separate sections of Gerda's life.

Despite all the paper records packed into the five suitcases, what is missing from the oeuvre vastly exceeds what remains. Gerda was a diarist, but an unreliable one. Much of her war is missing, either because she kept no regular record, or she did but (for reasons known only to herself) ripped out the pages. As evidenced by the thick stubs left behind, more pages were torn out of the wartime diaries than left intact, and apparently nothing happened worth noting on many of the remaining disconnected dates as they are blank. It seemed to me, as I went looking for my mother through her diaries, that she was erasing herself as she went along.

Looking For Lewinsohn remained the working title of the first book almost to the end; unlike the family it referred to, it was there to stay. Lewinsohn sounds both Jewish and German – which of course they were – though such connections were soon uncoupled in a country where you couldn't be both, especially after the Nuremberg Race Laws of 1935. In less than a decade the Nazis broke up this family and many others like it, as well as most of Europe. So, a big subject, but viewed through a family lens. And there was another attraction. The search for a disappeared Jewish-German family started on 2 January 2021 – the exact half-centenary of my mother's suicide, so no coincidence – and took me through vast tracts of unread diaries and letters. Opening them for the first time promised to open up previously closed lives, disclose secrets, and surprise me; all to the good in a 'lockdown' year. Essentially, I was looking for Gerda. After all, she was my mother. Of course, I was also interested in the wider family and what happened to them, but always with a view to catching her reflection in every letter she kept and put away for posterity. The correspondence revealed aspects missing from her diaries, for in the old family letters I sometimes glimpsed unsuspected sides of my mother. Having found out so little about her while she lived, it felt like being granted a second chance.

It was only as I approached the end that I noticed the shift in focus in the material I had compiled in good faith as some kind of partial family history. It was subsequently reflected in the last-minute change of title to *Remember Who You Used to Be*. A line taken from an anxious father's letter (30 May 1939) to an errant daughter at risk of forgetting her own history and identity (as well as him), it applied as much to Gunther as to Gerda, for he could never forget the loss of the family fortune and the life he might have had if not for Hitler and history. It in fact applied to both brothers but (like Tatta) it was Gerda I had mostly in mind because, of the siblings, she tried hardest to forget who she 'used to be'. Gunther never forgot his lost heritage – the status, the standing, the assets stolen by the state, his rightful future forfeited. Gerda, meanwhile, spent the rest of her life trying to forget. Getting to know anything about my mother was always on a need-to-know basis and, luckily for her, children are incurious about their parents. Only in retrospect can I see how anxious she was not to expose her history. The past, it seems, was too painful to remember. Unfortunately, it was also too painful to forget.

The book's title had changed but it remained a 'family history' and as such a justification for reading and eventually publishing private diaries and letters meant for her eyes only. Despite an initial twinge of guilt, discovering who she really was seemed a reasonable thing to do in my seventieth year: better late than never.

Burn the diaries. Allegedly her last wish – though I recall no written authorisation in her own dead hand, or my father informing us of it at the time, or (if he did) anything being done about it. Anyway, the secret diaries remained unburned, untouched, and unread, in the attic of my father's house until (during one of my many subsequent explorations) I found them, plus decades of correspondence and other private papers, and removed them without the family particularly noticing or caring.

My mother had packed her history into those suitcases, but had she the right in perpetuity to withhold it? I thought not. It seemed that by ending her life she had forfeited any further claim to it; I was slightly uncomfortable with that line of reasoning but, after all, none of it could hurt her now. She was beyond being hurt. Also, after revealing so little of her life before ending it without so much as a goodbye, at least she had something to offer by way of compensation.

An unbequeathed inheritance of five old suitcases of documented family history, left undisturbed and dormant for five decades, had become something for me to look forward to in my retirement. Yet two years after the project commenced, I was impatient for it to end and let me get on with the remainder of my life. An old European family at risk of extinction but for my timely intervention – that was something surely worth salvaging, but I was also glad to see the back of the whole lot of them, including my mother. To go on ingesting her diaries suddenly seemed a sickening prospect.

But the sense of closure soon gave way to doubts and misgivings. From my mother, I had expected more. More what? Not more unanswered and probably unanswerable questions. More disclosure, yes, because surely that's what private diaries are all about. Perhaps, too, I had unrealistic expectations of her because she was still my mother, though long-dead, and often more is expected of mothers than they can give. After all that hard work and my almost undivided attention for two years, which (on reflection) she had done little to merit, then to be left at the end with a sense of unfinished business was very disappointing: either she had failed me or I had failed her. It was all to do with expectation. Leaving her diaries for so many years to mature had not improved them as much as expected. Unlike Gunther, she is seldom a light or entertaining read, being disposed to darker thoughts especially as she got older. Also, I couldn't deny that her later diaries could be as mundane as her life; and as repetitive, if not more so. Nearly every day for two years my hands were literally full of her, and by January 2023 I was echoing the words so often on her own lips: *Genug ist genug*.

Enough is enough.

What she mainly had in mind with that useful phrase were the piles of jumble sale and charity shop clothing she accumulated through the postwar years once she had a house to accommodate them. 'I have too much junk', the Gerda of the later diaries chided herself, 'and you can't take it with you'. She probably had other things in mind besides heaps of second-hand clothes when complaining that *Genug ist genug*, for by then she'd also had enough of most things. Enough of scrimping and saving with no prospect of any other life. Enough of children getting on her nerves. Enough of people upsetting her when she was out shopping, and family upsetting her at home. Enough of piling on the weight (she recorded an increase of '17 lbs' in one horrified diary entry) despite 'pecking like a bird' and repeated 'starvation' diets.[4] By the 1960s she'd also had enough

---

[4] Among the paper debris of her past is an easily missed miniature 'weight card' measuring two inches by one, picturing a trim Boxer dog with WEIGH DAILY stamped diagonally across his lean body. The card is before me now, on my desk, and scrutinising it again I realise how much my mother weighs on my mind and what a weight of meaning I attach to such emblems. On the reverse side of the little card

(certainly more than her fair share) of history, which was coming back with a vengeance with 'the world hating the Jews all over again'.

By the end of that last decade, which others remember more as an expansion than contraction of possibilities, *Genug ist genug* had other useful applications, neatly summarising her life as the half-century marker approached. As age fifty neared, she no doubt thought *Enough is enough*, and calculated the quantity of pills required to end all her difficulties.

What I had in mind, as another 'ending' approached with the publication of *Remember Who You Used to Be* in 2023, was also a sense of surfeit: That is definitely enough of her for now. *Genug* of Gerda. It had been good getting to know her at long last, but she was best taken in small doses, and after examining her daily for two years and poring over the minutiae of her life, I had overdosed on the diaries. She had let go of the family, apparently without a second thought (except for the dogs, who got an honorary mention in her suicide note), and I could as easily let go of her. So, we were even.

And yet, for somebody with an ingrained habit of leaving when things turned bad, Gerda was perversely staying put this time – only not in the suitcases where I

(issued by the British Automatic Company, Ltd) is the date: 9 NOV 53. Public weighing scales were in chemists, Woolworths, and railway stations in the 1950s, and for a penny you were instructed to 'stand still on platform until red hand stops.' On 9 NOV 1953 it stopped at 8 stone 13 lbs for Gerda – 13 lbs too much. After she became a mother, Gerda was at war with her weight. In a lifetime of losses, it was the one thing she couldn't lose.

had packed her away, but in my head, where I kept turning her over like an unresolved problem. The diaries were responsible. Through them a more intense and uninterrupted relationship had grown between us than ever seemed possible while she was alive. There were other unsuspected and much more interesting Gerdas tucked away inside my mother all the time, but it had taken her suicide and most of my adult life to notice them. Just as well that I had delayed opening the suitcases and diaries. The extended interval had given her time to mellow. Half a century is time enough for anybody (the most restless of souls) for the disturbance of life to subside. Gerda had needed a good long rest after her life.

It wasn't love exactly, but I couldn't stop mulling over her, recalling the things she said – or rather wrote – since I picked up her voice and foreign intonation audibly through the diaries. One particular entry kept echoing in me. It was actually the first one I had read, back in January 2021, and also the last entry in her last diary (30 September 1969): my mother complaining that the pills prescribed by her doctor had made her feel 'sicker than ever' – 'I'm sure that man is trying to poison me!' She had few happy times if her diaries are the only evidence, and reading my mother had given me nearly as few; but recalling my first excitement as I set out on a long-postponed journey of discovery, I wanted it back again. I remembered my expectations at the outset of the project.

When I first read my mother, I was older than her and our relative positions were reversed. She was the one who needed looking after. She seemed so vulnerable; more so as she aged in her diaries, and I wondered what I could do to help so late in the day. Parents are remembered very differently by ageing children, especially by a son older than his mother and much more sentimental about her past. Half a century after her death she lacked body, and without the diaries and letters to hand, I could not have summoned back the woman who was once my life.

Of course, I was afraid of losing her again. But what more could I do? The diaries had been duly digested – apart from early indecipherable passages where a barbed German script barred access – and I had scrutinised the entire corpus of correspondence, plus every stray scrap of paper down to old receipts. For two years my mother had been my more-or-less constant companion, far more communicative and forthcoming than when she was alive, and I was sorry to see her go, but the book was behind me and there was nothing more to add. Not many mothers, unknown outside the family and not much better known within it, end up in books, and she had herself as much as me to thank for that, having left so much 'evidence' and the shadow of a life behind. When my turn comes, written evidence that I ever existed will barely fill a shoebox, and I'll leave no shadow.

So, goodbye Gerda. The future project had become the past. Impatient to close her down, pack her back into the old brown suitcases and forget about her again, I had welcomed her coming absence with relief; yet perversely, no sooner had it arrived, than I was missing her. And I missed her in a different sense, too.

Though I had given Gerda every opportunity for direct and unmediated self-expression and allowed her all the space she needed to come out and show herself, I had somehow missed something of vital significance. Having let her speak for herself, the woman emerging from her own diaries should have been Gerda unadulterated, and if something vital was missing, that was more her doing than mine. She was a poor advocate for herself at the best of times. Not that she often had the best of times.

If the negatives outweigh the positives in her history, that was only to be expected. Gerda told her own story in her own words. They were her diaries, after all. I never altered or excluded a word or date but simply reproduced them, word for word, alongside other primary sources. As for the suicide, I'd have preferred a different ending, but that was the only one available. If all the darkness in the book gravitates towards it and collects there, suicide has that kind of draw. She had sidestepped the Holocaust, but it got her in the end. That's how it seemed to me. Gerda had told the truth about herself, because that's what people do in private diaries. All I did was watch from the sidelines while the inevitable unfolded.

Anyway, if I had really missed something crucial, it was too late. The book was out there and other people (luckily for her, not many) would be reading her and probably thinking what an odd woman she was, especially towards the end. Doubts and misgivings were unavoidable in the circumstances. Having steeped myself in her for so long, I was still lost in Gerda-world. Yes, she was certainly an odd and interesting woman, and it was never my intention to misrepresent my mother (I had left that up to her), and if that was what had had happened despite weighing up and reporting almost every word she wrote, so be it.

It was all to do with letting her out of the diaries in the first place. She was such a private woman. They were her protection. Reading them was betrayal enough. So there was that. And there was another consideration, more niggling than any residual guilt at having drawn her out of her cubbyhole.

The later diaries, while she was a wife and mother, outnumber the earlier ones, when she was free of such encumbrances. For some reason she had neglected her diaries during the war and was making up for lost time with sometimes daily postwar entries. As a young mother with a new family she maybe had more need of a diary as a safe place, a refuge where she could just be herself. If she is to be found anywhere, it is in the later diaries, where she often reveals more than she intended, because once they are let out, words have a life of their own. By turning my late mother into a book, I had somehow done her a grave misjustice. How she comes across in the later diaries is accurate enough and corresponds to my own memories, but something important had been left out. Those diaries positively bristle with agitated, 'nervy' life, and yet more than five decades after her death I felt her absence more keenly than just after her suicide.

Too late to go back and infill. Too late for me and certainly too late for her. There she was, and there she must stay, to be picked up and pored over by others or (more likely) put back on the shelf, unread. From her point of view (if she could be said to have one), it no longer mattered. She wasn't around to see what I had been getting up to in her absence or consider her latest incarnation. She was long past caring what others read into her dispensable life, and if readers soon lost interest and donated the book to a charity shop, so much the better. At least she ended up where she felt most at home.

But I kept turning her over in my mind. You can't just

erase someone with whom you have just shared an intense if belated and one-sided intimacy, and in retrospect I can understand her reluctance to leave. She still had more to disclose.

My mother was too hard on herself, too quick to pass judgement, and that wasn't just my view. There is evidence enough in the diaries. A notable example is the entry for 4 January 1960 – notable as the only time she reflected on what she had done to her father and Aunt Bertha, but also because it had left her with the conviction of her own 'wickedness'. Typically, she hadn't gone on to explain why she felt so wicked. It would have been interesting to know her thoughts on the subject, but she was always more given to statement than to analysis or explanation in her diaries. I can guess the reason. With the world turning against her again, she had internalised external hatreds and turned them on herself. Unfortunately, analysis (including self-analysis) was a missed opportunity in her diaries. Yes, she spoke for herself in them. Without fear of anyone ever finding out, she recorded her experiences in her own words, but she had also spoken ill of herself and more often shown only the shadow side. Thinking about it, that is where she let herself down, and where I also let her down.

We hadn't always seen eye to eye. In fact, towards the end, silences stretched between us, and I remember how unkind and even cruel I could be in my callow years: telling her, for instance, that she looked 'like a witch' (Gerda's diary 29 April 1968). She could be hard on me too, wishing I 'would bugger off to Australia' (same entry). That memorable entry in a memorable year closed on a climactic note: 'Good riddance to bad rubbish'. At least I got a mention in her diaries – an emphatic one at that. She didn't expect it to be read, of course. If gifted with such foresight, my mother would have unwritten much that I later read in her diaries. As it happened, those words from a mother to a son were a gift, passed on to me many years later, when such estrangements stretched behind us and I had a more considered and considerate view and understood that the hurt was more hers than mine. My poor mother, what have I done to you? As if you hadn't enough to put up with (Hitler and the Holocaust) without me adding to it.

That was the nub of it. The book I had compiled to commemorate and make something of her life before it went the way of other lives was my gift (if unwanted) to my mother: my way of making amends for all she had gone through. A reasonable, reconciling thing to do – putting her vulnerability and hurt before mine, before anything else – but also a mistake, for it made a victim of her. She had inadvertently colluded with this, leaving a residue of herself in the last diaries as a disturbed, depressed, damaged woman. Yes, she was all those things, and it seemed an unfortunate yet fair reflection of the mother I half-remembered, but it was only half of her. It is easier to lose a mother than find one. She had already taken up two years of the limited retirement stock available to me. If losing a mother is 'a misfortune' (to paraphrase Oscar Wilde), finding one is worse. The diaries of her last two decades are a depressing reminder of things best forgotten, and she had been right all along about wanting them destroyed after her death, for even as a young mother she had a poor self-image – as the crude faces drawn at the end of her 1957 diary suggest. With their wrinkled brows and bulbous, mostly bald heads, they were evidently how she viewed herself then, and if I supposed she was just doodling for fun, what she wrote against the gargoyle heads – *'Ich bin.* I am' – suggested the ugly truth.[5]

In November 1879 the American essayist, Ralph Waldo Emerson, then in his mid-seventies and in the grip of advancing dementia, described the cohesive and connecting power of memory to link past and present and give some continuity to our lives and hold families together. As he himself was losing or had lost the essential human quality he was celebrating, it struck me as a poignant and brave choice of subject for a lecture. It also opened up a new line of inquiry.

Among the many (unanswered or unanswerable) questions raised by *Remember Who You Used to Be* was one concerning connection and continuity. When Gerda left Germany, she left more than a country behind, yet in all her subsequent diaries she seldom referred to it or acknowledged her Jewishness except as an unfortunate inheritance. That indelible mark of identity was to be kept hidden from the children, from other people, and as far as possible from herself. As mothers do, she was protecting us from the harm of knowing too much and for the best of reasons revealed nothing about the fate of her first family. If relevant information escaped her internal censor – like the story about the diamonds she had smuggled out of

---

[5] That she had herself in mind when she doodled these gargoyle heads is also evident from several diary entries towards the end of 1957 concerning the loss of hair, teeth, and good looks. If her diaries are to be believed, her beauty soon left her once she became a mother. By the age of 36 she was turning into a gargoyle of herself.

Hitler's Germany and then lost – it was (as it turned out) unreliable. Her real reason (I now suspect) for discouraging Gunther from visiting her, as he kept promising/threatening to do during the 1960s, was not that he was a 'bully' and her flamboyant opposite; no, it was that he remembered their German past and would bring it up again if they met, and she could not have borne that. 'The past is a foreign country', L. P. Hartley wrote, and so it was for Gerda, though not quite in the way he meant. They certainly did things 'differently there' in the Third Reich, and my mother wanted no reminders.[6] Sadly, the good memories were tainted by the bad, the rot having spread through the whole lot, so she blanked out those years, except occasionally, as in 1960, at the start of the new decade, when the pressure of external events brought up the past in sickening spasms. There was no escaping memory, after all.

That my mother so misread her own life as to implicate herself in the worst crimes ever is not surprising in the circumstances, considering what history had done to her and seemed to be about to do again. That I could have misread it too (despite suitcases stuffed with evidence

---

[6] The opening line of the Prologue to *The Go-Between* (1953) by L. P. Hartley. The full quote is: 'The past is another country: they do things differently there.' There are deeper connections with *The Go-Between* than I first realised. Leo, the ageing narrator, revisits catastrophic events via a diary written over half a century before – a 'Christmas present' from his mother - and I am reminded of my mother's suicide in December 1971 and her unintended Christmas present to me of her diaries. Like Leo, I found myself, fifty years later, sorting 'stacks of papers' through 'winter evenings', exhuming a 'buried past'.

and her history in my hands) was the bigger surprise. If anyone knew my mother after all the posthumous opportunities she had provided, it had to be me. By the time I was done with her, I remembered my mother better than she remembered herself. Yes, she was unfinished business – how could she not be? – but starting a second book about her within days of finishing the first needed some explaining. It was beginning to look like an obsession, which is never a good look – especially in an ageing son preoccupied day and night with his mum.

Sue, meanwhile, watched me withdraw again into my attic study at 9am and emerge nine hours later at wine-time for further Gerda-related introspective musings. Yes, I wanted my mother to leave, but not before time, and was actually rather glad of an excuse to delay her departure for another year (certainly no more than that). It would allow enough time to explore our new relationship.

The by-now familiar diaries and letters had lost their first attraction but still mutely called to me from inside their suitcases: *Come and see what you have missed.* Nothing important could have escaped my attention after two years of close study, but on the off chance that something had been overlooked, missed, I had to go back and check. Fortunately, there were also more entertaining places to look.

For want of a suitable category, *Remember Who You Used to Be* is a fragmented family history. With no pretensions to biography, my intention was that this follow-up should focus on Gerda alone. The others – Tatta, Tante Bertha, Gunther, Kurt – had all run out of history. There was more to be found, no doubt, but not by me, as I was not researcher enough to look beyond the suitcases stacked up on the old oak-floored landing outside this attic study. Anyway, it was Gerda I was after. The relative absence of her family would make more room for her.

Gunther actually took up much more space in the first book with his lighter letters than Gerda did with her darker diaries. Rereading the correspondence, I recognise him as the livelier, more exuberant, and more memorable of the two. With his '227 lbs' of German-Jewish-American packed into 'a Bavarian outfit with real short Lederhosen', his 'Boogie-Woogie' and 'Honky-Tonk Piano', and his imagined 'stick' for recalcitrant women, he was always going to get more attention than Gerda, and I was sorry to say goodbye.[7] But with nothing to add to his story, and with the others at the edge of her life also absenting themselves after relatively brief appearances, this second book would be about Gerda sans family. Putting her at the heart of things seemed the right thing to do for another reason, though what I am about to write next is only supposition. As a mother she saw herself as incidental to the needs and demands of the family, an adjunct to it with no separate life of her own and no other function. She had delayed her suicide until the children were grown up, leaving home and no longer in need of her. For Gerda, timing was everything: she had found the optimum time

---

[7] Gunther often humorously referred, in his letters to Gerda, to his 'stick' for disciplining the women who got close enough to feel it. All this was apparently imaginary – the 'stick', which he called his 'Prugler', and the intimate women needing it for their good and his. What was behind such repeated references would take too long to investigate, and I don't like to speculate, but certainly Gerda was at times on the receiving end of a pen-lashing from a big brother ever mindful of his duty towards her. In this sense his pen was also sometimes his Prugler.

to disappear, when she would be least missed.

If writing one book about a long-dead mother wasn't bad enough, a second seemed worse: a further and unwarranted intrusion calculated to scare her off for good. Privacy was as precious to her as life itself and she simply wanted it respected in perpetuity. Her only wish was not to be remembered. Was that really asking too much? Actually yes, it was, but that wasn't my main concern this time. A 'follow-up' risked repetition.

With five casefiles of 'evidence' to hand as before, I might yet uncover fresh information, interpret things differently, find new connections. Equally, nothing might come of it. That was the risk, with the focus just on her, and already it looked like a fool's errand. After all, she had disappointed me before. Reading a mother's diaries, you expect to see a life lit up at times, illuminated, where all was darkness. And I won't deny it, that did happen. But when it didn't, the letters (Gunther's especially) were an alternative source of light. This time with the spotlight on her alone, Gerda would have my undivided attention, and I was not sure that I would see any more than before.

Marginalising her family would leave Gerda more exposed. Me too, for that matter, because as the only 'narrator' I couldn't withdraw for pages at a time as I had done before and let the diaries and letters get on with it in my absence and carry the story without explicit interference or direction from me.

A more oblique, imaginative-intuitive approach was taking shape, in which the Hollywood films and movie stars she loved would say as much about Gerda as her diaries – more, probably. *Remember Who You Used to Be* was diary-centric, for obvious reasons: they were there, at my disposal, asking to be read, repositories of her most private thoughts. Most were large hardbound 'Scribbling' diaries from Boots the Chemists and Timothy Whites and (unlike Gerda) 'British Manufacture Throughout'. Who could resist reading a mother's diary? If those closest to us ever disclose the murky truth about themselves, it is in the dark where they think they can't be seen. Also, if she really wanted her diaries to remain unread, she shouldn't have told us to burn them. That last sonorous wish had the opposite effect, of course, drawing to my attention a previously unsuspected opus crying out to be read, and was a further incitement to pore over every private word. The diaries had to be a good read if she was so desperate to have them destroyed.

They remained a key point of reference when I set out on this further search for her. Having exploited, if not quite exhausted, all available resources and unsure where else to look, I still had the diaries to fall back on. Actually, I was rather looking forward to reading them again. It was an act of intimacy, from which she could hardly recoil after two years of close contact.

Already I was viewing them differently, more in regard to their missing than their actual content. What intrigued me as much as (or more than) the diary entries were the blanks and gaps and missing pages when Gerda unaccountably absented herself from her diary or ripped out whole sections of her recorded life. Absence featured disproportionately in her history and suddenly appeared the key to understanding it, so absence must be my starting point.

The *Oxford English Dictionary* on the shelf above this desk defines absence as: '1. The state of being away from a place or person; the time or duration of being away. 2. Non-existence or lack of. 3. Inattention due to thinking of other things.'

All apply to Gerda.

When she left fatherland and father on 23 May 1939, she met the first definition, for she was 'away' from 'a place' (Germany) and 'a person' (Tatta). The 'time or duration of being away' was important too, for she was unlikely to return and the duration of absence stretched into the distance with no end in sight. Then there was the question of how her 'absence' affected her father. By May 1939, he had lost nearly everything – assets, status, rights, and identity other than 'Jew' – but the loss of his daughter hurt the most, leaving him abandoned, bereft, and in the dark. How deeply his absence (from her life) affected Gerda remained unexplored and merited a much deeper dive than before. As to how her later 'non-existence or lack of' affected her 'English' family – that too invited closer inspection, though I was determined to keep us mostly outside the margins of this second book. No less consequential than when she and her first family parted thirty-three years earlier, my mother's suicide was the culmination of a life of absences and the source of my ongoing intense interest in her.

The idea of 'absence' and its special place in my mother's story informed the working title of this present book: *Absences*. Both as title and main motif, it seemed to sum up her life, but titles do more than shape books; this one was soon eating into her, rubbing out the edges, erasing entire sections. There was less of her to find, as if the effort of retrieval and recovery had scared her off. She was becoming more a woman of absence than a woman of substance, and it is difficult to connect with absence.

Death can mean permanent disconnection. For many years that was my mother's lasting legacy, and that was fine with me. If she was done with us, then I was done with her.

For the following five decades I was in no hurry to rouse her from her long sleep inside the suitcases. Waking her up meant raking her up. It meant trouble. Let sleeping Gerdas lie. And I won't pretend that the back of my neck prickled with a preternatural awareness of my mother looking over my shoulder as I read her diaries. That never happened. It wasn't a ghost story and I had no unnatural visitations to report.

Much of her is missing from the first book, and I have outlined the risks of this second approach: that I might get no nearer and it would be another year of my life gone with nothing to show for it. After ingesting the entire contents of her suitcases, I was still used to thinking of my mother as somebody with whom anything more than a fleeting connection is unlikely, even posthumously.

Connection? Was that what this was all about? Following that line of inquiry, a quick internet search came up with E. M. Forster's famous phrase, 'Only connect!' For all my scrupulous attention to her, we had so far failed to connect, but a further clue appeared in the last line of the quote: 'Live in fragments no longer.'[8] It gave me the direction I was looking for and led me to Barthes, the French

---

[8] *Howards End* (1910) See Chapter 22 for the full quote. The novel concerns disconnection, with the protagonist, Margaret Schlegel, a force for connecting otherwise parallel lives. My mother had difficulty connecting with others, including herself.

semiotician, who had also spent a lot of time looking for his mother after she died. It was the one thing we had in common, but it was enough. Searching for her in old photographs, Barthes was unable to recognise her 'except in fragments'.[9] His long search brought my own mother closer, for she too appeared in 'fragments' and had failed to cohere even after being painstakingly pieced together. She preferred it that way, it seemed.

All this was more encouraging than otherwise. Continuing the search, as Barthes did, in itself signified a live connection with my mother, albeit one-sided. Suicide was a good enough reason to remember her for longer than usual; it set her apart and to that extent was consistent with how she felt about herself in relation to others. But in the half-century since leaving me, she had come close to achieving the one thing she wanted: not to be remembered.

Gerda must have concluded that her life amounted to nothing and was best forgotten. It was a realistic self-appraisal. She could be dismissive of others (family included) but equally dismissive of herself. For me to have compiled one book about her was evidence enough that her life had not amounted to nothing. Curiously, in my early seventies, my mother seemed to matter and mean much more to me than when I was younger, and she was alive; to write two books about her attested to her lasting presence.

That I should 'leave the poor woman alone' and let her rest in peace has been a repeated self-reproach

---

[9] Roland Barthes, Camera Lucida (Vintage, London, 2000), pp. 63 - 68), originally published in French in 1980. Looking for his mother after she died, Barthes missed 'the essential being' he sought.

throughout the writing of this present book. What could she possibly have done to deserve such unwanted late attention? Considering this further, I reframed it more positively. Gerda wasn't a 'poor woman' at all. Compared to the overblown lives of Gunther and Kurt she was modest, didn't regard her life as interesting or unusual despite the evidence of history, and erred safely on the side of low self-esteem.

In a last letter (1963) to Gunther, who hadn't heard from him for thirty years, Kurt referred to his 'adventurous and raging life'. That was the opposite of what my mother claimed for herself.

I don't know what Kurt had in mind as unfortunately he provided no further details before dying a few months later in a Buenos Aires hospital. Gunther, who lived longer and left more letters for me to read, had many more opportunities than Kurt to evidence his own adventurous life. It wasn't 'raging' (Gunther particularly disapproved of his brother for that reason and several others); self-aggrandising would better describe it.

After arriving in in Quito shortly after the start of world war, Gunther 'found quickly the way to glory' in 'the smartest Bar of this country, leading there the Band'. For the next thirty years, his letters kept Gerda as close to him as distances and their differences allowed, while also providing opportunities to exhibit the great success he was making of his refugee life, first in South America, then in the US, despite the series of furnished rooms and his factory job as 'a slave of Heinz'. What Gerda wrote to him is lost, but I couldn't imagine her making half so much of herself – at least not until I discovered a previously overlooked reference to her 'magnificent' letters.

Not Drowning but Waving

And there lay my opportunity: to find more in her extraordinary past than she found or chose to remember. By her own account (or lack of it) hers was certainly no 'adventurous and raging life'; she didn't front a band or boogie-woogie in South America, or swell as a citizen of the US. Yet her life, too, had been touched by momentous events, the magnitude of which I could have no real measure. The woman who rode off to jumble sales on her old black Raleigh bicycle and came back with bags of clothes was also the woman who once smuggled diamonds out of Nazi Germany.

To my surprise and delight, I recently came across, in the local antiques centre, a vintage black Raleigh bicycle almost exactly like hers – curved handlebars and crossbar, bell, Brooks leather saddle, basket in front with leather straps, rear rack, dynamo, chain guard. 'Worth in excess of £1000' according to the seller. 'Bought, alas, with a youthful heart. Could be yours for £375 cash.' I was tempted.

Peter Thornthwaite

She had emerged fully-formed as a mother in the 1950s: a woman without a past worth remembering, her life shaped to the needs of others more than her own. Yet as the diaries revealed, she had passed through history at its most convulsive, and history had passed through her. The mother I knew was only the last in a long line of Gerdas. The best part of her history had already happened before she became a mum.

Maybe she was content for a while, for all the 'scrimping and saving', the 'making ends meet' among 'the poor and the proletariat' (as she referred to them) housed like her in ex-army Nissen huts and raw new council estates. She had done her best to leave history behind but it came back for her in January 1960.

It knew her as a Jew and was coming for her family too, and although there are few further explicit references to resurgent antisemitism (aside from Colin Jordan as Hitler reborn in Birmingham) in the last decade of her diaries, history sought her out in other ways. She kept seeing people she hoped 'never to see again'. A young charity shop assistant made no secret of her detestation of my mother by accusing her of 'pinching a brown jacket'. Then there was 'that horrible woman in the 'Spastic shop again', who was 'ever so nasty' and 'started to pick a fight with me'. Her own son said some terminal things. Isolated instances, maybe, but they coalesced and came to the same conclusion. There was no getting away from history once it had it in for you.

So, if I needed a further rationale for another book about my mother, it would be that I owe her this, partly as posthumous apology for reading her diaries in the first place, partly to make amends for what history and I had done, but mostly to make more of her life than she did. Flicking through earlier diaries, looking for a fitting phrase to end this chapter, I came across this from 28 September 1939, a few weeks into the war: 'I hope I can be strong and brave enough to take up the fight with destiny.'

CHAPTER TWO:

TITANIC

Eyewitnesses observed the stern rising high in the air as the ship tilted down into the black water to an angle of fifteen then thirty to forty-five degrees until 'almost perpendicular' as the flooded bow pulled it down. After the lights went out, it reportedly 'split apart' although a first-class passenger, Colonel Archibald Gracie, who survived the sinking and just had time to complete his own eyewitness account, *The Truth About the Titanic*, before dying later that year (1912), maintained that it remained intact as the sea swallowed it. This 'marvellous ship' and 'floating palace' – the 'perfection of all vessels hitherto conceived by the brain of man' – had not yet broken in half. Like the inseparable couple, whom Colonel Gracie made a point of observing in his account of the sinking, Mr and Mrs Isidor Straus, who had steadfastly stayed together on deckchairs (referred to as 'steamer chairs'), the ship also stayed together until disappearing from view. The wreckage now lies on the seabed in two sections over two thousand feet apart, the bow and sumptuous interiors still recognisable after 112 years, the stern ruined. One internet source memorably described the depth (12,500 ft or two-and-a-half miles) to which the world's most remembered ship sank as '9 Empire State buildings stacked on top of each other'.[10]

The two main sections are virtually back together again. A recent full-sized digital scan has reunited them in a 3D view of the entire ship, revealing both its vast scale and details such as serial numbers on a propellor. Until a year or so ago, my knowledge of the *Titanic* drew on the 1997 James Cameron disaster film. I now find myself (alongside countless other internet explorers) peering down the gaping hole in the boat deck into the virtual black void where a wrought-iron and glass dome once admitted light to the first-class Grand Staircase with its great crystal-and-gilt chandelier.

It doesn't take a deep internet dive to learn that every aspect of the Titanic – from conception and design to its famous iceberg moment – has attracted increasing interest since the discovery of the location of the wreckage in 1985 and controversial salvage operations. The size and splendour of the ship (the largest passenger liner and largest ship ever built at the time); the wealth of its first-class passengers (it was known as 'Millionaires Special'), who hurriedly deposited their diamonds, jewellery and valuables before leaving the comfort and security of the ship for the night and the boats; the ghostly undersea images of the wreckage at the bottom of the North Atlantic:– these will ensure lasting interest long after it

---

[10] I read Colonel Gracie's *The Truth About the Titanic* (1913) at the British Library. The following day was absorbed by the Holocaust Galleries at the Imperial War Museum, and the juxtaposition stayed with me for many months. The initial quotes are from Gracie's account. The 'memorable' internet source to which I refer is CBS News (cbsnews.com), 23 June 2023.

has disappeared and has only a 'virtual' reality. I have read of deep-sea diving operations, equipped with the latest technology such as robots roaming the sea floor to take close-up images, scanning the remains in desperate attempts, before the *Titanic* finally disappears, to recover diamonds now worth hundreds of millions of pounds, and searching for the jewellery deposited with obliging pursers as the ship sank. Such salvage operations, which have brought thousands of precious items to the surface and into auction rooms, have been likened to 'grave-robbing', though no bodies remain in the crushing dark. As for the drowned – the unrecovered bodies of the nearly fifteen hundred bodies sinking in the icy sea that night – it was initially supposed that the extreme pressures at that depth would have compressed them into jelly. Evidently much of the debris sought by salvagers has not decomposed beyond saving (if only in spectral images), with new technology like the miniature remote-operated vehicle ('a flying eyeball') looking for and photographing remains. What interests me as much as the actual wreckage is the wide field of debris mapped by these seabed searches. Unopened champagne bottles and women's lace-up boots are readily identifiable in the seabed sediment of internet images. The field of debris is much more extensive than the wreck itself, and this has a personal relevance.

In the summer of 2022, the 'largest underwater scanning project ever' was undertaken by Magellan Ltd, a deep-sea mapping company, and Atlantic Productions, with 'more than 700,000 images taken by submersibles'. Much of the *Titanic* is now open to virtual view, including portholes still with glass in them, great chandeliers hanging from ceilings, and the collapsed bathroom of Captain Smith, his bathtub full of stalactites of rust. If the most opulent and unsinkable of ships hadn't sunk when it did, and in such an unforeseen way as to jar 'two hemispheres', as Thomas Hardy put it, it might still interest but hardly fascinate after 112 years. For me (and for many others, I imagine) the enduring attraction of the *Titanic* is more to do with its journey down and its unseen transformation on the otherwise unvisited deep seabed where, ironically, it remains better preserved than if it had stayed afloat as expected and sped past icebergs on its maiden voyage to New York. The ship's lasting appeal has much to do with the surreal wreckage and debris spread wide across the ocean floor in the deepest, darkest 'midnight zone' of underwater night – where, I have read, marine worms and giant sea spiders sift through the muddy sediment and bacteria form and feed on the rotting iron remains.

Visualising the ship down there among all its debris, including the hundreds of thousands of artefacts spilled from the cabins, saloons and smokerooms, I think of my mother. Having the misfortune to be German and Jewish and growing up with the Third Reich, Gerda was born a month before Hitler began to lead the Nazi Party in 1921 and she turned twelve six months after he became Chancellor in 1933. It may seem an unlikely association of ideas but there is much in her situation to connect her to the disaster of 15 April 1912.

The story of Gerda's life and history, in which I remain immersed, and the better-known story of the *Titanic*, have remained deeply but obscurely interconnected for me over the past year. As the two stories are in no way analogous, the interconnection remained murky, though

Peter Thornthwaite

I clearly recall what prompted me to find out about the *Titanic* and so join the many deep-sea divers of the internet in search of sometimes abstruse yet strangely resonant areas of lasting interest.

The *Titanic* sank two years before the First World War also jarred 'two hemispheres'. Stefan Zweig, remembering the Europe he knew before the two world wars, sought 'some faint reflection of my life before it sinks into the dark'. Those words, written shortly before he and his wife killed themselves in Brazil, sank into my own semi-subliminal depths when I first read them a year ago and was unusually susceptible to such things because of my own deep dive into old diaries and family letters dating back to a rising Third Reich as it approached its zenith. Around that time (April 2023) and while still deep into Zweig's memories of Europe before the wars, I read an online newspaper article describing the deep-sea digital scan in 2022 of 'the world's most famous shipwreck'. Already well primed to connect ostensibly disparate things, I thought afresh about my mother's life and history and death. Zweig's words, at the end of his foreword to *The World of Yesterday*, published in 1942, suggested a man drowning or about to drown but also someone salvaging what he could, in the little time left to him, of his old European life before it sank 'into the dark' with the rest of old Europe.[11]

This in turn brought up my mother's history of persecution, exile and diaspora. The newspaper article on

---

[11] In losing Europe, which he regarded as his 'true home' and any place in it, Zweig had 'nothing left' of his past but what he carried in his 'head'. *The World of Yesterday* was published soon after his suicide.

the full-sized digital scan of the *Titanic*, and the possibility – the 'hope' – that it 'might yet give up its secrets', touched on my own, admittedly more personal and limited, salvage operation. In my own little way (unlikely to make newspaper headlines or grab global attention), I was doing something similar. The story of the *Titanic* lent my mother's own history a magnitude I had previously missed. Hitler and history had broken her family and countless others apart and most, including my mother's, are no longer remembered, but in Gerda's case (in five cases, actually, as five old brown suitcases of history survived her death) she left a 'wide field of debris' behind for me to pick through at my leisure.

That full-sized digital scan of the *Titanic* on the seabed achieved – on an admittedly grander scale – what I had attempted in the first book about my mother's life and history. It was not unlike what I tried to do for Gerda and her family: examining every detail that came to light, assembling the scattered evidence, putting together fallen pieces of history, looking for connections, making sense of the whole. The *Titanic* broke apart as it sank, and so in a sense did Gerda when, on 23 May 1939, she left her younger self behind; her life broke into two widely separated halves and, more than half a century after she died, I was still putting her back together again. It was all about making connections: reconnecting her German and English lives, and at the same time reconnecting with my estranged mother after fifty years of separation.

What broke Gerda and her family apart also broke Stefan Zweig. Not much else associates her with the most famous writer of his time, but the Jewish and special historical connection was enough to align two figures who would otherwise never come together in a thought. Zweig was famous in the 1920s and 30s, a 'free man' of Europe as he described himself, when Gerda was growing up in Breslau, until Hitler changed both their lives. For a while Zweig had a distant view of Berchtesgaden, where the man lived who would 'destroy' him and much of Europe. It pleased him that his own 'modest' connection with Hitler was to cause him 'great annoyance' (Zweig's name and books being particularly reviled by the Nazis and the subject of 'endless debates in high places' including the Berghof). He left Austria for England in 1934, five years earlier than Gerda. As a noted enemy of the state – he featured in the so-called 'Black Book' listing persons to be detained following the German Reich's imminent conquest of Britain – Zweig went to the US in 1940 and settled in New York. There he loses any significant connection with Gerda and her widely dispersed family until the double suicide with his spouse, Lotte, in Brazil in February 1942. When that internet search ended there, I naturally thought of my mother and her suicide, also from an overdose, nearly thirty years later. It took her a while to get there, but she got there in the end, albeit with no 'kimono' or well-dressed spouse to keep her company.[12]

But what really brought her to mind while reading *The World of Yesterday* was Zweig's sense of recent history and 'the almost constant volcanic shocks' suffered by Europe, first with World War One, then with the rise of the Third

---

[12] Formally attired for the occasion, Zweig and Lotte, who wore a Kimono, were found dead of a barbiturate overdose in Petropolis, Brazil, on 23 February 1942.

Reich and the start of World War Two. Together, they amounted to too much 'history': 'more radical changes and transformations' than 'in ten normal human generations'. By the time she left Germany for England in 1939, young Gerda had already experienced enough history to last her a lifetime. That line of thought led me back to the *Titanic*.

There are occasions when history seems more concentrated – when more can happen in a single night to change and transform lives than normally happens in wider spans of time. The sinking of the *Titanic* was one such night, its ripples undiminished 112 years later. Much more than a big ship, it symbolised a certain conception of 'civilisation' and unstoppable human progress, since lost. The world is a different place with the *Titanic* rotting on the bottom of the North Atlantic. It was, as the 1958 film described it, *A Night to Remember*.

An equally memorable night featured in Gerda's family history: that of 9-10 November 1938, the 'Night of Broken Glass'. *Kristallnacht*, as it was called, also drew worldwide attention, revealing the brutal reality of Nazism more publicly and violently than any other marker of the Reich's progress in the five years preceding it. This was when Gerda determined to go while the going was good.

That decision led to yet another night to remember – 23 May 1939 – as seventeen-year-old Gerda boarded an American ocean liner, *SS President Harding*, at Hamburg docks. It was also bound for the US and (unlike the *Titanic*) it reached New York, though Gerda disembarked at Southampton. Also (unlike the *Titanic*'s passengers) hers was a night to remember for its sheer delight, life-changing in a good way, and her excited 'Journey Note', written as the ship was preparing to depart, is testament to that. Whatever wonderful things awaited her in England, nothing in her future matched that first euphoric night of freedom.

When I started putting these various memorable nights together, other connections then occurred to me – mostly spurious ones but nonetheless compelling and convincing, especially when they came to me at night. About two thirds of *Titanic*'s passengers were drowned, and a similar percentage of approximately nine-point-five million Jews living in Europe in 1933 were dead by the end of the Third Reich. Eighty-five per cent of the mass of the iceberg was below the surface, and some such percentage probably applied to the Nazi menace at the outset. For Gerda and her family – and for Germany, Europe, the world – the hidden depths of Nazism were initially unknown. Much of it soon became visible – in book-burnings, the Nuremberg Race Laws of 1935, the nationwide pogrom of November 1938 – more than enough to sink her family and many others, but the true extent of its inconceivable depth and darkness remained partly hidden even then.

There is only so far you can go with such a metaphor. The Iceberg was a force of nature. For Germany, Europe and the world beyond, the looming 'iceberg' of Nazism was a force of nation.

The *Titanic* received repeated serious ice alerts from other ships, including a Morse code message less than four hours before it sank, warning of several large icebergs ahead. Gerda and her family, and others in the 'same boat', were receiving enough warnings too. Public notices throughout Germany informed them that *Juden* were not wanted, not allowed, *nicht erwunscht*, and told them to go away. *Juden haut ab!* Jews go away. And many did. An exodus after Hitler became Chancellor in 1933, more after Nuremberg in 1935, still more after *Kristallnacht*. That tinkling word, more suggestive of German Christmas preparations than a pogrom, brought to mind the glassy wall of ice scraping against the starboard side of the Titanic and the long-drawn out rending of steel plates. As the Titanic went down, its lights all aglow, Colonel Archibald Gracie heard 'a noise no one had heard before and no one wishes to hear again'. The same could be said of *Kristallnacht*, which was heard beyond Germany and made headlines in British and American newspapers: the *Daily Telegraph* reporting the burning 'to the ground' of synagogues, the wrecking of Jewish shops, the government-led 'outbursts of frenzied barbarism'.[13]

The *Titanic*'s 'Night to Remember', the Nazi 'Night of Broken Glass' – no, they are not analogous, but when I set out almost exactly a year ago to write a second book about my mother, having only just finished the first, I was intent on finding 'connections', even in the least likely places, in the hope of viewing her differently. If the 'story' of the *Titanic* has helped me do that, I don't yet know, but I can

---

[13] In its report (11 November 1938, Issue 26036) on the November pogrom, *The Daily Telegraph* stated that the 'entire Jewish population of Germany was subjected yesterday to a reign of terror.' On 12 November, in an article on the 'Nazi Pogrom', it described it as 'the most ferocious pogrom which Europe . . . has witnessed since the Middle Ages' and blamed the German government for having 'permitted, and even instigated, such vile outbursts of frenzied barbarism.'

see why that 3D digital scan of the ship so resonated with me. That was something I could do for her, albeit in a circumscribed and subjective way. Writing about, reconstructing – in a sense 'recovering' – her lost life, would be my equivalent of 'deep-sea mapping'. And in return, like the *Titanic*, she might yet give up her secrets. Also like the *Titanic*, for all that I can see of her, she lies two-and-a-half miles down on the ocean floor, in that deepest, darkest of midnight zones, and nothing might come of yet another search.

At times I wished she would stay there, mysterious to the end, undisturbed by my scanning and salvage operations even as I followed the 'comet-like trail of debris' like a robotic deep-sea vehicle equipped with sonar and camera.

CHAPTER THREE:

ABSENCES

A perceptive reader of *Remember Who You Used to Be* explained in a recent Zoom meeting what it is about. As the author, I should have known, but it wasn't until he summarised it so succinctly that I understood what I had written. He began by paraphrasing a famous English diarist: 'It's not so much the things that happen to us which represent the greatest tragedies in life, it's the things that DON'T happen'.[14] That pithy and memorable summation of a life marked by absences summed up a mother who also missed out on things of the utmost importance to her and who spent much of her life awaiting some life-changing event. In her case, 'life-changing' meant money: her 'Big Win', as she called it, which actually (and ironically) materialised shortly after her death. It was one of the things that should have

---

[14] W.N.P. Barbellion was B.F. Cummings' pen-name, and the reference is to *The Journal of a Disappointed Man* (1919). The exact wording of the quote is: 'The real tragedies in the world are not the things which happen to us, but the things which don't happen.' I have also come across another Barbellion quote relevant to my mother: 'For nothing can alter the fact that I have lived; I have been I, if for ever so short a time.'

happened to her but didn't until too late. Picking up on that potent word 'Absences', which seemed to encapsulate much of her life, the perceptive reader pointed out that Gerda's wealthy and respected German-Jewish family had everything going for them – an established business, property, assets, status, a stake in society, good economic prospects – until it was taken away, stolen by the state. For those that survived the break-up and dispersal of the family, and whose subsequent lives in London, Buenos Aires, Quito, Oxford and Pittsburgh I had tracked and traced following a paper trail of diaries and letters, there was always an absence behind their achievements and aspirations, a sense of what might have been, what ought to have been. It was like being 'haunted, even if subconsciously' (the perceptive reader suggested) 'by a counterfactual, an idealised alternative life in different circumstances that is always, by definition, much better than the life we end up living, and their actual lives could never compete with it.' Referring then to the title of the book under discussion, he suggested that Gerda and Gunther might have been better off 'forgetting who they used to be' and 'accepting, appreciating what they had and not measuring it against what might or should have been.'

As *Absences* was the original working title of this present book, and this current chapter (also entitled Absences) was written before that Zoom meeting, the idea of 'absence' had been there from the start. Actually, it was there from as far back as I remember. My mother has been an aching absence for the best part of my life. I was twenty when she died. By the time I got round to 'reading' her, I was twenty years her senior and the balance of power between us had changed. She was a diminished figure, more or less forgotten without her diaries to remind me that she was once the only woman in my life. Last seen (Christmas 1971) in hospital, she hadn't looked much like herself. It had not occurred to me until I saw her that a massive overdose could change even a mother almost beyond recognition. When the nurse drew back the plastic curtain, I expected a face and shape familiar enough to require no further examination, and was unprepared for what lay there. Whatever I absorbed, before looking embarrassedly away, certainly had 'presence' in that curtained-off bed, but it was somebody else, not her. Her blue remembered eyes, shut tight as clams, saw no surprise in mine. After all these years it is difficult now to bring back exactly what I observed, but I have retained an impression of bloat and puffy folds of flesh and sunken closed eyes, and thinning strands of dark hair exposing more scalp than even she would have expected to find in the mirror at the age of fifty.

In December 1957, perhaps in a prevision of the more frightful appearance to come, my mother (then thirty-six) noticed in her diary how her hair was getting so thin that she could 'hardly hide the 'baldness in front', and the last pages of that year are covered with multiple crude doodle drawings of shorn heads with staring faces, and 'I am' written underneath.[15] Maybe she had her later, post-overdose appearance in mind, though the face I saw in late December 1971 – before looking away in

---

[15] This looks like a repeated reference to the heads my mother doodled at the end of her 1957 diary, and it is, but those shorn heads with staring faces keep surfacing when I think of her. It is how she saw herself then.

embarrassment and out of consideration for her vulnerability and exposure – was sightless. What I now see is absence. She had not expected to be there – somebody to be observed and her unusual appearance noted – and fortunately she was unconscious and so spared that further and final shame. The eyes squeezed shut, swollen face and bloated body had nothing to do with her, nor she with them. She had absented herself. She was there but not there.

With the benefit of hindsight and her diaries, I had come to see her differently. Thankfully, in the interim, she had cast off that unsightly bloat and thinned to something more suitably diaphanous, ghosted by long absence, and even in her last comatose incarnation could be viewed with equanimity. She had frayed to filaments and threads of memory. Gerda had kept her distance long before she died. She got what she wanted in the end – erasure. Never having really mourned her death, I didn't begrudge her that. She was a mother I had not expected to see or hear from again – until, that is, I read the diaries. I had her suicide to thank for them and the unique opportunity they offered to bring her back in some form or other. In the event, she did not cohere in them – any more than she did in memory – but I recall my curiosity, excitement even, to discover what I had missed, and my impatience to go back to before we met. With years of my mother to go – all the way back to Gerda and the Third Reich – the sense of her absence was, from the outset, the ineluctable attraction, and so it remains.

She had recorded in black and blue and occasionally red biro the familiar phrases and fears that once formed my idea of a mother. It felt like eavesdropping, for I could hear her mouthing them, and while memories are vague on dates, her diaries specified the day, the month, the year: I could precisely locate my mother in the certain knowledge that she was there. So, for instance, on 23 November 1964, she mourned in real time her beloved short-haired dachshund, Sandy, sadly put down earlier that day because 'unhappy and in pain' and she 'couldn't bear to see him suffer so'. With the salutary reminder of her diary, that special day came back to me, and I was thirteen and in shock at the sudden and irreversible absence of one of the family. But when I first read that entry, it was my mother's nearness I sensed, not mine, and as she mourned Sandy she broke through. She wasn't dead after all, but had returned from a long absence in time to tell me about her life and reinstate herself and put the record straight.

Absence defined her. If one day more than any other in her history marked the meaning of absence, it was 27 December 1938, when she recorded in her red Tagebuch: 'The future looks quite black. We Jews are an unhappy people, violated, badly treated.' This is the first time 'we Jews' appears in her diaries. Gerda realised, as that climactically antisemitic year closed, that she couldn't stay, that sitting it out in Germany was no longer an option. When I came across that seminal entry (inscribed thirty-three years before her suicide), and checked her red Tagebuch for any previous reference to the November pogrom but found none, I supposed that Gerda paid minimal attention (at least in her diaries) to external events, no matter how momentous, being more interested in herself. But when I recently reread it, I realised that the absence of *Kristallnacht* from her red diary actually attested to its breaking impact on her life. From my extensive reading and research, it is now clear as glass to me that, from an early age, Gerda made sustained efforts to avoid mentioning, let alone dwelling on, the most difficult things. I think I know why she dared not allow the November pogrom into her diary. When things got too bad, she shut them out.

Her father was well established in Breslau, a fixture of its commercial life, despite being a Jew. Herr Elkan Lewinsohn amounted to something with his shops and properties, and you can see it in the earliest photographs, not just in the physical size of the man but in his presence and self-possession. He was there to stay. Before Hitler took over, the Jews of Breslau were sufficiently assimilated for Elkan not to consider himself an outsider or pariah. In 1925 (when Gerda was four), 23,000 Jews lived there, a proportionately higher percentage than in other German cities. Breslau also gave a proportionately higher percentage of its vote to the Nazis in 1933 and showed leadership in excluding Jews from society. By the start of the Second World War, over half the Jewish population of Breslau had left. The suitcases of diaries and letters my mother unknowingly left me contain no evidence of shattered shop windows or of anything else affecting her father during the night of 9-10 November 1938, but the absence of any reference to the state-instigated pogrom, or indeed to other encroachments on normal Jewish family life under Hitler, is just as telling. By December 1938, the first Kindertransport had left Berlin, her brother Gunther had departed (a week before

Kristallnacht) for New York, and Gerda was determined to leave and do something about it. She might not have known about the Kindertransport, but I expected some mention, if only in passing, of Jews leaving en masse after the 'Night of Broken Glass' and of Gunther having already left for the US. What I now know is that the absence of certain things from her diaries does not mean that they were absent from her thoughts but just the opposite.

The diary entry for 13 February 1939 ends memorably with: '*Morgen – Fruh – Ge-sta-po*': an appointment with the Gestapo early the next day. Though a date to remember, 14 February is blank in her diary. On the day following, she said goodbye at the Breslau Bahnhof to her 'boyfriend', Gerd, who was too young for her and was also going to Bolivia, so the relationship had no future. Leaving 'forever', 'little Gerd' gave Gerda 'a golden pendant' – a heart with a door in it and a miniature letter inside with the words '*Ich liebe dich*' – and in their almost identical names and that parting gift, I felt the shared moment as they separated for good. Love was what mattered to her then, at seventeen, even if Gerd was a boy love and not the 'Big Love' she was looking for, and for that reason he has a place in her diary, whereas the previous day's appointment with the Gestapo has none. The last place she wanted to see the secret police was there, in her red Tagebuch. It would be like inviting them into her home. She had to see them – not doing so wasn't an option, and she needed to progress her emigration plan – but they should take up no more space than necessary. Already in her diary, absences had a special meaning. Not mentioning something unpleasant or painful was a way of getting past it and as it left no trace in her diary it could not act as a reminder. So, the Gestapo was less of a threat if left out, and similarly whatever pain was associated with saying goodbye 'forever' to Gerd was also best left unwritten.

There were other notable absences that year, things that didn't make it into her diary, such as the absence of a future should she, like so many others in her situation, fail to get someone to guarantee the only position she would be likely and lucky to get: domestic service in an English household. She couldn't suppress her fear entirely, and it surfaced in an undated draft letter to an unnamed agency: *Having no chance to get out of here at the moment and being much afraid to be left here alone, I entreat you to get me a chance for I am quite desperate about my future.*

Something she had taken for granted until Gunther left and *Kristallnacht* happened – that of course she had a future – was no longer a certainty. She might not have one after all. A German-Jewish girl at that time and in that place, with absences accumulating behind her could only look forward to her own absence. In a sense, she was absent before she left, for she no longer had a place in Germany or a right to remain. In her own house, she was occupying living space needed by the more deserving 'Volk' entitled to it, but not for much longer.

As if anticipating his own absence from her life, Tatta – the portly patriarch of the early beach photographs, stern-faced, dignified even in the absence of clothes – has no place in Gerda's diary in the months before her departure. He is briefly seen escorting his daughter from Breslau to Hamburg, where she boarded the *SS President Harding*, but then he falls off that turning page of her life. There is no mention of Tatta in her ecstatic 'Journey Note' on the eve of departure. Gerda could be forgiven for forgetting her father after delightedly waving goodbye to the diminishing figure on the docks. She was getting away. She had a future again. Already he was the past.

It is another example of Gerda excluding difficult things from her diary. During her last year in Germany, Tatta had become one such difficulty. He irritated her more, which earned him an occasional if unfavourable diary entry but otherwise he isn't there. Considering what he was going through as an established man of business of the wrong 'race' in the era of 'Aryanization' and 'penalty taxes' for being a Jew, I hoped for glimpses of the paternal presence, if only in passing, but already he was disappearing from the family records. Possibly he kept his troubles to himself, shielding his beloved daughter from external realities. My appreciation of what Tatta meant to her – his omnipresence in her early life after her mother's death – comes more from photographs than written words. The sepia and the black-and-white pictures are where Tatta takes up the space befitting a proud German father and prosperous Kaufmann, and in them he remains an imposing figure.

That her Tatta loved her above all is evident from the pre-1933 beach photographs, in which no other family ever comes between them, and I can see from his powerful and protective presence how jealously he guarded the space he alone shared with his dark-haired doll of a Gerda. His fatherly love informs the few letters he sent Gerda following her arrival in London on 12 June 1939, although there it comes across as fear and reproach. That Gerda loved him after she left is less obvious. Before the permanent break in their relationship, he perhaps kept from her the full extent of his losses, careful not to distract his daughter with his problems while she was so busy resolving her own. Studying his stern face and fleshy figure in the early German photographs, I see a man who kept certain things to himself as a matter of paternal pride, and so he remained even as his life broke in half under Hitler. With *Kristallnacht* the sections further separated, and then he knew for sure he was going under. Always his thoughts were for Gerda. Both sons had left. Up until 20 May 1939, when an official letter arrived for Gerda, and she could be more confident of having a future again, all that mattered to Tatta was that Gerda got away. It was a selfless act. She was the only one of the family, I think, whose absence felt visceral to him.

And when she left, he felt huge relief. She had got out, she was safe, she was free. Relief was soon succeeded by an overwhelming sense of absence as he found himself in a still darker place than before. What he didn't know (though he suspected something) was that within weeks, even days, of her leaving, he had been eclipsed by Joe, a Jewish refugee from Berlin, whom Gerda met on the ship. Withholding this information from her father was possibly her first big secret, for she could not have been unaware how utterly Joe supplanted him in her affections. There is no diary evidence that this troubled her unduly, but Tatta felt the loss without ascertaining the cause of it. All he knew was that when his daughter left, light left his life.

From her arrival in London, up to Chamberlain's announcement to the nation on 3 September, and for the first four months of the 'Phoney War' (so-called because little actual fighting brought the reality of war home to Britain), Gerda's 'Big Love' (as she capitalized it) occupied every day of her diary, leaving no space for Tatta, who was out of sight and apparently out of mind. Gerda turned eighteen on 26 June; she was in London and in love, and suddenly being Jewish didn't seem to matter or exclude her from anything, and the attractions of the big city were there for her to enjoy as well. Her father's letters were an unpleasant reminder of difficult things she had left behind (including himself) and even made her feel bad about having a good time after all the privations of the past year. 'I forbid you to waste so much time uselessly,' he wrote on 30 June. Gunther, writing to Gerda from New York on 2 July, appreciated her situation and simply wished her 'enjoyable days' with her friend Steffi going out to 'movies, theatre, dance etc'. Tatta, meanwhile, sent reproachful and rather bitter letters, advising her to remember who she 'used to be'. She was too easily distracted by trivia and her own pleasure when instead she should be using all her 'power' to help him get out of Germany. What could she do? As a Jewish refugee and domestic in a foreign land, she was doubly diminished and anyway, as she wrote on an undated and unsent postcard, she was 'fully occupied'. She didn't specify what or who so 'fully occupied' her in London. Tatta's letters held enough truth to make her uncomfortable. She was sorry, of course, that he felt abandoned and bereft and afraid, but why must he keep reminding her of it and expecting her to do something? Gerda didn't want to remember who she used to be. That girl was gone, never to return, but her father wouldn't let her go.

Such 'insights' into how Gerda felt after yet another unwelcome letter from Tatta and Tante Bertha are mostly supposition on my part, for there is nothing in her diary to evidence her feelings about anyone other than Joe, except for that rather shocking 'I hate Tatta' entry in her diary around this time. It surprised me when I first came across it and would have surprised Tatta, yet it was at least proof that he still figured massively if entirely negatively in her life. Apparently, Gerda preferred living with his absence and they might have got on much better, with less rancour, without those persistent reminders of his and Tante Bertha's difficult situation in Germany. They only upset her, and she was having enough problems of her own.

By December 1939, the 'Big Love' with Joe was over. 'Deep within' her, she was still 'waiting for him to call', but she also remembered what an 'arsehole' he was and how the 'Big Love' was much smaller than it first appeared. What she didn't know then (but I do) is that slick, dark-haired Joe from Berlin wouldn't call, and this would be another absence she must learn to live with. Fortunately, four months into the war, Gerda could still fall back on the important things. She had only to look in a mirror to cheer herself up, for she was 'beautiful as a picture' and had 'lots of luck in love'.[16]

There then followed a two-year gap in correspondence with her father. On 20 January 1942 he wrote briefly to announce his arrival in Ecuador and inform her of his ill health throughout the long journey. He also inquired in

---

[16] It was a comforting self-image she could not fall back on indefinitely, of course, but at least it saw her through the war.

his letter about the so-called 'goods'. It was a disguised allusion to the diamonds she had somehow smuggled out of Germany. What remained of Tatta's 'huge fortune' (as Gunther later remembered it), the shops and properties and declarable assets, had turned to diamonds (cut, colour, clarity, carat unknown) by the time Gerda left Germany, and they don't appear in any correspondence until her father's brief letter announcing his arrival in Quito. What Tatta didn't know in January 1942 (but I do, having read his daughter's diaries and later unsent letters) is that by then the diamonds were no longer in her 'possession'.

Her relief in hearing from him after so long and knowing he was safe with her brother was probably complicated by the reminder of 'the goods'. Apparently, Tatta had entrusted the diamonds to her safe-keeping and she had sold or lost them in London (she herself could never decide exactly how she had parted with her only inheritance of any value). It was a dilemma for her – whether to answer his letter and communicate her delight at his safe arrival, or delay while she decided what to confess. In the end the decision was taken out of her hands, because Tatta died a few months later, as Gunther promptly informed her. Distressing news for a daughter who lit up her father's life and left him in the dark, though his death conveniently obviated any further need to answer that awkward question about 'the goods'. Maybe she thought it was just as well he never found out.

If Tatta's death amounted to an absence equal to others she had experienced by the age of twenty, there is no diary evidence of it; but then she left so many important things out of the very place you'd expect to find them. It came as no surprise to me that it took Gerda over two years to respond to Gunther's letter informing her of their father's protracted and painful death, and to add another layer of mystery, she actually never did reply. The two nearly identical draft letters of January and June 1944, referring to Tatta's demise and scripted as though she had only just learnt of it, were never posted, and I can see why. It must have sounded strange, even to her ears, to express how 'sorry' she was 'to hear the bad news about Tatta' and give no explanation for the two-year delay in acknowledging it.

When previously reviewing her likely relationship with her father before and after she left Germany, it appeared that Gerda stopped caring or thinking much about him. If so, I sympathise. She had arrived in England just two weeks before her eighteenth birthday. She was no longer the girl he remembered, but with everything else gone from his life Tatta wasn't ready to let her go. It happened too suddenly, before he could adjust to another immeasurable loss. More than anything he wanted her to go – get out while she could – and more than anything he wanted her to stay. Gerda, meanwhile, was only too glad to let go of everything. She had taken the initiative, got out of Germany by her own unaided efforts, while unfortunately Tatta had to stay behind. It seemed unlikely, in the circumstances, that she would see her father again. Writing to him from London, her casual reference to a man she had met in transit, and who meant 'nothing' to her, was not reassuring and might have subsequently seemed tactless even to her. She also mentioned (and perhaps later regretted her candour) that she had gone to Paris en route, but gave no further details and left her father still more perplexed. The new uncertainty between them turned to mutual exasperation and heightened emotion. 'You've shot for the moon and now you are helpless and powerless to help me,' he wrote on 30 June. His daughter was so busy enjoying herself that she couldn't even write 'punctually'. Though his letter ended with 'a thousand kisses from your loving father', the damage was done when he got too close to the truth: 'You have forgotten everything, my child, because you are relatively well off over there'. Gerda's response was to stop writing, and in a letter dated 17 July Aunt Bertha mildly chided her for this break in communication: 'Your "Tatzelwurm" was grumpy from the start today as he is long missing a message from you. Hopefully one will arrive tomorrow.' One didn't. There is no further reference anywhere to the longed-for and long-awaited 'message' from Gerda to 'grumpy' Tatta. In an undated postcard she wrote a 'quick few lines as I am fully occupied', but 'Lieber Tatta' never read them as the card evidently remained unsent, since I am reading it now.

It appeared she had indeed 'forgotten everything', including her father, and that his absence was less of a problem the longer it persisted; that she could live with it more comfortably if not constantly reminded of it. I was wrong.

The word itself, 'Absences', must share some of the responsibility for my mistake. So long as it remained the working title of this book, it subtly influenced how I 'read' the evidence. Did Gerda realise what her wordless absence was doing to her father? Did she fret, agonise, over it? There is no evidence of this. For Tatta it was unbearable, and I wonder if she realised that or (if she did) resented the responsibility. Probably, any underlying sediment of sympathy for Tatta was soon overlaid by other sentiments, and until recently my 'reading' of their relationship was that her father first irritated and finally incensed his distant daughter with the truth as he saw it – that she was thoughtlessly enjoying herself in London while he was persecuted daily by the Gestapo. As for Gerda, she naturally resented being made to feel guilty and useless. Tatta was a changed man. This wasn't what she expected of her father. After all she had been through, and considering her young age and circumscribed scope of action, it was undeserved and unfair. There were good reasons for Gerda to cut off all further communication with him. He was asking the impossible and she could never meet his unrealistic expectations even if she tried.

Unfortunately, Gerda left no diary entries exposing any conflicted feelings about her father and her efforts to unknot them, whereas his affecting letters are there to be read. His love for her demanded, at the very least, that she allowed the same space for him in her life as before, and that was never going to happen. Her London life was too full of new experiences for Tatta to get much of a look in. From his point of view, as I see it, she inhabited every beleaguered cell of his being. It took him a while to get the measure of her absence, and when he did he saw no end to it and (rightly, as it turned out) feared the worst. It is easy for me to sympathise with a father who made no secret of his feelings, while all that Gerda revealed of hers was the 'I hate Tatta' entry in her diary and the heartfelt hope that her desperate and demanding father would never join her in England. As a solitary marker of her changed attitude towards him, that entry alone skews the evidence against her. Evidently, she had not yet learnt to remove from her diary entries she might later regret or fear might be one day read by others.

But as I say, I was wrong. She missed Tatta terribly. The evidence is there if you look for it, and I missed it. On 1 December 1940 she wrote to Gunther: 'It is impossible for me to get any news about Tatta. I worry a lot how he is getting on and would be awfully happy to hear something about him.' Rereading that draft fragment of a letter, I sense again her delight in describing the impact of the Blitz on the household during nightly air raids, but also notice how she is reminded of her father's much worse situation and how 'terribly thrilling and exciting' war is 'if it wouldn't be for Tatta'.

Her 'if it wouldn't be for Tatta' seemed an afterthought on my first reading, as if it suddenly occurred to her, mid-letter, that the war wasn't 'thrilling and exciting' for her father. She evidently wanted Gunther to know that she never stopped thinking of Tatta, even in the midst of the Blitz. Now, though, I read an entirely different meaning in her unsent words. He was always there, her Tatta, at the back of her mind, even as she cuddled up on the floor with her employers during night after splitting night of air raids. As the Luftwaffe sought her out in SE15, her thoughts were with him: 'I would be ever so much happier if he would be with you or another safe spot'. That, too, was considerate of her. In the changed circumstances of war on the home front, she hardly wanted Tatta here with her in the unsafety of London.

Her brother never got to read that letter fragment of 1 December 1940 because it ended up with me. Of course, she might have written a similar letter, which she posted, though I suspect she thought better of it, censored herself, and wrote something more calculated to please or placate Gunther, omitting what he might consider improper sleeping arrangements with her employers and the add-on about Tatta. There are several such remnants of unposted letters to her brother, and his loss is my gain as they provide invaluable insights into my mother and who she used to be. Without this one from the Blitz, I might never have guessed that her thoughts were with her unfortunate father even as German bombs fell.

My assumption, when I drafted this chapter, was that Tatta was an absence she had come to accommodate with the others. With him out of her life for good, there was no further need to think of home or Germany or what might have been. No longer his little girl, she had to get by without a Tatta. The world had flipped, and actually she rather liked it that way. That was how I viewed Gerda at that critical juncture in her life, and I didn't blame her. She was struggling to get out from under father and fatherland. They cast a long shadow. But she was young and had a future again, and there was no place in it for him.

It was a misinterpretation, which happens with just the 'evidence' of diaries and letters to go on. They are the least reliable of primary sources and yield different meanings at different times, depending on what I am looking for and 'read' into them. In this case, though, and less forgivably, I had paid insufficient attention to her words. In the above letter from the Blitz she also mentioned to Gunther that it was 'impossible' for her to get news of Tatta. That set me thinking and reminded me of his earlier letter to her, dated 6 May 1940:

Not Drowning but Waving

Father asks to you that from now on your writings to him shall be all remitted to me and I shall forward them from here directly to him.

The 'from here' meant from Ecuador, and I suddenly understood what had happened. All further correspondence with their father in Breslau was to go via Gunther – not because Gerda had stopped writing to Tatta, but because of wartime censorship. She couldn't write to him directly from England as the countries were at war. As a Jew in Germany, he was under close observation: an enemy of the state with no right to be there and a betrayal of the Reich by his very existence. Correspondence with a daughter in London invited scrutiny, censorship, and worse. Gerda and Tatta could have shared no information about their respective situations; she certainly could not have mentioned the diamonds she had smuggled out of the Reich, or how much she enjoyed the Blitz after months of nightly bombs. Ecuador was not then at war with Germany, so Gunther could continue the correspondence without further endangering their father.

Actually, it was Gunther who also misled me. His early wartime letters to Gerda reminded her (lest she forget) how much he was doing for Tatta, and it appears that he alone as the only dutiful son was doing his best to keep the family together, and of course he was right. Unlike Gerda, Gunther did his duty; helped their father when no one else did; facilitated his escape from persecution at the last moment. And he succeeded. Elkan Lewinsohn did get out, in October 1941, a month before his sister Bertha was deported and killed. He arrived in Quito on the first day of the Wannsee Conference, where high-ranking Nazis were gathering to consider and coordinate the 'Final Solution of the Jewish Question'. He was concerned with another urgent question, which remained unanswered in the time left to him. Gunther had no answer to give, but at least he was there with his father at the end when he needed the comfort of family. Later he informed Gerda of Tatta's last wish: that he could die happy if only Hitler died first. It was Gunther who paid the funeral costs and future upkeep fees at the cemetery and later complained that Gerda had contributed nothing. All that is true.

The available 'evidence' of the letters and diaries is that Gerda took no responsibility for her father or thought much about him after she left. Soon, war also divided them. All she could do was make the best of things. Most misleading of all was Gunther's unsparing accusation in a postwar letter (February 1949), to which I attributed particular significance. Gerda had written to her brother, complaining of her degrading circumstances in a camp of Nissen huts alongside 'filthy people' who also had nowhere better to live. Far from commiserating with his sister in her distress, he wrote in reply:

Dear sister, you always made your own decisions in your life, neither you paid attention to my opinion or suggestions nor you cared for your daddy who loved you so much.

For a young woman, who by the end of the war had come to regard herself as a 'useless being', Gunther's harsh judgement (no doubt meant to administer a good moral shake) merely edged her nearer to self-negation as a defining attitude. His accusation stayed with Gerda for years, surfacing in January 1960 when she recalled her 'wickedness' to her father and aunt. Naturally, as her son, I was inclined to side with her against her brother's vindictive verdict, but I couldn't entirely disagree with it. Gunther had a point. There was little evidence that she cared for her 'daddy' after she left him. It really did seem a case of 'out of sight and out of mind'. The less she thought about him, the less she worried and could get on with her own life. Not that she cared nothing for him after she left – Gunther was wrong about that – but she had to let go of everything when she left him at Hamburg, and Tatta was a big part of everything.

That was where I got her wrong. She worried dreadfully about her father, I'm sure. His shadow never left her. She might give the impression that Tatta was far from her thoughts, but then she seldom used her diaries to admit, let alone resolve, contentious issues. And there are all the missing pages in the wartime diaries to consider, too: if they provided evidence that she missed her father terribly, it is lost as she apparently ripped them out, wanting no reminders. In the absence of evidence, I can only speculate.

What Gerda was thinking when she read her father's letter of 20 January 1942 is not recorded, and her reaction to Gunther's news several months later of Tatta's death is also a matter of conjecture. She could have shown herself in a better light but she wasn't that kind of diarist and withheld almost as much from herself as from others. My impression is of a woman who brooded on bad things and preferred to write nothing rather than commit herself to words. It is a strange diarist who leaves mostly blanks and the stubs of torn-out pages behind, but then my mother was strange. Was Tatta brooding on her as he died? Yes, of course. The absence of a daughter who meant so much, and whom he missed more than life itself, took up residence in him at the end, more so as the intestinal cancer consumed and hollowed his once great girth. Her consoling absence was there, I am sure, waiting patiently by his bedside, looking down at the prostrate body with the love of a daughter to whom he once meant everything. And recognising his part in what went wrong between them after she left, Tatta finally had the opportunity to apologise for his earlier reproachful letters and explain that they were written out of fear; but of this I am less certain, not knowing him very well. One thing I do know for sure: her absence stayed with him to the end.

And what of Gerda? Between news of her father's safe arrival in Quito and Gunther's confirmation several months later of Tatta's death, there are no surviving letters or diary entries, so if she even knew that he was in hospital and dying is unknown.

This is what I now think: she was dreadfully upset that she couldn't be there at the end to say goodbye, and she was sorry. *Sorry, Tatta, that your letters really irritated me; sorry I wrote that I hated you in my diary and hoped never to see you in England; sorry I was too busy to write; sorry I seemed to forget you. Sorry you are now the one to leave.*

'It's not so much the things that happen to us which represent the greatest tragedies in life, it's the things that DON'T happen.'

I doubt if Gerda ever imagined herself there, in that hospital in Quito in April 1942, at the bedside of a wasted and shrunken father consumed by cancer. It was one of the things that didn't happen in her life, and because there was no *goodbye* or *sorry* or *I love you*, the memory of what she had not done and of what hadn't happened came back years later to condemn her.

CHAPTER FOUR:
ANNE FRANK

Collins ROYAL DIARY for 1940. Most pages missing or blank. The entry under 'Memoranda' begins, *'Ich bin in London und ich bin glucklich fast'* (I am in London and I am almost happy), and ends with wishing herself *'ein gluckliches Neues Jahr'* (a happy New Year). The first day of 1940 *'war nicht sehr zufriedenstellend'* (not very satisfactory) because *'ich esse zu viel und arbeite nicht schnell und gut genug'* (eating too much, not working hard enough). A certain *'blode'* (stupid) Herr Egon Wolfsohn, thirty years old, wearing dark glasses (*'schwarze Brille'*), and *'aus Breslau'* like herself, has hinted he wants to marry her, but she is *'immernoch entschlossen HD zu heiraten'* (she is still determined to marry HD).

Having entered her diary, HD leaves it at the same point. Between 2 and 15 January pages have been ripped out, with nothing more about Herr Wolfsohn or HD in 1940 and beyond; if they reappeared, it was in the missing sections. The following months are blank, and flicking through to December I see from the last entry that a year has been skipped and it's suddenly 1941:

Not Drowning but Waving

Heute ist der 31. Dezember 1941. Paper is very short and expensive, so I should buy a new book and use this backwards. My brain is so full of things that I think to write diary will do me good. Life is not all honey and I think there are ever so many more troubled hours than happy hours. It is now getting near Christmas and I wonder what the new year will bring.

What it brings, when I go to the next entry, isn't January 1942 but 3 January 1951 and not a good start to the year:

I am restless and hurt when people ignore me and women don't like me. I should so much like to have a lot of nice friends and be popular with everybody. I did have a friend in this camp, but I have fallen out with all and I am very much on my own.

Having missed a decade of diaries and wondering how I got through her war years without them, I searched her suitcases and found S.O. Book 135, G.R. Supplied for the Public Service. The first entry, 22 July 1945, describes a wedding, which Gerda considered *very dull and boring. There should have been more life in the party. English people are awfully dull and uninteresting. I don't like them much, except for my little Jacky of course who is really one of the best fellows in the world and don't you ever forget this, Gerda. He'd do anything on this earth to make me happy, and he has to bear a lot of me really.*

Her worries turn to her weight and women serving in the ATS (Auxiliary Territorial Service): *all bossy, mean and catty, or perhaps it's me.* S.O. Book 135 then jumps a year to August 1946, then on to 1947 and Oxford, and finally to 24 May 1949, when she is 'nearly 28' and worrying that she hasn't heard from Gunther since *I wrote and told him about the diamonds. I still dream about them an awful lot, I don't think I'll ever be able to forget about them, I seem to be always in trouble.*

1949 stops there.

These fragments of diary – months and often years apart, with no attempt at continuity – show that for extensive and undoubtedly eventful periods in her life Gerda was at best a sporadic and indifferent diarist. What is missing from the record – vast tracts of unrecorded life – is at least as intriguing as what is there, not because what she wrote is uninteresting, but because the unwritten or excised records are wide open to speculation. The scarcity and cost of paper alone hardly explain these prolonged absences from her life. Was she covering her tracks in transit? Of course, my mother never expected her diaries to be read, so she could delete as much of her life as she liked without anybody particularly noticing. Unlike Anne Frank, she wasn't writing with future readers in mind. Her diaries were private. Also, considering all the gaps, she couldn't have written them with any intention of connecting up separate sections of her life, and I don't suppose she ever re-read her diaries. Gerda was never one for looking back.

In January 2021, with the outer world locking down, but her inner world about to open up to me with unrestricted access to the diaries and letters, I hoped to find the hidden woman in those suitcases of hers. Undaunted by the quantity and confusion of papers, I was a researcher – any residual guilt arising from intrusion, trespass, disregard of her wishes, was soon subsumed by other things. There was work to be done here and not before time.

What a mess she had left me. Sifting through the

evidence of an unremembered life, I had no preternatural sense of any response to my respectful touch and probe, yet something stirred and seemed aware of my fingers in her papers as if urging me to press on regardless of scruples. Having started, I had nowhere else to go but on with the project, and if it achieved nothing more, at least it would see me through a lockdown year. Two repeated capitalised words from her later diaries were as much a guide to me, through this first phase of the project, as they were to my mother at the time: UTILISE and ORGANISE. Like her, I was determined to utilise everything, so that nothing of hers that she had valued enough to keep – not a scrap – was wasted. By the end of her life, she had no further use for these diaries, letters and papers, which merely increased my curiosity. As for her second guiding principle – ORGANISE – that had been the first imperative at the outset of the project: aligning diary entries and correspondence in more-or-less date order and filing everything in blue folders with lists of contents. That her systematic approach could be exemplary is evident from her 1965 'Plan of Suitcases', whereby she packed and catalogued more than a hundred suitcases of second-hand clothes for the family's future; but it failed to follow through when it came to these written records. If she had deliberately set out to mislead and thwart a future reader, she couldn't have done a better job, and I rather suspected she had done it on purpose to protect her posthumous privacy. More likely, she was just careless, not expecting her diaries to be read by anybody and not wishing to go back over them herself. Maybe they were in rather a mess because, if diaries reflect a life, the mess she made of hers was what they mirrored.

Peter Thornthwaite

Was her life any more of a mess than most? Probably not. It is only when you construct a family history and 'story' that, for ease and coherence of narrative, you sequence and link the sections in ways that seem to make sense. My mother and her first family had lain undisturbed inside her suitcases for more years than they had lived, and I optimistically supposed (wrongly as it turned out) that she was all there, just a bit jumbled up – as befitted my idea of a mother of the 1950s and 60s who spent her diarised life obsessed with jumble sales. They were the prose and only passion of an otherwise tedious existence. So, it seemed entirely appropriate that the diaries and other paper remains of her life were also a 'jumble', only this time it was my turn to dip my hands into it.

Just as she never knew what might turn up at the next jumble sale, so I anticipated some unusual finds – pleasant or otherwise, I hardly minded, just so long as they piqued my interest and kept me going through her life – but what surprised me from the outset were the wide gaps in the written record, including family letters (Gunther's especially), which were generally a much more reliable source of information than Gerda's diaries. Such gaps were inevitable, in view of family breakup and dispersion, and tell their own story. Such breaks in correspondence can be as revealing as the surviving letters. When Gunther anxiously wrote to Gerda's domestic service employer, in October 1940, asking for news of his missing sister – *Unfortunately, my father and me, we are without news about the fate of my sister. Has she come in a concentration camp or has she had an accident?* – he heard nothing and by early 1941 was urging the Jewish Refugees Committee to help. Gerda, meanwhile, was complaining that this was *the third letter I write to you without getting a reply.* Such disconnects were normal for war and diaspora and an essential part of the story. More concerning were the gaps in Gerda's diaries, her unexplained absenteeism. What was happening between entries?

It is instructive to compare Gerda with another wartime diarist – a rather better known one who wrote a diary for just two years. When Anne Frank started hers in June 1942, she didn't know the short time span available to her, and it is the more poignant for being interrupted, arbitrarily cut off. *Anne Frank's Diary* (which, unlike Gerda's, deserves a capital 'D') is a model of compression. If Anne had outlived her Diary, she might well have written others but abandoned them for lengths of time as more pressing matters absorbed her energies and interest. Like Gerda, she might have gone missing from diaries, with nothing much to report on her return. She might have turned into the kind of housewife and mother she never wanted to become. If Anne had outlived her wartime Diary, few (if any) might have read it. What happened to her following arrest and deportation to Auschwitz and then Bergen-Belsen, where she died, is absent from the Diary for obvious reasons. The unwritten death camp end of her story adds terrible poignancy to it. As it is, she wrote 'the world's greatest bestseller', made it (posthumously) to Hollywood, was big in Japan and even in Germany, and became, I read somewhere, the 'poster girl of the Holocaust'. The story of how the diary was salvaged – how her bereaved father found in it another unsuspected Anne – adds to the legend.

As for my mother, I didn't 'discover' another Gerda in her diaries, letters, etc until long after she died, and unlike

Otto Frank, my interest often faltered and I felt disinclined to continue a frustrating and seemingly fruitless task. The discovery and salvaging of Anne's Diary, scattered across the floor of the 'Secret Annexe' after she and the others were taken away, and the circumstances in which it was returned to her father on his return from Auschwitz, and how much it meant to him to get her back if only on paper – these subsequent events, though outside the Diary, added immeasurably to it as a story of miraculous survival against the odds; whereas the 'discovery' of Gerda's diaries is of little interest to anyone but me.[17]

I first read *Anne Frank's Diary* in German at A-level. Reading it in translation, nearly a lifetime later, for the purpose of comparing Anne and Gerda as 'diarists', I read it quite differently. My remembered impression was of entries packed tightly into a small space with minimal time gaps. With no life outside the Annexe to interrupt or divert her, Anne had more time for her diary and probably more need of one than normal for a lively, sociable teenage girl. In fact, the time gaps are often so wide that you wonder what unreported events and reflections are happening outside the Diary. There are long continuous sequences of daily entries in February, March, April and May 1944, almost as though Anne knew she was running out of time and needed to source each day for fresh material, but elsewhere gaps widen to a

---

[17] On the morning of 4 August 1944, SS and Dutch Security Police arrived and arrested the occupants of the Secret Annexe who were subsequently transferred to Westerbork transit camp, then Auschwitz. Anne's Diary had been left among other books and papers scattered on the floor and was eventually handed to her father when he returned home from the death camp.

week – two weeks – three weeks – as much as a month on the three occasions I have counted. Resuming her diary on 14 August 1942, after one such extended break, Anne admits that nothing happened worth mentioning. It is easy to overlook such omissions when the overall impression is of an eager young diarist with too much to tell and too little time to tell it, and her readers see something she could not foresee: the end day, 4 August 1944, when she would be parted from her diary.

Twenty-five years on from that end date (30 September 1969), Gerda left her diary, also never to return. There was no suggestion in her last entry that over thirty years of diaries would end there, without explanation. Bringing Anne into the equation, the similar timescales are intriguing. Gerda's terminal two-year absence from her diaries is the same amount of time it took Anne to write hers from start to finish. Unless there are missing diaries from 1 October 1969 to December 1971, it appears that Gerda had no further use for the safe place, the refuge, or whatever they once provided.

When Otto Frank was given his daughter's diary by Miep (one of the staff assisting the Franks during their two years in hiding), he was already aware that both daughters had died in Bergen-Belsen. A diary is not a daughter, but it 'returned' one of them to him – the Anne he remembered – and there was an unexpected bonus, for alongside her was someone he knew less well, the Anne of the Diary. It 'restored meaning' to his life. Thrilled by the discovery and soon 'obsessed' with it, even he could not have foreseen that it would be translated into sixty languages and that five pages of missing Diary would one day sell for £300,000.

Peter Thornthwaite

There are more than five pages missing from my mother's diaries, though I would not expect them to fetch that much at auction. In fact, entire diaries are missing. As an assiduous reader of highly personal records, I would not compare myself to Otto Frank. Thankfully, after Gerda left Germany and wrote more in English, my mother's thoughts are accessible, but I could not claim anything like the excitement of Otto Frank as he discovered a deeper and more reflective Anne than he remembered. If there are revelations in Gerda's diaries (and sometimes there really are), they were reluctant to announce themselves. Her German diaries predate Anne's by six years. There are points of comparison: both German, born in Germany in the 1920s (Gerda near the beginning of the decade, Anne near the end), both Jewish, both diarists. That was probably the extent of it, though.

Gerda was no Anne Frank. She had an interesting story to tell – indeed, I wouldn't be writing a second book about her if I didn't believe that – but hardly as interesting as Anne's, given their widely differing abilities, temperaments and circumstances. With its background of Holocaust, war, diaspora, Gerda's story might be of occasional interest to people outside the immediate family, though she is hardly the best narrator of it, and unlike Anne's it is not a story ending in a death camp and so lacks the poignancy of a life cut horribly short. So, for all the apparent connections between the two, they appear more unalike than alike.

For two years, 1942-44, Anne Frank was 'in hiding', in the 'Secret Annexe' at the top of her father's business premises in Amsterdam. To suggest that my mother was also 'in hiding', though not in a literal sense, stretches a point, yet such tenuous associations can be the most tenacious. Gerda needed no actual 'Secret Annexe', no 'back house', when she already had one in her diaries. Actually, I could go further and suggest that Gerda had no need of a 'Secret Annexe' since she herself housed one. Anne – outgoing, gregarious, a 'chatterbox', unlike my mother in almost every way – also found in her diary a place where she could be herself, but she was also happy to be with others.

Connections are there to be found if you look for them, so I decided to do what my mother did in her later diaries when uncertain and confused and make a list to clarify things and find a way through. The following, an exact copy of the list heading my notes for this chapter, significantly extends the limited 'points of comparison' above:

- German, from middle-class families.
- Jewish, which in Germany and occupied countries was the only identification that really counted.
- Fled Germany.
- Loved film stars, cinema, and *Gone with the Wind*.
- Loved clothes.
- Preferred father to mother (admittedly, Gerda had no mother to dislike after age six).
- Their fathers preferred them.
- Hated Germans ('no greater enemies on earth', Anne wrote and Gerda thought).
- Inveterate diarists from teenage years (Anne had only two years to establish the habit).

- The secret lives of Anne and Gerda have been revealed only after their deaths.

A Jewish pharmacist, Arthur Lewinsohn, one of several friends enjoying the Franks' Saturday afternoon social gatherings in Amsterdam before they upped and left, was asked to move his equipment into another room when they moved into the Secret Annexe at 263 Prinsengracht. No evidence of any connection with my mother's family, the Lewinsohns of Breslau, has yet emerged, but the name alone is enough to suggest one. A quick internet dip comes up with a 'Stolperstein' (a Memorial Stone) to one Arthur Lewinsohn, deported 3 March 1943, 'murdered in Auschwitz', but as he was deported from Berlin, I assume he wasn't the pharmacist friendly with the Franks, though I can't be sure.

Gerda apparently felt some connection with Anne Frank. I can almost see the famous Diary among the few books lining my mother's shelf in the homemade oak bookcase, next to the Harold Robbins, and I seem to remember her going to the pictures to see the film. Like Anne, she loved movies, followed the stars, and she viewed her life inside a cinematic frame. Also, my mother's diary entries for late 1959 and early 1960 were veined with news of resurgent antisemitism in Germany and Britain, so Anne Frank and connections between their stories could well have been uppermost in her mind then.

Of course, they related to their diaries differently. A bright, vivacious, chatty teenage Anne playfully addresses her diary double as 'Kitty', seeing her as a 'best friend'. For all I know, young Gerda also thought of her diary as a 'friend' who listened patiently, uncritically, accepting the impress of mood and emotion without answering back. Finding herself more friendless in England, maybe she sought one in her diary. It's a reasonable surmise – a diary often functioning, I suppose (never having tried one myself) as an uncritical friend who comes when summoned. 'Don't tell other people your troubles,' my mother wrote in December 1967. 'Keep it all to yourself.' Her diary (her only confidante) remained an exception to that rule. She confided things she could never disclose. But towards the end of the 1960s she was, unfortunately, falling out with her diary too, and by the end of the decade it went the way of other human contacts.

Anne told her diary what she couldn't say outside it, for example how much she disliked her mother. Generally though, she was a cheerful, positive person. She lacked the temperament but also the time and experience to grow into anything like a Gerda. Some differences seem more marked at points of apparent connection. When Anne talked with Peter about the difference between the 'inner' and 'outer' self and her 'mask', my mother sprang to mind. Gerda too had her 'inner' and 'outer' selves, though the thinnest of membranes separated them. Anne explains, in her last 'letter' to Kitty, that it's the 'lighter', 'more superficial' Anne, the joker, the clown, who masks the deeper, 'better' Anne. 'I'm split in two,' she tells Kitty. My mother was also 'split', but not quite as Anne meant. Last impressions overshadow first ones, but it isn't my mother's light and jokey side for which she will be remembered. Young Gerda was probably learning to 'mask' her innermost feelings, but the older mother I recall was an inside-out woman and, if stressed, could have as readily masked her hurt and pain as peel off her face. The deeper Gerda of the diaries she kept from us, and I don't think she ever considered it her 'better' side.

Her brother, Kurt, writing to her from Buenos Aires in May 1939 just as she was leaving, saw from a distance the little girl he remembered and as she had come across in her last 'lovely' letter to him 'from the mountains' – idealistic, overflowing with illusions. That sounds more like Anne Frank. Evidently, my mother once had another lighter, brighter, more hopeful side to her, until the world darkened it.

How many readers, I wonder, have compared or are likely to compare their mothers to Anne Frank. The world has heard about the famous Diary, read it in sixty languages. Eleanor Roosevelt praised it, and of all the voices in history speaking out in times of suffering and loss, John F. Kennedy heard no voice 'more compelling than that of Anne Frank'. Gerda's diaries are known within a circle of one (me) – two, if you count Gerda – and remain a more-or-less private legacy. No one has heard of Gerda in Japan or Germany, and she remains virtually unknown outside her immediate family, and even within that smallest of circles she is now largely forgotten. No German school has been named after her, and I am unaware of any interest from Hollywood.

There is little to connect them, Anne and Gerda, other than persecution and war, heritage and history. As they reveal their inner selves (Anne eagerly, Gerda tardily), they could hardly differ more in character and outlook. If Gerda was 'born happy', she had time (unlike Anne) to grow out of it, and the mother I remember tended not to see the goodness in people, just the opposite. Anne wanted to go on living after her death; Gerda most definitely did not. Anne was joyful and optimistic, Gerda gloomy and pessimistic. Anne felt spring awakening inside her, my mother felt winter. Memories meant more to Anne than dresses. This could not have been said of Gerda, who had no time for memories.

You can tell what sort of person Anne was from the Diary. Even in hiding, with all the restrictions and frustrations of confinement and daily dread of discovery, she displays an ebullient attitude. Lively, energetic, interested, amusing and likeable in her frankest moments – everything, in fact, that my mother was not. And she was as keenly attuned to the outer as to the inner world. Almost from the start, with future readers in mind, Anne provides helpful background information about her parents, family composition and ages, emigration to the Netherlands, father's position as managing director of a Dutch firm, antisemitic decrees after May 1940 and how the Holocaust came to Holland. There is even a detailed description and map of her father's office building and the location of the Secret Annexe. All this helps future readers locate Anne and family in time and place, and this is something Gerda might have considered in her early diaries to assist future readers (such as myself) in mapping her family, its history and rise and fall. She could have saved me a lot of time and trouble. Of course, unlike Anne, she anticipated no future readers. All she ever wanted was a future, and though the same could be said of Anne, it also defines the difference between them. Gerda did have one. Anne, fearful of losing hers any day, longed not to have lived 'for nothing', whereas my mother had no such expectation or hope. Indeed, I think she expected that nothing was exactly what her life amounted to. And in a way she was right.

Had Anne outlived her teenage diary, she could have become more Gerda-like as the future to which she looked forward failed to live up to expectations. She might have survived, as her father did. When Anne Frank died, around early March 1945 (precise date unknown), liberation was just a month away, with British soldiers finding about 67,000 prisoners, most of them half-starved. Had Anne lived, she might have found her way back to her beloved father in Amsterdam and to her unfinished diary and completed it. After the war her Diary might still have been published, her survival no doubt adversely affecting sales and public interest. Not because it was of no interest or relevance to them, but because by the end of the war most people wanted to look forward, not back. Perhaps Dutch people especially turned their backs, given the abnormally high wartime death rate of Jews in the Netherlands and the assiduous participation of some Dutch citizens in gaining that distinction for their country.[18] Anne might have survived and returned from Bergen-Belsen, as her father did from Auschwitz, and picked up the pages of her diary and her life from where she left off. But for her famous Diary to succeed as it did, she had first to die in a Nazi death camp. It is observant, insightful, reflective, full of life and longing, and would be unread and forgotten but for what happened to her after she stopped writing it. It is forever framed by

---

[18] It has been suggested that collaborators with the Nazis facilitated a higher percentage of the country's Jewish population to be killed than in Belgium or France. I have read that, after the war, more than 300,000 Dutch people were investigated as collaborators.

atrocities beyond the diary: a young girl's terrible suffering and death a month from liberation.

When the Hollywood film came out, details of the real end of the Anne Frank story were evidently considered a necessary excision, sparing cinemagoers grisly death-camp scenes while drawing on general public knowledge of the sort of thing that went on in such places without unnecessarily reminding audiences of the actual horror or rubbing their collective face in it. The Anne missing from her own Diary – shaven-headed, naked, emaciated, covered in sores from scabies, 'selected' by Mengele, feverish with typhus – she would have been hard to reconcile with the hopeful innocent at the end of the film looking up through the attic skylight and dreaming herself outside. Death Camp Anne's absence from the film leaves the optimistic Anne of the Diary intact and an inspiration to us all as she looks up at the sky of the attic window, knowing that, 'in spite of everything', people 'are really good at heart'. The Anne of the Diary (not the film) who hated the Germans (though one herself by birth), would have surely excepted the Nazis from that last idealistic generalisation.

If my mother had read the Diary and seen the film, she might have noticed (as I did) the greater prominence of the Yellow Star in the latter. Film is a visual medium, so the repeated focus on that familiar symbol of antisemitism is understandable. It reminds the audience that the occupants of the Secret Annexe, who otherwise appear and act like ordinary people, were uniquely set apart and stigmatised and that the 'Yellow Star' or 'Jewish Badge' enabled immediate identification of difference, segregation, deportation and death. Otto Frank's big Yellow Star stands out against his double-breasted herringbone coat, with another Star revealed on his jacket breast-pocket when he takes off his coat. Young Peter Van Daan (more of a 1950s American teenage rebel in the film than a Dutch Jew) rips off his Star, much to Anne's concern; asked what he then plans to do with it, he savagely replies, 'Burn it!' Anne, more attached to hers, reminds him that 'after all, it is the Star of David'. Needless to say, none of this dialogue is in the written Diary.

After noticing how the film repeatedly draws attention to the six-pointed Yellow Star, I checked the Diary for comparable evidence. Reference to it appears early on, 20 June 1942, when Anne recalls how life had become much more restrictive for Jews, with multiple exclusions and 'anti-Jewish decrees' including the requirement to wear a Yellow Star. In fact the order to do so appeared in Dutch newspapers on 29 April 1942, stating that Jews aged six or over must wear the Star in public, and detailing its exact size and location and the word identifying them. In the Netherlands the word was 'Jood'. After Anne's initial reference to it in the Diary, the Star is seldom seen or mentioned – hardly surprising, since the occupants of the Secret Annexe couldn't go outdoors anyway, so weren't obliged to display it. It's probably something Anne disliked drawing attention to. When she tells 'Kitty' that Mr Dussel the dentist has arrived, she observes that he is asked to remove his coat, thereby covering up the Yellow Star. In the film, however, he wears a Star-less raincoat, which he takes off to reveal a prominent Yellow Star on his dental tunic.

If she did see the film, Gerda might not have noticed such details, including Otto Frank's double-breasted herringbone coat. For me, having once worn a similar one

– genuine British wartime with distinctive zigzag weave and CC41 Utility identifying mark, a real charity-shop find – the herringbone coat has as much a starring role as the Star itself in the film. After they hear a siren, Otto Frank comforts a frightened Anne before removing his coat to go to bed. Later, she's seen wearing it – a visual connection between them and a reminder that their winter is indoors, not outdoors. Interestingly, an almost identical double-breasted herringbone coat is currently displayed behind glass in the Imperial War Museum's Holocaust Galleries, which I visited around the time I watched the Hollywood film of Anne's life on a streaming channel. A father had bought it for his son, who was then about the same age as Anne, buying a coat several sizes too large so that the boy could grow into it. This story instantly connected me with my own memory of a much-loved, vintage double-breasted herringbone coat, which I inexplicably lost, and these are now interwoven with Anne's story and the coat she wears to keep warm in the film.

My maternal grandfather, Elkan – always 'Tatta' to his children – must have worn the Yellow Star for about a month before leaving, as it was a requirement in Germany from 1 September 1941 and he left that October. By then the Nazis had curtailed all Jewish emigration so he was lucky to get out when he did. He was bound for Ecuador, via Cuba, to join his son. Elkan's three-month passage to Quito, the capital, long remained a vexing gap in family history. Despite my previous two years of research, involving the closest scrutiny of extant diary fragments and correspondence from that crucial period, as well as deep internet dives, Elkan's journey was a blank. The name of the ship, its passenger list, exact date and point of departure were missing, whereas Gerda's departure in 1939 is well documented. The internet did reveal that more than twelve hundred ships carrying eleven thousand Jewish refugees arrived in New York between March 1938 and October 1941. The statistics seemed unlikely given the severe restrictions on immigration to the US, and I could find no details of ships from Germany to Cuba after 1940. But leave he did – not for the US, of course, but for somewhere that would have him – and I was relieved to have this confirmed, having long supposed from what my mother said (or rather didn't say) that Tatta stayed in Germany and died in undisclosed circumstances. Recently, however, as I began writing this second book about my mother, I found new information – new, that is, to me.

Rereading Gunther's letter of 30 April 1942, I discovered fresh details of Elkan's momentous journey (see Chapter One, footnote 3). In that landmark letter to his sister, informing her of their father's death, Gunther also disclosed the name of the ship Elkan had boarded – the *Isla de Tenerife* – and the trying circumstances of Tatta's arduous journey from persecution. After discovering what I had somehow overlooked during multiple previous re-readings, I then found more reliable information from the internet about the *Isla de Tenerife* steamship – notably that it was built in 1921, Gerda's birth year. These details partly filled one of the bigger blanks in family history, but of course others remain – such as the two years between Gerda's departure and his own. He was subject to 'daily persecutions', of course, before getting away, but unfortunately, they are nowhere specified other than a relentless pressure to leave. That was, of course, easier said than done. There is no mention anywhere in the surviving family records of the Yellow Star, so it is only supposition that Elkan had to wear one for a while before leaving his once beloved country. As all Jews still in the Reich were required to do so, it was probably Elkan's younger sister – the 'Aunt Bertha' of the letters – who sewed the 'Jude' Star onto his breast, as well as onto her own. Whether she was living with him or close by is unknown, but she was near enough to provide his morning coffee. Sewing the Yellow Star onto his coat was another little service she could do for her distressed brother. If my grandfather actually wore the Yellow Star, if only for a month, I am touched. This isn't just history; this is family history: family connection with some of the worst atrocities in history. Distanced as Gerda then was from their situation, she was surely aware of the tightening restrictions although, having stated this, I begin to doubt it, for I don't know what news trickled down to her, and anyway, she had other distractions at the time, and her father probably avoided mentioning the matter, from shame or humiliation or fear of his letters falling into the wrong hands.

Tatta meant at least as much to Gerda as Otto Frank did to Anne, despite all evidence to the contrary – the 'evidence', that is, of Gerda's diaries. Comparison with the apparently much closer relationship between Anne and her father has reopened for me the vexed subject of Gerda's changing relationship with hers after she left. As ever, the comparison is not in Gerda's favour. The younger girl's affinity with her father never faltered, and being forced apart after arrest and deportation only reinforced it. This was hardly Gerda's situation, but willing to give her the benefit of the doubt and revise former misimpressions, I eventually realised that she never stopped worrying about Tatta in all the months and then years after she had got away. Given my present search for the positives in her life, it was only a matter of time before such insights appeared. It suited me to find that I had yet again got her wrong, misjudged her attitude towards her father. I was primed to read their relationship differently. If she was at fault, then so was he – though that was also understandable in the circumstances. When Tatta wrote that her departure had drained all the light from his life, he appeared to attribute the darkness of his situation to her absence rather than to Nazi Germany. He could see she was having a good time in London and didn't like it. Tatta was in a dark place in his life and he visited it on her.

Gerda naturally had other things to think about: her refugee status and role as a domestic servant in a foreign household, and the more pleasurable but (as it turned out) frustrating and unsatisfying role as a young woman looking for love. Tatta wasn't alone in his disappointment. Gerda was disappointed too. With Joe, she had half-believed she was getting somewhere, in fits and starts, but the 'Big Love' hadn't lived up to expectations and she was on her own again. Yes, Tatta's situation was dire but hers wasn't easy either.

This is all supposition. It was never easy to fathom my mother, alive or dead, but I imagine she adopted a pragmatic approach to Tatta's predicament and did nothing about it, since there was nothing that could be done. She had done more than enough already, getting herself out of a bad place. From necessity she had moved on; got by without a Tatta to make the decisions; found a Joe to love and lose.

Anne and her beloved father were never reunited – at least not until she came back in her diaries. Whether Gerda expected or even wished to meet Tatta again can't be known but, like Otto Frank, he never let go of his beloved daughter. Though Gunther probably kept her apprised of their father's situation and last-minute hairbreadth escape from Germany, there is no written evidence of it. Did Tatta's letter of 20 January 1942 surprise her? Was she kept more in the dark than I realised? Had she been expecting to hear from him any day? But if his short message didn't surprise her, its final question probably did. What had happened to the diamonds? – 'the goods', as he called them from a long habit of secrecy and concealment. At a distance of over 10,000 km from Germany, Elkan still feared the long reach of the Reich. I have considered this matter many times, but never before with Anne Frank and her father in mind. Tatta had not seen Gerda for over two years. Leaving, she had taken the sun with her. Yet the urgent question in his letter is not about his daughter but about something else almost as bright she had taken with her: the diamonds. Were they still in her 'possession'? It was the sort of difficulty Anne never had to face with her father.

When twenty-year-old Gerda opened that letter from Tatta, she might not have seen it as one of the special moments in her life. To me, it is one of those moments when an abyss opened up before her and if she never got to the bottom of it, I will. Again, the comparison with the loving relationship between Anne and Otto Frank appears to show Gerda in a bad light. If she delayed responding to Tatta's last letter and urgent question, it is understandable. As things turned out, it was a sensible and even considerate course of action, for it saved him unnecessary worry and upset before dying, but it leaves the impression of something unresolved between them. Life without Gerda had been dark enough. With the double loss of daughter and diamonds, there would be even less sun for him in Ecuador with his son.

Then it came to me. Unlike Anne, Gerda had time to grow up. Leaving Germany, leaving Tatta, falling in and out of love, enjoying the Blitz, losing or selling the family diamonds, forfeiting her father – she had grown up fast.

Anne Frank died in Bergen-Belsen some months before her sixteenth birthday. In the Diary her love for her father is still the love of a girl. She did not live long enough to leave him or discover how different circumstances can come between daughters and fathers. It is inconceivable that the Anne of the Diary could have written: 'I hate Daddy.' That was inconceivable to Gerda too, a year before she wrote it. What she thought when she got his letter from Quito after a gap in time I can only guess, but a lot had happened since they were last together, and in January 1942 she was almost 21, he nearly 65.

Within a year of the release of *The Diary of Anne Frank* in 1959, my mother was worrying about antisemitism everywhere, while packing her biggest old brown suitcase with belated newspaper accounts of Nazi death camps. Names like Eichmann, Mengele and Himmler were again making Holocaust headline news. So it seems likely that she also saw the film around that time. She liked Audrey Hepburn, who had been asked to play Anne but declined, considering herself too old for the part, but Millie Perkins, who looked like a young Audrey Hepburn, had the same appeal, and my mother saw young Gerda in her. Anne Frank was enjoying another big moment of world attention, with the film winning three Academy Awards, and my mother must have been drawn to it in spite of herself: the subject was still too close for comfort, and to her this wasn't just history, but she couldn't keep away.

Assuming she read the Diary while it was again making news, or saw the film at the cinema, Gerda surely felt a close if uncomfortable connection with Anne, and it is more than coincidence that in her diary for 1960 she revisited her unhappy relationship with her father and felt the shadow of his love again. Like Otto Frank, he had come back for her, but with a vengeance.

For me the underlying connection between Anne and Gerda is undeniable, despite all the differences of character and circumstance. Gerda got away. Anne didn't. The Wannsee Conference was still three years away when Gerda left for England. During her last year in Breslau, things had been bad enough for the family, but not nearly as bad as they would be for the Franks from 1942. The date of Gerda's arrival in London, 12 June, was also the date of Anne Frank's first diary entry, although Anne's was written three years later. The Diary, which Anne had time to write but not to finish, is so shaped and contained by its historical circumstances, so complete in its incompleteness, that it is hard to imagine further diaries (had she survived) adding anything to it. She enjoyed growing up but lacked the opportunity to continue doing so. Anne was still fifteen at Bergen-Belsen and she stopped at that age. Gerda stopped at the age of fifty. It is difficult to think of Anne going the way of Gerda, but then my mother had more time to go to pieces and out of her mind. She also had more time to heap blame on herself for past sins. 'Dear God, I know I have been wicked, especially to my father and Aunt Bertha', she admitted on 4 January 1960. What she singled out for special censure, she didn't clarify, but it was evidently to do with having a carelessly good time in London, going out to 'movies, theatre, dance etc', and not answering those letters from home while Tatta and Aunt Bertha were housebound and unvisited except by the Gestapo. 'Wicked'? My mother was always too hard on herself. As she turned eighteen, safely out of Germany, in London and in love, it was impossible to suppress her natural exuberance. She knew what was happening to Tatta, but it wasn't something for her diary, and it took her another twenty years to find a place for it.

CHAPTER FIVE:

'DER WEISSE ENGEL'

Within a decade or so of her death, Anne Frank was being idealised, even in Germany, where in 1957 over two thousand teenagers walked to Bergen-Belsen to remember her because she died 'for all of us'. Hollywood's reinvention of her starts with Anne opening a box of collectible film star cards as well as a new diary on her thirteenth birthday. An apt opening scene (I made a note of it) for a girl destined for film stardom herself. Anne Frank had finally arrived, albeit posthumously, at a celluloid presence unimaginable to her on 12 June 1942 when her diary begins. In the film, towards the end of her life, Anne refers to 'the miracle happening in her body as 'a sweet secret'. She is almost a woman, yet young enough for her ideals to remain intact and to believe in the essential goodness of people. Before arrest and deportation (off-screen) Anne invites us all to 'Look at the sky. Isn't it lovely?'

It is at Auschwitz-Birkenau that the Anne outside the Diary meets another legend of the Holocaust who, for different reasons, would also long outlive himself: Josef

Mengele. Actually, it is misleading to say that she 'meets' him, since apparently the doctor, being well-practised in his work and with an eye for the interestingly abnormal, had no need to look closely at individuals during the selections and he could hardly single her out from among the 400,000 nameless people who passed before him during the best two years of his life . To some observers, he appeared dispassionate, as one might expect of such an educated and cultured man, impersonally involved in a process necessary to the advancement of the race and vital to his career and professional prestige.

Mengele was remembered for the barely perceptible movement of a white-gloved hand indicating right or left. Life or death. He was there as usual (September 1944) when cattle trucks bearing the Frank family and others arrived at Auschwitz-Birkenau, and again, end of October, for a further selection (involving Anne and her sister) in the women's camp. Had Anne Frank survived the two death camps and returned to Amsterdam, as her father did, and picked up her Diary from where she left off, it would be interesting to know what she made of Doctor Mengele; how she would have described him with his black SS unform, good looks, the elegance of a man in control, and the white-gloved hand of a conductor.

There is another link, admittedly slight, connecting the two. Anne's family came from Frankfurt. It was where she was born, on 12 June 1929, and where Mengele received his medical degree and joined the Institute for Hereditary Biology and Racial Hygiene. His subsequent 'research' at Auschwitz-Birkenau served the Aryan ideal, of which he was considered an exemplar. When Mengele joined the SS, he declined a 'blood-mark sign' (to confirm his Aryan blood had been vetted), being 'too vain' and too certain of his superiority to need one.

Mengele would have disagreed with nearly everything subsequently written about him – except his legacy as 'the right man in the right place at the right time'. Auschwitz-Birkenau was heaven-sent, an ideal setting for his interests and the specialised medical research that could only benefit from the vast living laboratory at his disposal: one in which he had untrammelled choice, an almost endless supply and range of patients, and unrestricted freedom to do whatever he wanted to advance Nazi medical science unrestrained by medical ethics. Though 'subhuman', the numerous subjects of Mengele's 'experiments' were evidently human enough to give credence and validity to the knowledge gained from multiple amputations, planned infections, vivisections, and the injections that included turning children's eyes blue with methylene dye. It is well known that twins were his area of special expertise. Normally in short supply to a genetic researcher like Mengele, if they could be found anywhere in plentiful, replenished numbers, and from more than one source – Jew or Romani or disabled – it would be Auschwitz-Birkenau. Some of his 'patients' appear in photographs taken shortly before dying from experiments, starvation, infection, or gas. He could do anything he chose: clear camp infections by eliminating the infected; operate on twins in an attempt to join them together. One twin was sewn to the other, back-to-back. For such services to science, Mengele was awarded the War Merit Cross, to add to his other medals for bravery.

It has been pointed out that Mengele was only one of many Nazi doctors involved in such selections and medical input. Also, that he gained distinction through his devotion to duty and 'frequent presence on the ramp where selections took place', and that even when he was not on 'selection duty', he was there anyway, on the lookout for twins and specimens with visible deformities. Though sometimes appearing aloof and dispassionate, bestowing little attention on any one individual link in the chain of queues, he was also remembered for his smart attire in neatly pressed uniform and gleaming boots, and for conducting the selections with a flamboyant air, often smiling and whistling classical tunes. These snapshots of Mengele suggest a man who was there because, really, he could think of no better place to be, who enjoyed what he was doing and was totally relaxed about it, while ever on the alert, of course, for something curious enough to catch his eye. Another Mengele was always there, too, less visible perhaps to those on the receiving end, but one he himself never lost sight of or ceased to regard: the dedicated doctor, the brilliant researcher who, though he had been here many times before on the ramp, could hardly believe his good fortune in having endless opportunities to advance his own career and reputation while working for the greater good and thousand-year future of the Reich.

There is, too, yet another Mengele, as remembered by some survivors. No frigid, imperious, sadistic 'doctor of death', but 'Uncle Mengele', who gave the children chocolate and sweets before injecting and slicing them. They feared him but some also responded to the kind and sympathetic bedside manner. It might have been genuine, this other side of Mengele, and it might have amused him to assume the face of a doctor recognising a common humanity and dispensing kindness and comfort as he stood by the beds of his little patients, reassuring them before operating, often without anaesthetic. Mengele was a sensible enough doctor, I imagine, to avoid unduly alarming or distressing children about to be infected or injected, cut up or killed. And for him, this was science, not sadism: through him, they could be of assistance to the advancement of the German Reich. Unlike another Nazi luminary, Franz Stangl, Commandant of Treblinka, who saw the children of the camp as a 'huge mass' and 'rarely as individuals', Mengele in his role as doctor and scientist got up close and personal when the situation demanded it. Perhaps his sympathy, if real, for his victims was that he had the foresight to see that, though they themselves were unworthy of life, with the help of his medical expertise and vision they could still make an important contribution to the betterment of the race.

Every so often I watch *The Wizard of Oz* – my go-to film when I need a little 'Oz' in my life, as well as a pleasant way of combining escapism with necessary research. I mention it now because, when I last played the DVD, it reminded me of Mengele. An internet article I came across recently compared the Oz of the film to the United States of Donald Trump. It likened Trump in his 'Tower' to the Wizard in his Emerald City. *The Wizard of Oz* was released late August 1939, shortly before Chamberlain's declaration of war with Germany. If the film had been available to German cinema audiences following its release, they might have seen Hitler in the Wizard, for both could be viewed as miracle-makers. At his height then, Hitler was regarded in his own country as 'great and powerful' – not just by words but deeds 'because of the wonderful things he does'. Having already performed miracles at home, in 1939 he had yet more to perform abroad. And this is where Mengele comes in, for as I watched Judy Garland singing and dancing among the Munchkins before following the 'yellow brick road' with her straw, tin and leonine companions in search of the only man capable of helping them, it occurred to me that the good doctor could also be seen as the Professor Marvel/Wizard of his own magical time and place.

It is unlikely that Josef Mengele saw this or any other Hollywood movie available to Goebbels, or that he would have recognised himself in the Wonderful Wizard, yet the comparison with the doctor is still more compelling than with Hitler. In the film, the Wizard is a kind of doctor, supplying the Scarecrow with a brain and the Tin Man with a heart, and Mengele also dealt in body parts. In the film the Wizard makes much of testimonials and awards, and Mengele had his fair share of them, including the War Merit Cross for his experimental work, free of medical and moral constraints, at Auschwitz. There he enjoyed, in his version of the Emerald City, the unassailable power and authority of the Wizard, and now that I think about it there is even a suggestion of Oz in the first two letters of the Polish name for Auschwitz: Oswiecim. To Simon Wiesenthal, who later hunted him, Mengele's name 'was known throughout our world'.[19] With his neatly pressed uniform, gleaming boots, white-gloved hands and baton, Mengele certainly had presence. He was noticed; he could

---

[19] See P. 234 in *Nazi Hunter, The Wiesenthal File* (2002), Alan Levy, Robinson, London.

not fail to be noticed. Among all the death camp doctors, he stood out. Decades later, Auschwitz survivors could still see him standing there. He was a more visible and commanding presence than the Wizard, who hid behind a curtain. In Auschwitz-Birkenau no such concealment was needed, and by the time the 'curtain' was whisked away to expose the reality, Mengele had also whisked himself away to a life under cover. But he always had fond memories of the death camp and had he seen the film later, during his post-Auschwitz career, the little Munchkins (though only 124 of them) might have reminded him of the place he had never really left. It is known that Mengele 'adored midgets and dwarfs' and he couldn't have been more delighted (except by twins) when a transport delivered a family of them 'from a circus in Budapest' complete with their 'miniature furniture'. He evidently had a soft spot for such little people, letting them slowly bleed to death in relative luxury. The Munchkins of the film, had he watched it, would have evoked pleasant memories, and it might also have amused Mengele to learn that they were paid less than Dorothy's little dog, Toto.[20]

Anne Frank had two years of life in the Secret Annexe. Mengele also had two years to make a name for himself. Two years for legends to be made: very different legends (they could hardly be more different). Much can be achieved in two years by the right people in the right circumstances, and their sudden absence – Anne from her Diary, Mengele from Auschwitz – added to the legend.

---

[20] Actors playing the Munchkins were reportedly each paid $50 per week, while Toto (and his trainer) were paid $125.

His was the more intriguing disappearance since he was still living, somewhere – here, there, anywhere he could be sighted – only to vanish again when they closed in. Anne's was more final, though her death was also the beginning of an illustrious if posthumous career. Mengele's disappearance was the ending of his, though that didn't stop him making a name for himself as the war criminal who got away. Anne Frank would be mourned and missed for years to come. One could hardly say the same for Mengele. His heyday was behind him, but not his reputation. *Der Todesengel* or *der weisse Engel*, as he was nicknamed, became as infamous, as legendary for his absence after Auschwitz-Birkenau as he had been for his former distinguished presence there.

For a man like Mengele, who occupied his time and place with such panache and made the most of it with the plentiful opportunities provided by the Holocaust, it must have been a bitter disappointment to be forced to spend the rest of his life after the war in hiding. After two illustrious years at the cutting edge of medical research, not to be there, never to be there again, must have been hard for a man of his reputation and gifts. From a recently viewed TV documentary and multiple internet sources, I have pieced together facts about Mengele's subsequent career, yet found little about how he himself viewed his life after Auschwitz-Birkenau and the drastic downturn in his fortunes. He left the death camp and his black SS uniform behind in January 1945, disguised as a Wehrmacht officer, and was twice arrested that year under his own name by American troops who (luckily for him) failed to select him for interrogation because he had no identifying Nazi 'blood-mark' tattoo. With a new identity, the first of many aliases, the disappearing doctor, disguised as an agricultural worker planting and harvesting potatoes, went into hiding at a farm in Bavaria for three years, while his wife willingly became a widow and his family faked his death with a funeral mass.

Helped by his family, the 'doctor of death' was erasing his identity with the same determination he had shown at Auschwitz-Birkenau when making a name for himself, a name to be remembered.

In 1949, under a new alias and inconspicuous among the millions of displaced persons throughout Europe, Mengele left for Buenos Aires aboard the *North King*. He found work first as a carpenter, then a salesman for his father's farm machinery business, also finding time, it appears, to practise medicine without a licence, including abortions. His later impersonations included becoming himself again – in 1956 obtaining a passport in his own name from the German Embassy in Buenos Aires, without difficulty. Armed with his own identity, Mengele was then confident enough to visit Europe. No doubt he was missing home and family, and if being introduced to his son, Rolf, as 'Uncle Fritz' seemed odd even to him, it went some way to restoring what he had lost. Behind this and other post-Auschwitz aliases, Mengele was, it seems, looking for family, and during that visit home he also met his sister-in-law and wife to be, Martha, in an idyllic Alpine setting. Things were looking up.

Of course, I am omitting much from this cursory account of his later life in my impatience to reveal what interests me most about Mengele. There were more aliases to come, more reinventions, more assistance from Nazi sympathisers in South America. Mengele's years 'in hiding' stretched to thirty-four – unlike Anne Frank's two. And unlike the naked, nameless girl who passed before him in one of his many 'selections', Mengele had Argentina, Paraguay and Brazil to confine him, not secret rooms in an old warehouse annexe. When Eichmann was abducted outside his home in Buenos Aires in 1959, Nazi hunters hoped to catch Mengele too; he was no longer there but in Paraguay, protected by his new nationality. It seems that, whenever history closed in on him, Mengele – like 'Macavity the mystery cat' in T. S. Eliot's poem – wasn't there.

His elusiveness and absence only heightened his stature, though it appears that physically he fell short of the blond, blue-eyed Aryan ideal. As narrated in that TV documentary about him, he was once 'spotted' in Brazil, out walking by the farm where he lived with a family; the man suspected to be Mengele was described as an 'Austrian-German, 6' 3" tall'. Another Mengele look-alike was seen, with his binoculars and 'fourteen to fifteen dogs', climbing hills north of Sao Paulo, scouring the area for Nazi-hunters. Such sightings give the impression of a tall man of powerful and imposing build, if also a little paranoid. Yet, according to 'Nazi-hunter' Simon Wiesenthal, Mengele was actually of medium height and build, dark, with eyes 'like Peter Sellers'.[21] His skeletal remains, when finally unearthed and examined following what was referred to as his 'seventh death' (having 'died' so often before), revealed a man about 5'8" tall. My height, in fact. So, it seems that even at his peak, in his element at Auschwitz–Birkenau where he was having the time of his

---

[21] See P. 242 in *Nazi Hunter* (as previous). Wiesenthal described Mengele as 'a small, swarthy, dark-haired man'.

life and growing daily in stature as an SS doctor of distinction and servant of the Reich, Mengele was missing the very attributes belonging to the Aryan superman. Yet his subsequent absence was also the making of him.

There is little enough to connect Mengele with Anne Frank, other than during 'selections', when he no more noticed her than any other Jew passing before him, and his two-year career was the reverse of hers. While she remained in hiding, Mengele was on show. There wasn't much to occupy a lively and articulate teenager besides writing a diary, which she must have assumed only she was ever likely to read, while he was free to do whatever he liked and establish a reputation that could only flourish beyond even his expectations. When Mengele left Auschwitz-Birkenau as its function and his were coming to an end, it was his turn to go into 'hiding', and it was then that Anne came out in ways Mengele could hardly have foreseen when the nameless fifteen-year-old girl passed by unseen and unremembered. I sometimes wonder if, in his many years on the run, he ever heard about Anne Frank and her posthumous fame, and if so, whether he reflected rather bitterly on their reversal of fortunes. Of course, he could not have recalled her – an undernourished anonymous girl filing past, just one of the many bodies to pass briefly under his dispassionate gaze. That somebody like her should be so feted and famous, a global name, while he hid behind an ageing mask of a face, bush of a moustache, and string of aliases, and had to deny and disown the more questionable aspects of his own past when his son probed him about them, could not have been foreseen.

Nor could Mengele have foreseen – for all his vision of a glorious *Judenfrei* future, to which his own racial research robustly contributed – that in a different future, far beyond even his conception, a company with offices in major European cities would be advertising something that would have surely appealed to him in life after Auschwitz. 'We erase your past' is a tagline to catch the Mengeles of the world. According to an article in *The Guardian*, this company specialises in providing a 'deep clean' of damaging internet information including 'mistaken identity'. Like its many current clients, Mengele might have benefited from such erasure. If anybody needed a complete clean-up, it was the *Todesengel*. As for the company's promise – eliminate the past to rebuild the future – it could have had Mengele specifically in mind. Since this useful service was unavailable in his day, all he could do was deny everything – as he did in conversation with his son Rolf, who had come from Frankfurt to South America in 1977 to meet and find out a bit more about his long-absent dad. Mengele was a surgeon, he told his son, like any other in a field hospital; the purpose of 'selections' was simply to identify those capable of work; as for the three thousand twins that passed through his hands, they owed their lives to him. The infamous doctor of death and Mengele were not the same person, as a trusting son should have known without having to ask.

A year before his son's visit, Mengele 'starred' in an American film, *Marathon Man* (1976). It is unlikely that he saw it or would have recognised himself in the fictional Nazi war criminal Christian Szell, as portrayed by Laurence Oliver. The title refers to the Dustin Hoffman character, Babe Levy, who is seen running at key moments of the film, but Mengele himself could also be considered a 'marathon man', given his many years on the run. Though the character of the dentist and diamond-lover, Szell, with his concealed retractable knife, was based on the 'Doctor of Death', Mengele would have doubtless viewed Szell as a grotesque and vulgar distortion and debasement of himself. *Der weisse Engel* had done what he could, in the time allowed, to perfect the race, and he had expected to be thanked and honoured as one who decided his own destiny and helped shape the world. It must have been a bitter moment for the doctor when his son visited him and he had to deny his once-great mission in life. Following the release of *Marathon Man*, Mengele had only three years to go – or nine, if you count his six posthumous years still (apparently) on the run.

To mark the fortieth anniversary (1985) of the liberation of Auschwitz-Birkenau, Mengele was tried 'in absentia' in Jerusalem. He had in fact already died in 1979, following a heart attack or stroke which left him paralysed and flopping in the sea off the coast of Brazil. Holidaying with a family, the Bossards, he had gone for a swim to cool off, when one of the children noticed something was amiss with 'Uncle'. But they were too late to save the most infamous of the Nazi war criminals never to be tried.

The description of Mengele's eyes as they appeared during that last sighting of him – 'fixed and staring' - suggests a fitting end for a doctor who had lined a wall of his laboratory at Auschwitz-Birkenau with human eyes 'classified by colour' and 'pinned like butterflies'.

When tried 'in absentia', Mengele was still, as far as the world knew, in hiding, his death a secret except to family and a few faithful friends. Simon Wiesenthal was still hunting him, and 'sightings' of the most elusive of Nazi war criminals continued unchecked by his actual demise. Remarkably, Mengele was hunted for six years following his death and did not emerge from hiding until 1985, when his skeletal remains were discovered in another man's grave. It was a year also memorable for the discovery of other legendary remains – those of the *Titanic* seventy-three years after it sank in the North Atlantic.

I was thinking about Mengele during a recent visit (early 2023) to the Holocaust Galleries of the Imperial War Museum. My mother, too, was on my mind (when is she not?) as she had sometimes remembered the Elephant and Castle from her wartime years and I had once gone back there with her in 1968, just the two of us, for an unplanned outing the more memorable for its spontaneity and exclusion of other family.

That Mengele was absent from his own trial was only to be expected of a man who had built a second career on not being where he was supposed to be and never at any of the places in which definite 'sightings' of him had been reported. Had he been caught by Nazi hunters and brought to trial – like Eichmann and Stangl – the fascination with him as one of the looming faces of the Holocaust and the limitless horrors of Nazism would have survived, but there is no doubt that his evasions and disappearing acts from 1945 until his exhumation forty years later added to it. And forty-five years after his death people still search for him online.

Mengele remained at the back of my mind when I visited the Galleries, for earlier that morning I had also searched for him on the many internet sites where he can now be found. The Imperial War Museum opened in June

1920, a year before Gerda was born, but the Holocaust Galleries opened over a century later, in October 2021, fifty years after her death. It was with no expectation of glimpsing so much as a ghost of her Breslau girlhood that I wandered through the connecting rooms, pausing to wonder where and how she fitted in; looking for connections; visiting her pre-war Germany and imagining it through her eyes. I couldn't help remembering my last sightings of her, around Christmas 1971, when my mother lay inert and unresponsive in a narrow hospital bed. Led there by a nurse who suggested I try speaking to the body as 'she might be able to hear you', I thought at first that she was showing me the wrong woman, a case of mistaken identity.

Mengele's fugitive life reminded me of hers. It might seem perverse to look for and find connections between Mengele and my mother, yet their situations were not entirely unalike. Both in permanent exile from the countries of their birth. Both mortally afraid of being 'found out' for who they really were, especially in their later years. Mengele had good reason to be afraid. For him, having his true identity revealed meant arrest, deportation, trial and likely execution. After years on the run his appearance, as his son observed when they met again after a gap of twenty-one years, was that of 'a broken man', a 'scared creature'.

Of course, my mother was never 'on the run' or literally 'in hiding'. For most of the post-war years she lived on the edge of Oxford as an 'English' housewife and mother. And if she was at all unusual, it was her immersive interest in jumble sales and charity shops, and her eventual collection of over a hundred suitcases stuffed with old clothes, that marked her out as 'different'. It is only now that I more clearly see how history affected and veined her life to the end. No, she was not remotely like Mengele, but she also had a big secret to hide and, looking back, I see the fear of exposure in her eyes.

Her last diary entry (30 September 1969) was 'that doctor is trying to kill me', but she was evidently referring to another doctor. The only explicit link between them is the newspaper cutting circa 1960 concerning Mengele and the boys on the football pitch at Auschwitz-Birkenau, which she kept in that large brown suitcase with other newspaper reminders of the Holocaust.

Yet connect them I do. History has strangely brought together two people who were in almost every way the utter antithesis of one another. As Mengele concealed a past identity which, if revealed, would be the downfall and death of him, so my mother concealed hers as a shameful secret which, if it ever got out, would also mean the end. Not that Mengele was ashamed of his past; just the opposite. Probably he reflected on the irony of his situation: the highest authority and most advanced ideology, which had so praised and awarded him for work done to advance the Aryan state, and elevated him to such prominence, had given way to a new world order where, reviled and hunted, he hid and lived in daily fear of discovery. The man at the top of his game had become game.

Mengele feared exposure as an infamous Nazi, my mother as a Jew. She considered her inner Jewishness as a fatal inheritance, an underlying identity at risk of raw exposure once the outer layers of 'English' wife and mother were peeled away. Revisiting her early 1960s diaries is like entering the world according to Gerda (though she wasn't wrong about its antisemitism) and finding how profoundly she had internalised antisemitism and turned it against herself, castigating her past 'wickedness' and pleading with God to 'turn the Jews into good people so they don't get so disliked'.

Reflecting on my earlier attempt to track Gerda down through diaries and letters, I realised that (like Mengele) she keeps disappearing from her own life. The paper evidence suggests that she tore out more diary pages than she retained, and I can only regret that she discarded so much of her inner self. In a speech from 1940, Hans Frank, the Governor General of occupied Poland, who (unlike Mengele) was tried and executed for his crimes, asked 'nothing of the Jews except that they should disappear'. Yes, I thought to myself, that's what Gerda did. It took her a while to complete the job, but she got there in the end.

She could not have foreseen that her 'remains' (the 'written remains' of diaries and letters) would surface, like Mengele's bones, and suffer such prolonged examination. It is one of the ironies inherent in remembering my mother in not just one but two books about her, that her loving son (no irony intended) would exhume and go through them with a fine-tooth comb. After all his years on the run, Mengele had six years of posthumous respite and rest, disappearing entirely from view before being dug up and identified as himself. My mother had fifty posthumous years of peace before I pulled her old brown suitcases out from under my bed, opened them up and turned her whole life inside-out. If Mengele was finally 'unmasked', his real identity revealed following exhumation and DNA analysis of his skeletal remains, it could be said that, by looking into her history and heredity, I have done the same for Gerda, whose story did not disappear with her as she wished.

There is one last thing worth mentioning about Mengele which has some relevance to my mother. Once analysed for DNA identification and confirmation of identity, his bones were left unclaimed inside a blue plastic bag in Sao Paulo's Legal Medical Institute. The doctor leading the team that identified Mengele in 1985 saw an opportunity some thirty years later to put them to good use in forensic medical courses. Doctor Mengele was finally assisting medical science, though not in a way he might have foreseen or approved. Nor could my mother have foreseen my use of her 'written remains', and though I don't suppose that she'd have approved of what I have been getting up to in her absence, I think some good will come of it in the end.

If such 'connections' occurred to me as I wandered through the Holocaust Galleries during that repeat visit a year ago, I don't recall, though I see from the notes I made at the time that I was trying to track her down. Opening the black A4 notebook, which records highlights of my visit to the Nazi Germany of her teenage years and the history she kept from us, I come to my notes concerning the public notices outside population centres throughout the Third Reich as antisemitism gripped the nation:

Wir wollen keine Juden sehen – We don't want to see Jews

Juden haut ab – Jews go away

Juden sind hier erwunscht – Jews are not welcome here

Though such notices were ubiquitous, my mother never mentioned them (or any other distinctive feature of the Reich) or referred to them in her diaries; yet she could not have missed them. Gerda was a girl then, and Germany was still her country, and it must have been difficult to adjust to the new reality, so perhaps she looked away and hoped for the best.

That I was also thinking of Anne Frank during my visit is evident from the initials *A.F* repeated in the margins of the black notebook, and as I have Anne's Diary readily to hand these days, and because something has just now occurred to me that urgently needs checking, I flick through it to July 1943. That day in Amsterdam, the occupants of the 'Secret Annexe' were discussing Anne's eyes and her need to see a specialist. The thought of 'going outside' and 'walking down the street' petrified the girl at first, but then she felt 'glad'. There is nothing like this, I reflect, in Gerda's German diaries – apart from that one stand-out entry of 13 February 1939, with its reminder (as if she needed reminding) that first thing tomorrow (*Morgen - fruh*) she has an appointment with the Gestapo. The day of the appointment comes and goes in Gerda's diary without description or comment. Anne Frank could have written pages about such an experience, if marked in her Diary, telling 'dearest Kitty' all about her encounter with the Gestapo in chilling and graphic detail, for she was as much an observer of others and the world outside herself as of the world awakening within. Gerda was no Anne Frank.

On 15 April 1945, the British Army entered the camp at Bergen-Belsen, and I see that this date is asterisked in the black notebook alongside a note to self that by mid-April Anne Frank and her sister Margot were already a month dead. A contemporary 'Sketch of Belsen' by war artist Bryan de Grineau, who worked for *The Illustrated London News*, might have included the sisters in his sketch had he arrived a month earlier, as it was done in one of the camp's women's sections whose starved inmates were 'just alive'.

Information boards in the Holocaust Galleries apprise visitors of the extent to which the Nazis attempted to conceal their programme of mass murder and 'cover up what they had done', by dismantling camps, burning millions of documents, and making Jewish prisoners (afterwards murdered) empty the mass graves and burn all the bodies, with any remaining bone fragments crushed in grinders. Despite the Nazis' best efforts to erase history, the liberated camps provided ample photographic evidence and film footage of what the Nazis had achieved – including the image of a blackened skull lifting up its head as if staring at the camera through empty eye sockets.

Returning from the Holocaust Galleries by the Northern line, under the City to Euston, I sat back, tired after visiting the Holocaust but satisfied that I had made good use of my time there as a 'researcher' with a more than academic interest in such matters. Possibly I was thinking of those other trains and tracks and enlarged black-and-white photographs of long queues of people at a transit camp waiting for the night train to Auschwitz–Birkenau. Perhaps I was also remembering lines from the last letter a woman wrote to her husband while she waited there, with her youngest son, for the order to board the trucks, when a female voice interrupted my dark reverie with the announcement: "This station is Angel. This is a Northern line train terminating at Morden."

Angel. Engel in German. Mengele, *der Todesengel*. Mengele, der weisse Engel. Incredibly I had not, until that moment, made the connection between 'angel' and the 'engele' tucked inside Doctor Mengele's name, hiding in plain sight with its darkly folded wings. My discovery was duly noted and marked with a double asterisk, and just as the train was leaving the station I added the further observation that 'Morden' is German for murder.

CHAPTER SIX:

SORRY

One of the things I noted while visiting the Holocaust Galleries was part of a speech given in October 1943 by Heinrich Himmler, Reichsfuhrer of the SS, second only to Hitler and so-called architect of the 'Final Solution':

"This we will never refer to in public. I mean the evacuation of the Jews, the extermination of the Jewish people. And to have withstood this – apart from some exceptions due to human weakness – to have remained decent has made us tough, and is a glorious chapter that is never mentioned and never will be mentioned."[22]

It is the final phrase that interests me. The 'Final Solution', the 'elimination' of six million Jews in Europe (more if the Nazis had won), is a 'glorious chapter' in German history yet must never be mentioned, never openly acknowledged. Instead of boasting of their achievement, they must say nothing and behave as if it never happened. What Himmler does proudly acknowledge is that achieving extermination on such a

---

[22] From speech by Himmler, 4 October 1943, to high-ranking SS officers. Himmler acknowledged the character-building challenges involved in genocide.

scale can only be character-building and that only people like themselves could do it and remain 'decent'.

It never sank in until I read her diaries how much my mother internalised the Holocaust – which she had, after all, escaped. Perhaps this was because, like Himmler (though obviously for different reasons), she never mentioned it. There was one notable exception to her rule of silence on certain subjects: when she once let us stay up late (way past our bedtime) to watch what I now recognise as documentary footage of the 'liberation' of Nazi death camps. It wasn't the television treat I was expecting, but (reversing the usual order of things) she was the one who insisted we stay up and follow the camera past various heaps of things to the heap of bodies at the end.[23] That alone was odd enough – not just letting but *making* us stay up late – for it to have embedded itself amid earliest memories. She didn't refer to it the next day or ever again, as if it had never happened. The words 'Holocaust' and 'Jew' never passed her lips in my hearing; not that they would have meant anything anyway. I have since learned that she once told my elder sister, 'Never tell anyone you're a Jew.' She had no need to tell me because I didn't know I was one, and remained untroubled by my hidden inheritance. Indeed, I don't think my sister knew

---

[23] In 1945 the Allies filmed the liberation of the Nazi camps, with 8000 ft of footage submitted from eleven camps, but it was so shocking that it was shelved. According to Alfred Hitchcock, who was involved in the filming, 'Nobody wanted to see it.' That went for me, too, that memorable but mostly forgotten evening in the late '50s, when we were allowed to stay up late to watch television. After more than six decades I barely recall the documentary. What I mostly recall is my mother's insistence that we stay up and watch it to the end as something never to forget.

it either, until she was told not to tell anyone. Being secret; something to hide; shameful, it evidently stuck in her memory. Looking back, I see now that suicide was my mother's definitive way of having nothing more to say on the subject, though there appeared no obvious connection between her Jewishness and her sense of difference, exclusion.

In the few explicit diary entries on the subject, there is a palpable sense of being ostracised, avoided, disliked because different. Paranoid? Perhaps. But she didn't just imagine women crossing the street when they saw her coming, or invariably interpret their words (when they did speak) as insult and abuse. The later entries record all the nasty things people (including me) said to her. Had she diarised her life to the bitter end, she might have recorded more evidence of the world turning against her, and I would have welcomed this, for I wanted to uncover everything that distressed her. It was a big disappointment that the last entry, 30 September 1969 (oddly coinciding with my eighteenth birthday) predates her death by over two years. She was again withholding things I needed to know, though it must hurt me to discover them. I have often wondered why she stopped writing a diary. Perhaps because it was a refuge from nothing, an unsafe place, where even she had turned against herself. Her loss was mine too, because I dearly wanted to know everything, however bad – indeed, the worse the better, for only then would I get at the truth.

If a diary is a mirror, reflecting the inner as well as the outer person, she increasingly disliked both. That became more apparent in the late 1950s, when she observed that her hair 'was getting thinner than ever' – she could 'hardly hide the baldness in front' – and wondered 'how long it will take before I have to wear a wig'. That year she also noted that she couldn't get used to her new teeth ('they still feel a mouthful and make me sick'), and at the age of thirty-six, she was 'really growing old with a vengeance'. Around this time, the hand-drawn hairless heads with horns and a scribble for a face make their first appearance, floating free of words, and she was drawing herself, for under one such doodled head she had written: 'That's the devil in me.'

Antisemitism was soon rearing its ugly head in her diary:

There is more antisemitism in Germany. I don't think there will ever be an end to it. Only hope it doesn't happen here. (January 1960)

It did, in the shape of Colin Jordan, second 'World Fuhrer', who enters her diary, 20 August 1962; it took a while to clarify and confirm the date because my mother (as if anticipating my future intrusions into her life and setting little traps for me) reused an earlier and almost empty 1958 Timothy White diary for 1961 and 1962 entries.

The 1960s diaries, though often repetitive, tedious and mundane as a record mainly of what she bought (her 'bargains' and 'blowflies', as she described them), nonetheless absorbed me, for they always reflected her state of mind and I could sometimes glimpse her face ghosting the glass. Then there were those other revelations in the piles of newspaper cuttings from the late 1950s and early 60s. Having written at length about this Holocaust hoard, I won't repeat myself, except to say that they all concerned what went on in the Nazi death camps. The actual horrors exposed (as though for the first time) in newspaper headlines fifteen years after the event weren't the revelation. It was the fact that my mother had devoted so much time and trouble selecting and cutting out those headlines and articles before packing them away in suitcases for posterity. The big story was the trial of Adolf Eichmann in Jerusalem in 1961. Mengele, the good doctor of Auschwitz, also put in an appearance. Without having to go back to the suitcase of cuttings to refresh my memory, I still recall that article about the doctor describing how he had a plank nailed across a goal in a field at Auschwitz-Birkenau to decide those, among the two thousand boys paraded there, short enough for the gas chamber that day. A good half were selected.

Gerda had a lot on her mind as she entered a decade more often remembered for changes, innovations... the focus on the future. For my mother, the 1960s would be all about the past and history repeating itself. She had other things, too, on her mind – like the further depredations of age, and there was no concealing them. Hiding the Jew in her was also more difficult. Days into the new decade, it wasn't just ageing that advanced with a vengeance. By 4 January, the sounds of *Kristallnacht* were returning with 'windows broken, the whole business starting all over again', and she blamed herself, believing that 'God' was punishing her for past sins. By 10 January, she couldn't 'believe that the Jews are all evil', but she seemed to doubt her own disbelief. Gerda had escaped the Nazis twenty-one years earlier, but they hadn't forgotten and were coming back for her.

Not Drowning but Waving

It is 2023 and I am revisiting the 1960s, or rather her 1960s, a different and much darker decade than the one I remember – not for pleasure, but because it has to be done to check if I overlooked anything important when I first read her diaries two years ago. Self-disclosure is what I'm after – the darker the better, for where darkness collects in her diaries, there she is to be found – and I know from previous readings that it collects on certain dates more than others. 9 October 1968 is one such instance. That was the day she bought me a second-hand transistor radio – for which I remain grateful but don't recall despite the diary reminder. Like many of her other hopeful purchases, the radio turned out to be not the 'bargain' she hoped for but a 'blowfly'. 'Must atone for it,' she wrote – not a word often associated with second-hand transistor radios – and it is where the darkness in her again gathers. By the close of 1968, she had sinned repeatedly in the second-hand shops of Oxford. Another date stands out, 4 December, for its verdict on other 'bad buys' (chipped glassware and a blunt carving knife) and on herself as the person responsible: 'Must make amends for that.' It is more than the usual disappointment or regret about wasting money. Once again, she has done something bad and must somehow make amends.

There is no reference in her 1968 diary to events deemed newsworthy outside it. The external world rarely intrudes in her diaries, so I wouldn't expect 1968 to be an exception, but it is worth pointing out some of the more notable events of global significance that year just to gain a clearer understanding of where she was coming from. In 1968 a South Vietnamese general was photographed shooting a 'suspect' (hands bound behind his back) in Saigon. Martin

Luther King was shot dead in Memphis. Enoch Powell foresaw in the flow of immigrants coming to Britain a 'river of blood'. Senator Bobby Kennedy was shot dead in Los Angeles. Russian tanks crushed the Prague Spring. 'Gestapo tactics' were practised by police in the street of Chicago. Bloody street battles erupted in Londonderry. Nixon was elected President. My mother seldom noticed history happening around her – no reason why she should. She had selective vision, noticing only when personally relevant history intruded. On 20 August 1962, for instance, she noticed that 'Jordan got 2 months prison', adding: 'he deserves more than that'. My mother, never one to waste words, usually reserved them for essentials like listing the second-hand clothes she bought and regretted buying. For her to refer to the world outside her diaries suggests how intimately it touched her when it did, as in the case of Colin Jordan. There is no specific diary reference to the international conference he hosted in Gloucestershire, where he was elected 'World Fuhrer', or to his attempts to set up a paramilitary force modelled on the SA, the *Sturmabteilung* (Storm Troopers) of Hitler's Germany. Such details were too close to home. As she killed herself in December 1971, she didn't live to see Colin Jordan fined £50 for shoplifting three pairs of women's red knickers from Tesco's Leamington Spa branch in June 1975, which might have afforded her some small satisfaction as prurience unbecoming a 'World Fuhrer'.

The interior world of Gerda's diaries provided an inner space where she could be herself. It allowed no room for anything outside her immediate life other than events of special relevance. This isn't a new insight. I am drawing on the same primary sources as before. The difference this time around is in not knowing where this second reading of her life will lead me without the diaries and letters determining the direction of travel. I have more time to pause, look around, pay attention, take notice; and what I notice right now is the oddity of those words – 'atone', 'make amends' – when applied to a dud second-hand transistor radio, chipped glassware, and a blunt carving knife. To me, they are more revealing than passages of intensely introspective self-analysis, which is just as well as there are no such passages in her diaries. By the late 1960s, it didn't take much for her to realise she was letting herself down again and needed to atone and make amends. 'Don't be so hard on yourself,' I murmur, 'surely there is no sin to expiate here. They weren't the bargains you sought, but blowflies. So what? No need to ask for God's forgiveness for buying a broken transistor radio.' Brooding on her 'blowflies', I venture deeper: Blowflies scavenge carrion and dung, just as she scavenged jumble sales and second-hand shops, and this isn't my view but hers. 'Jumbles are fun but very degrading,' she wrote on 12 March 1965. She accumulated 'piles of junk'. The only activity – outlet – that gave her any pleasure and respite from her life, was also the source of self-disgust.

'Must atone', 'must make amends': they resonate all the more because they are diary words, private words, and as I now realise, they are the words that connect us, for I am my mother's son and must also 'make amends'. This present chapter – indeed, this entire book – is an apology long overdue, and now I think of it, there is such a long list of things to apologise for that I hardly know where to begin. As good a place as any to start is her suicide.

Peter Thornthwaite

Firstly, I am sorry for not seeing the signs, heeding the warnings, paying attention, but as she usually presented as 'nervy' and 'easily upset', nothing in her face or general appearance gave her away. Also, suicide had been intimated so often before, by means of a 'gas oven' (her preferred mode as more graphic and easily visualised), that no one took her seriously. 'One of these days I'll stick my head in the gas oven – then you'll be sorry!' It was just her way of making us feel guilty about something said or done to her; it was what mothers said if they felt unappreciated and unloved. Another of her favourite phrases was, 'You'll be sorry when I'm gone', and besides suggesting she felt disregarded and unnoticed by the family, it opened up the possibility of her future absence, though that seemed unlikely. 'When I'm gone' sketched a future scenario of my mother walking out of the house one day and inexplicably not returning, going missing – a disturbing but equally improbable prospect. So, yes, looking back, there were repeated forewarnings, but the very repetition somehow made her death or disappearance less likely, for the years passed and nothing occurred. So, her suicide was a surprise, and I'm sorry about that, for such inattention to a mother's misery is more forgivable if of brief duration but less so if prolonged for years.

On the subject of 'Sorry', I am reminded of something else she used to say: 'It's no good saying you're sorry. The damage is done.' She was right about that. My mother didn't die straightaway after her overdose in December 1971 but the damage was definitely done. My view of her then, as I dutifully visited her body over the Christmas period, is described in *Remember Who You Used to Be*, and

I don't want to repeat myself or summon up her rather repulsively fleshy appearance, but it is incumbent on me to revisit her once more in that hospital, if only to see if this time she affects me differently and we can recover some kind of connection – if we had any in the first place, that is, and I am not sure we did. Maybe I am repeatedly drawn back there, to a mother in a coma, simply because any such connection seems unlikely, given that most of the time during those hospital visits I looked away and could hardly wait to leave. But it also seems that, as no words could ever again come between us, we might connect subliminally. The coma was, after all, the last of the key transitional, 'in-between' phases of her life, and as such a very special time for us both.

The nurse who showed me to her bed drew back the curtain and said: 'Speak to her. She might be able to hear you.' She didn't know my mother, who could have been asleep on the deep seabed, her fleshy face crawling with sea spiders, for all that she could hear the muffled voices above. What I did say – a son's last words to a strangely transfigured mother – I have no idea. We weren't very good at communicating, and I'm sorry for that too, for she meant everything to me. But what I didn't say then, or during subsequent visits to her bedside, or when they finally switched her off, was 'Sorry'. At the time I probably thought that if anybody should apologise it was her, for leaving us like that with no goodbyes or explanation, and with no regret for what she was doing to the man who once thought of her as his 'Angel'.

It was a selfish suicide, with no sign of any consideration for the soon-to-be bereaved family and its lifelong consequences for them. As for the scribbled note she also left for my father to find, even now (over half a century later) I can't help comparing it unfavourably to the tender suicide note Virginia Woolf wrote to her husband, Leonard, in 1941 before walking into water and pulling the Ouse over her head. There is no mention in my mother's note of the happiness Jack had given her; in fact, it wasn't addressed to him and refers only to 'the dogs'. Unfortunately, her suicide note disappeared with her, so I can't check the accuracy of my memory. As I recall, apart from 'the dogs', her last words were a model of terminal indifference to the family she left behind.

Her suicide and note featured in my previous account of her life, and I am sorry to bring all this up again. I do so not out of any residual bitterness but (just the opposite) to find some lost connection. For, looking back, I realise I took her suicide too personally, as a rejection, and for that reason postponed opening up the five suitcases of diaries, letters, etc. It was a big sulk. 'You're cutting off your nose to spite your face,' my mother used to say, and yes, that was exactly what I was doing by not sticking my nose into her private affairs. As I interpret it now, the half-century delay and my apparent disinterest expressed disapproval of what she had done, punishing her for killing herself. 'If you wanted nothing more to do with us, then I want nothing more to do with you,' I was effectively saying.

She didn't answer.

CHAPTER SEVEN:

GONE

Gone with the Wind premiered in the US, 15 December 1939, shortly after Gerda, a domestic in London SE15, sat drinking tea in her room, missing but not mourning the end of her first 'Big Love':

Joe was not the right one. He was until recently still very much the big love, he was extremely in love with me and I also liked him very much, but the arsehole stank lately so much that I felt nauseous and, all of a sudden, I didn't love him anymore because I wanted to throw up.

(Gerda's Diary 11 December 1939)

Gerda was more outspoken inside her diary than outside it, and I am used now to her occasional bluntness, yet such marked shifts of emotion still come as a surprise. I remember a woman who showed but seldom articulated her thoughts, and the eighteen-year-old refugee drinking tea in her little room remains an unfamiliar Gerda: a pre-mother. Is there already a shadow in her of the Scarlett O'Hara she later went to see at a wartime cinema? *Gone with the Wind* was not released in the UK until April 1940, so it might have been around then, pre-Blitz, that she spent a shilling or two of her wages to leave the blackout outside the cinema for the luminous blackout within. But I have also read that in the US there were limited and advance-ticket-only showings until July 1940, with general release in 1941. Then another internet source stated that it played in Leicester Square for four years from the end of the 'phoney War' in 1940 until D Day in 1944. And according to a further source, the film was shown from the week beginning 28 May 1940 at three West End cinemas. In fact, I don't even know for sure if Gerda saw it during the war, though she probably did as she loved cinema (this is one of the things I do know about her from personal observation) and cinema audiences increased through the war, with people queuing outside them at the height of the Blitz with fires still visible from the previous night's bombing. Most likely, Gerda was one of the many Londoners seeking an escape for a few hours from rationing and privation, blackout and Blitz, and at over three hours and in 'glorious technicolour' *Gone with the Wind* was wartime cinema at its escapist best.

All I know for certain is that, at some point between her arrival as a refugee in London in June 1939 and the arrival of a family (1948- 51), *Gone with the Wind* blew through her life and in a big way, though I don't recall her ever mentioning it, and it didn't enter her diary until 1968 when she saw it again and for the last time. Some things are just known inside families without needing to be located precisely on any tattered map of memory. The special meaning she attached to *Gone with the Wind* was one of them, but as she seldom spoke of the things she most loved, what follows is conjecture.

A Berliner, Joe was German like herself but being Jewish

he was available to love and be loved. It might have surprised him (or maybe not) how completely Gerda fell for him. Having read her diary entry for 24 June 1939, perhaps I know more about her feelings for him then than he did, because she probably held more back when with him than when alone with her diary. At the start of the affair she was writing about Joe with a gushing effusion of love altogether unlike the mother I remember, before he became a 'stinking arsehole' and exited her diaries for good.

As I recall, Joe reappeared in the later 1960s when she recollected, apparently without regret, the end of a love affair intensified by war and their shared status as Jewish refugees in London. Nothing could have come of it, she concluded, though he was the man she loved with the depth of emotion Scarlett discovered too late for Rhett Butler, and I would not have thought of linking them – Joe and Rhett – but for a coincidence. That late diary entry remembered Joe as the Big Love of her life, and I would pin down her words with the exact date if I could recall where they appear. Losing her words is a not infrequent mishap as the year on the cover of the diary seldom corresponds to the actual date of the entries. It was presumably to save paper that she would use the blank pages of an earlier diary for the records of later years. It was typical of her thriftiness, though I can't help suspecting she did it deliberately to obstruct and confuse unauthorised readers of her diaries like me. The entry about *Gone with the Wind* is dated 17 November 1968:

Went to pictures, spent 11`/6. Gone With the Wind. Shan't go any more pictures. Too nervy!

Peter Thornthwaite

Though we often 'went to the pictures' together, that entry makes no mention of me. 11/6 seems a lot, so I could have accompanied her but have no memory of the event. The film wasn't shown on TV until November 1976, five years too late for her. I have since discovered that, for its 1967 re-release, the film was issued with updated poster artwork showing Rhett Butler, his white shirt open to the chest as he presses Scarlett to him, against a wall of orange flames – the burning of Atlanta. This was the embodiment of love my mother would have passed as she entered the wide foyer of the vast red brick Regal cinema. It is still there, the Regal, with its white columns and high stretched windows at the corner of Cowley and Magdalene Road, but currently a Christian Life Centre.

Shan't go any more pictures. Too nervy! Pondering her terminal words and their place in a long list of renunciations, I wonder if what she meant was that it disturbed and upset her to see again the greatest of Hollywood screen romances and to be reminded of her own Big Love. Of course, it might simply be that spending 11/6 at the cinema made her 'nervy'. If her later diaries reveal one thing of particular importance to her, it was that spending the money she should have been saving was distressing and yet her only source of fun.

To suggest that she identified with Scarlett O' Hara is probably going too far; there is no evidence other than my own intuition and some watery memories. Yet I can still see that fat book on her shelf alongside other bloated books with titles like *Never Love a Stranger* and *The Dream Merchants*. In fact, I have just finished reading it – for the first time – not for pleasure but research and in the hope of finding my way back to her through the things she loved. As she wasn't much of a reader, the jolt of connection is more likely to come through her favourite films: the classic Hollywood movies that were her escape route from family and everyday life. Actually (and this is the exciting thing) I never know when and where the jolt might come. It can happen in the least likely places or, conversely, not happen at all when most expected; but with my mother I have learned not to expect anything. It will come or not. What follows either makes something of nothing – and she never saw herself in Scarlett O' Hara's character or situation – or is a remarkable new insight.

If she first saw *Gone with the Wind* with Joe still in mind, its dramatic end – a distraught Scarlett running down the red-carpeted stairs crying 'Rhett! Rhett!' as he says goodbye, not giving 'a damn' for her love – surely reminded her of her own situation. For Gerda too, that once-in-a-lifetime experience of love was already behind her, and she only nineteen or twenty! And I also wonder if Scarlett's famous last line – 'Tomorrow is another day' – spoke to Gerda especially in the dark of a wartime cinema, and during the following days as she resumed her domestic duties in SE15.They were the same – wanting love, looking forward, ever hopeful – and I suddenly recall a favourite phrase of hers from later years, '*Manana, manana*', whether expressed hopefully or bitterly, I could never tell. Did Gerda see in Scarlett O'Hara's belated realisation of her passion for Rhett Butler –the only man in her life who had the full measure of her deeply flawed character and loved her anyway – something like her own twisted feelings for slim, dark-haired Joe Schwarz? Yes, but I wonder if, with Joe out of the way, she freed 'tomorrow' from past complications. The future was empty but hers.[24]

Whether their heightened emotional states were alike or not, there can be no doubt that Scarlett's experience (not just at the end but throughout the film) mirrored Gerda's. For all their apparent differences – Scarlett, a Southern belle in Georgia during the American Civil War; Gerda, a refugee in London during the Second World War – their situations could be transposed. Both beset by war. As Gerda had left her past in Breslau, so Scarlett leaves hers at the old plantation, Tara, and longs to return and restore it. Both Breslau and Atlanta are besieged. The siege of 'Fortress Breslau' was still to come, and I am not sure if, by the end of the war, Gerda was even aware of Breslau's fate in 1945 or cared, but she might well have later seen a connection with Scarlett's related experience. Both young women suffer and survive the passing of civilisation as they knew it – for Scarlett, the pre-Civil War Confederacy; for Gerda, Germany before 1933. When the insipid Ashley Wilkes asks Scarlett, 'What do you think becomes of people when their civilisation breaks up?' he could be asking Gerda the same question. Without stretching the point, Gerda, along with other wartime women and cinemagoers, saw in the wilful, independent, resourceful, feisty Scarlett O' Hara the embodiment of female resilience and energy, who could not only survive the war but thrive on it. An inspiration to women in her unfailing

---

[24] I have read somewhere that Vivien Leigh thought that women must secretly admire Scarlett O'Hara, despite her shortcomings. I think my mother admired her because of them.

selfishness, deceit, and manipulation of others to serve her own ends, Scarlett O'Hara remains undefeated. She might weep at the bottom of the sweeping red-carpeted stairs at the end of the film, because for once she can't get what she wants, but even as she realises her folly and failure she looks forward to 'another day'.

Was Scarlett a version of Gerda on the big screen? Pondering this, I recall my mother's stacks of old movie magazines with their news and gossip about the stars. Rereading them avidly, as I suppose she sometimes did, she might have learned how Vivien Leigh got the part of Scarlett O' Hara, and this insider knowledge might then have touched the nerve of memory. Just as Gerda had her own notable 'night to remember' (9-10 November 1938), when the Breslau sky and beyond was alight with burning synagogues, so Vivien Leigh had hers a month or so later, when the most spectacular set-piece of the movie, the burning of Atlanta, was first filmed. It was on that remarkable night (15 December 1938), as I myself have recently learned, that as one of a crowd of spectators Vivien Leigh watched entire blocks burn and wondered at the grandeur and confusion. That was the night she met the film's producer, David O. Selznick, who was still looking for a Scarlett O' Hara somewhere out there and found her.

Gerda resolved to leave the Third Reich after her memorable night, and Vivien Leigh became Scarlett after hers. Neither knew what lay ahead, but both must have sensed that their lives would never be the same again.

In view of the instant and enduring success of the film, Gerda was one woman out of many millions of admirers. *Gone with the Wind* has been described as 'the peak of

Hollywood'. The novel, published in 1936, was 'the best-selling novel in history'. The movie was the highest-earning film up to 1939 and for a further quarter of a century and ('when adjusted for monetary inflation') the highest-grossing film in history. It is 'the highest moment in the career of Hollywood, 'painted in glorious technicolour'. This was the 'Golden Age' of Hollywood, and it is telling that my mother not only saw the movie again in 1968 but made a note (albeit a brief and rather dismissive one) in her diary. What was it in the film that especially appealed to her three years before she killed herself? Did she see Scarlett as an earlier version of herself – self-willed, selfish, vain – yet for all those apparent defects (and perhaps because of them) determined, brave, unafraid of the future? In one notable scene, which immediately reminded me of my mother and her constant fear of getting fat, Scarlett measures her waist (all of twenty inches and no longer the eighteen-and-a-half inches she remembered) and decides 'no more children', and therefore no more sex. I could go through the film and find, without having to look for them, the myriad connections with my mother. Only now am I starting to realise how wilfully perverse are my mis-readings of my mother's character and situation and that she was, if anything, braver and more enterprising than Scarlett, who always had the old plantation to fall back on. Going 'home' to Tara, with its avenue of dark cedars leading to the white house and a black 'Mammy' waiting loyally for her – that is the repeated refrain on Scarlett's lips. But for Gerda there was no going back, no past 'home' restored. Scharnhorststrasse 31 – Gerda's home for almost all her early life – probably did not survive the siege of Breslau –

the fierce street-to-street and house-to-house fighting marking the end of the Nazi war. It had ceased to matter. Germany was over for Gerda. Finished. There was no going back for a German Jew.

It is most unlikely that Gerda saw any connection between the Jews of Nazi Germany and the black slaves of the Confederacy. As portrayed by Margaret Mitchell, the black slaves of the Antebellum South are happy slaves, and post-war liberation is their undoing. When the film premiered in Atlanta in mid-December 1939, about 300,000 residents came out to see the movie stars arriving in their limousines, but because of Georgia's 'Jim Crow' laws there were notable absences. Hattie McDaniel, who played the house servant Mammy, on whose ample bosom Scarlett longed to rest her head at the end of the novel, was absent, as were the other Black cast members. They were not allowed to attend. Gerda was almost certainly unaware of this, as I was (pre-internet) but had she known, I doubt it would have unduly troubled her. Nothing she ever wrote or said revealed any interest in slavery in the Antebellum South or the racial segregation in force until 1968 – the year of her last cinema outing. If she saw any connection between the 'White Supremacy' in 'the land of Cavaliers and Cotton' and the 'Aryan Supremacy' of the Third Reich, she kept it to herself. She was apolitical throughout her life, having done with history – until it came back for her.

Thinking about connections, the one at the back of her mind when she saw *Gone with the Wind* on 17 November 1968 had to be with Joe, her first and perhaps last 'Big Love'; for it was around then, as I recall, that he suddenly surfaced in her penultimate diary after an absence of nearly three decades – his comeback coinciding with seeing *Gone with the Wind* for the last time. Odd then that when I checked her 1968 diary for the entry concerning Joe, I could find no trace of him in November or any other month that year, or indeed in any of the diaries of that terminal decade. As far back as 1960, Joe was nowhere to be seen. I finally found him on 6 February 1959: *'Been sorting letters out lately. Made me think a lot of times gone by, and especially of Joe'.* My relief at finding him – finding, too, proof that her paper past reclaimed her more than I had realised – hardly relieved my consternation on finding that I had misremembered the date of the entry by nearly a decade! The connection between Gerda remembering Joe and seeing *Gone with the Wind* was evidently more in my mind than hers. Whether she thought about him on 17 November 1968, I don't know. She merely records: *'Shan't go any more pictures. Too nervy!'* That entry has the brevity of her suicide note, then just three years away. Knowing her as I do, her favourite movie brought to mind a younger, hopeful Gerda, for whom 'tomorrow' might change everything. It upset her, jangled her nerves; for it was not like my mother to renounce cinema – the only lasting 'Big Love' of her life.

In the year of her death, 1972, I left England for the US to attend a college for women – Smith College, Massachusetts – one of the so-called 'Seven Sisters', a group of colleges in Northeastern US. A limited quota of male students had been allowed that year into Smith, a college brimming with several thousand young American women, and I was one of only two Englishmen among them.

Not Drowning but Waving

During that year at Smith, I discovered that Margaret Mitchell, author of the original novel *Gone with the Wind*, was one of its more illustrious past alumnae. Gerda never knew of my American plans. I was probably intending to mention them to her that December, 1971, back from university for the Christmas break, but her own plans overtook mine and I came home to be told instead about the attempted suicide. Shortly after her death in January 1972, I received some better news: my application to go to New England had been successful. Probably this wouldn't have much interested my mother, who had no trouble adjusting to the absence of her grown-up children and indeed welcomed it. To be informed that my future absence would be extended by a year in the US could only have been good news to her. Had she lived, though, she might have been interested to learn of Margaret Mitchell's old connection with Smith College.

Looking back to that eventful year, 1972, I sometimes fantasise about the long, interesting letters in blue airmail envelopes I might have sent her from Massachusetts, with further instalments concerning Margaret Mitchell's time at Smith. My mother might not have cared about my studies or me, but finding out where Margaret Mitchell had once resided (Chapin House) and if its famous winding staircase actually inspired the great staircases of the grand houses in *Gone with the Wind* would have surely interested her. Unfortunately, as she never surfaced from her deep and dreamless coma, such future correspondence between us is hypothetical, and anyway it probably wouldn't have occurred to me to mention Margaret Mitchell, whose previous residence at Smith made no particular impression at the time. I recall nothing about Chapin House or its staircase. In fact, my recollections of that year are so nebulous that sometimes I wonder if I was actually there, and I keep going back to the internet as a substitute memory. It was my first year abroad. It was America. My mother had recently killed herself. Those things should have located that year on the unfolded map of memory. If any year of my life should stand out, it is 1972-73 at Smith. Yet when I look for my shy and easily embarrassed former self among the green lawns and gardens and exclusive groups of young American women conversing on old verandas, and the redbrick and ivy-clad houses, and the flaming trees of the famous New England fall, I see no sign of him.

As I write this, I am a week away from 72 and the coincidence strikes me. 1972 was a pivotal year, a seminal year, one of those years later remembered as a change of direction. Yet when I look back (and it seems I do nothing else these days), the years empty themselves, as though remembering is itself an act of erasure, rubbing out the landmarks by which I once mapped and located myself. Fortunately, I am only looking for her.

If she is to be found anywhere, it is in the movies she watched and in which she sometimes saw herself. If *Gone with the Wind* featured in Gerda's life to the extent suggested, I can't say, but it occurs to me that the 'Gone' of the title might have especially resonated with her. As I have read somewhere, that was how Clark Gable once referred to it – simply as 'Gone' – when recalling how 'the wind' blew through his life. 'Gone' blew through Gerda's life, too.

Hence my current interest in the Margaret Mitchell/Smith College connection, and I really think I could be onto something here and owe it to my mother to find out. Fortunately, rather than scanning my own scant memory for connections, I have the internet and its worldwide web of information to find them for me.

Internet images of Chapin House, built in 1903, show a four-storey red brick building, classical white portico. Women on wide green lawns. Trees turning red. It is pleasant and peaceful there, as befits students whose families could afford the fees for tuition, room and board at a classic American women's college established in 1875. Scrolling through these pictures won't bring my year back, though I half-remember the historic red brick buildings and resided in one such house myself. Chapin House, where Margaret Mitchell stayed, occupies 'the geographic centre of the campus', overlooking playing fields, Lyman Plant House, and Paradise Pond. Hence the motto for those Smithies fortunate enough also to reside there: Living on the edge of Paradise.

That was where, towards the end of the First World War, Margaret Mitchell resided 'as a proud Chapinite'. Chapin House is justly famous for that reason (though it bears no resemblance to the white plantation house in *Gone with the Wind*). Did its staircase really serve as 'the inspiration' for the one in Scarlett O'Hara's Tara? Staircases feature significantly in the movie, taking the drama to new levels. It is from the bottom of the grand split staircase at 'Twelve Oaks' plantation (where Ashley Wilkes, the object of Scarlett's love, resides) that the dark-haired and disreputable Rhett Butler leans against the long curving banister and looks up with frank admiration and desire at young Scarlett O' Hara as she climbs the great stairs. Later, at Tara, she will shoot a Yankee deserter halfway up the staircase, blowing half his face off. Later still, it is up wide red-carpeted stairs that Scarlett in her red dress is borne by a drunk Rhett Butler to the marriage bed she has so long denied him. And it is down the same wide red-carpeted stairs that Scarlett hurries at the end of the film, crying 'Rhett! Rhett!' to stop him leaving.

Looking again at images of the much narrower staircase in Chapin House, it is difficult to see how it inspired Margaret Mitchell. In one view of it, which I mistake as a photograph of Chapin's stairs since it appears with others under that heading, I see the wide split staircase of the movie, but actually this internet image shows the great staircase of another grand historic house in the old South and has nothing to do with Margaret Mitchell. It is possible, I suppose, that I visited someone in Chapin House without realising that the author of my mother's favourite film once lived there, but if so its white staircase with curving mahogany banister left no impression. While there is no dearth of internet information on Margaret Mitchell at Smith, the issue of the staircase remains unresolved. Then, as I search the sites for her, the uncertainty surrounding the stairs as a prime source of inspiration spreads beyond them to the house itself. According to one website: 'Despite many sources claiming that she lived in Chapin, Margaret Mitchell actually lived in Spanish Influenza quarantine housing during her one year at Smith.' So, it appears from this and other sources that not only did she not reside in Chapin, but that the 'proud Chapinite' went home after her 'freshman' year, returning to Atlanta to take over the household for her father following the death of her mother from the 'Spanish flu'.

CHAPTER EIGHT:

SMITHIES

Other notable Smithies include: Betty Friedan (class of 1942), author of *The Feminine Mystique*; two First Ladies of the United States, Nancy Reagan (class of 1943) and Barbara Bush (class of 1947); Sylvia Plath (class of 1955), poet; Gloria Steinem (class of 1956), noted feminist, activist and journalist.

Sylvia Plath went to Smith College in 1950 and exulted, in her early letters home to her cherished mother, in being a 'SMITH GIRL' and the camaraderie of living with a group of young women.[25] In the summer of 1953 she attempted suicide, taking her mother's bottle of sleeping pills and swallowing 'quantities' in the basement.

The camaraderie I never quite experienced with groups of Smithies included classes on Sylvia Plath, and thanks to my mother I am sure that the semi-autobiographical account in *The Bell Jar* of events leading to and from Plath's overdose, published shortly before her successful suicide by gas oven in 1963, had personal relevance. As she was such a name at Smith, having once been a proud

---

[25] See letter dated 28 September 1950 in *Letters Home* (reprinted 1979, Faber, London), edited by Syvia Plath's mother, Aurelia Schober Plath.

'Smithie' herself, her reputation as a poet further enhanced by the circumstances of her suicide, courses on Plath were popular. Her time there as a student, then (1957) as a tutor, were still remembered by some staff. The connections with my mother are clear enough, though in 1972 I was doing the opposite of what I am doing now and trying to forget rather than remember her. Sylvia Plath also had a German father, Otto, who died during the war, so that was another connection, and then there are the poems with their explicit Holocaust-inspired images. Gerda often threatened to stick her head 'in the gas oven', as Plath did one December – apparently thrusting her head far into it to make sure of dying this time – but like Esther Greenwood, my mother decided on pills as her way into 'the whirling blackness'. I recently reread passages from *The Bell Jar*, looking for anything to connect Esther's overdose with Gerda's – and unsurprisingly, I found something to note. The number of pills she takes from the locked strongbox after finding the key to it among her mother's hidden jewellery is 'at least 50'. That number is repeated twice for emphasis. Fifty. My mother's age when she took her overdose. Otherwise, there is little to connect the two. Esther Greenwood, a young college student, enters the 'dim, undersea light' of her mother's cellar in search of a hiding place while Gerda – her own college days thirty-three years behind her – chose to die in the comfort of her own bedroom with the dark curtains drawn against the December night.

Like Plath, Gerda also attended a residential women's college:

Not Drowning but Waving

Victoria College
Prag 8 (Liben)
Kosinka 502
C.S.R

That address from eighty-six years ago appears in thick black ink on an envelope among the papers from her past. Unfortunately, the letter itself is missing; most likely it was from Gunther or Tatta to the sister/daughter then attending Victoria College (1937–38). Evidently her father retained sufficient assets to fund a year at a college 'for young ladies' in another country. Gerda was fortunate, enjoying her 'beautiful Prague time' a year before Germany (with Britain's agreement) annexed part of Czechoslovakia and later occupied the rest. Her delight in leaving Germany in 1937 is unapparent in her diaries but I imagine she was happy enough to escape a time and place closing in on her. That I too had left home and country to attend a women's college might not have especially interested her had she lived, though possibly reminding her of a parallel experience when she was young and the future an open door. There is no reason why she should have heard of Smith and its famous alumnae, and her own distant college days must have seemed a lifetime away. As for Sylvia Plath, poetry had no place in my mother's life, and she would not have appreciated poems like *Lady Lazarus* and *Daddy* and the images of barbed wire, swastikas, Nazi lampshades, nose, eye pits, teeth, hands, knees and skin as they were too close to the bone of her own history.

Apart from tenuous Margaret Mitchell and Sylvia Plath connections, and the fact that we both attended a women's college in another country, nothing else about Smith and my mostly erased year there brings my mother especially to mind. No reason why it should. Yet I can't help thinking that something of great significance is still there for the finding, so it's back to the internet and its larger stock of facts about Smith than I ever stored.

At this other Smith College, students celebrate traditional events like 'Ivy Day' (a centuries-old tradition established by the prestigious 'Ivy League' universities and followed by other historic colleges) and 'Illumination Night', when the campus is lit up with coloured paper lanterns. Students stroll through 'the Arboretum, 127 acres of woody trees and shrubs', and out to the spreading sunlit lawns. 'The Botanic Garden' was designed for them by Frederick Olmsted, who also designed Central Park and whose end-of-century plans for Smith included 'verdant vistas over Paradise Pond through wooded groves'. There is a 'great glass house', and a green lane between 'yellow and purple banks of flowers, a shady bench', the 'Japanese Garden' with its stone lantern and rock basin, and 'Paradise Pond' in the background. As for the 'Japanese Tea Hut', I search my memory for afternoon tea, female company and conversation, but find it was constructed eleven years after I left. Unfortunately, because of the graffiti and trash from the 'recreational drug use' it attracted, and the shelter it provided for 'homeless townspeople', the 'Japanese Tea Hut' had to go. Back to the internet archives, I come to the 'iconic Grecourt Gates of SMITH COLLEGE', erected in 1924 as a replica of the gates at a ruined chateau in Grecourt, France, 1917. A contemporary photograph remembers Smithies from over a century ago in fur coats and hats: 'the Smith

College Relief Unit', which set sail for France to bring humanitarian aid to villagers after the Germans had left. 'These brave Smithies saved thousands of lives, brought help and hope to many, and defied those who did not believe that women belonged in a war zone.' They look the period with style and assurance in their military-type belted jackets, long skirts and big hats, gazing directly at the camera with serious faces befitting the occasion. 'Prior to setting sail for France, the Smith College Relief Unit contemplated what to wear and settled on a plain grey skirt and jacket with blue accents.'

Images of altruistic early twentieth-century privileged American women with their sense of a higher mission in life than their individual journeys could hardly be further from the Gerda of the diaries, yet something like her shadow passes through them. There is of course nothing to connect her with those Smithies who, united by altruism and education, country and class, banded together to help victims of war and Germany. But they led me to an earlier and much celebrated manifestation of Smithie solidarity and sisterhood – the story of 'Composita' – and it was there that I found a crucial connection.

It began in the winter of 1885/6, when the Senior Class had their individual photographs taken as an experiment in 'composite photography', then in its infancy but with the potential to advance the human race. The intriguing possibilities of this new use of photography were being explored by Francis Galton, the 'father' of eugenics and half-cousin of Charles Darwin, whose evolutionary theory could also be applied, Galton believed, to human genetic engineering. 'Composite photography' was a tool to identify common traits – whether between family members, criminals, inmates of asylums, members of different ethnic 'racial' groups, and other groups of individuals similarly subject to generic classification, such as 'Smithies'. Their idea, influenced by the man behind the camera and a favourite professor, John Tappan Stoddard (who was himself influenced by Galton's ideas), was for the negatives of individual photographs of multiple class members to be merged at a local photography studio into a single 'composite' portrait to mark and memorialise their collegiate and class sisterhood and enduring connection. So successful was this idea that the photograph gained flesh and blood as the lead character in the Senior Class play in 1886 about a young woman who embodied 'many souls into one being'. 'Composita' was further invoked in the 'Class Toast':

> But who has heard before of bits that were human,
> Being clustered together and forming a woman.[26]

By merging separate identities into one 'composite' image of womanhood of a certain class and status and moment in history, the 'Class of 1886' emerged as an ideal type. In the terminology of their time, 'Composita' was the eugenic ideal of hereditary and biological citizenship, the flesh and blood (in female form) of evolutionary theory. The face of their collective identity as an elite group of educated American women at the end of the century, she was no female Frankenstein monster made up of 'bits' of

---

[26] The Class Toast of 1886 was written by Mary Eastman, who also played 'Composita' in the performance.

others, but the ideal type of the new American woman. The Smithies who had come together to form 'Composita' remained justly proud of their creation and celebrated her in annual letters and reunions spanning the Boer War, First and Second World Wars, Holocaust, and beyond. 'Composita' stayed with the 'Class of 1886' for the remainder of their lives, the flesh and blood link between them and as much a matter of class as 'Class', since they were mostly upper-class women from New England, well-connected by their social, family and financial inheritance, as well as being among the first to access higher education. The last surviving member of the 'Class of 1886' must have been nearly a century old when she died in 1964.

There is nothing to suggest that Gerda came close to a 'Composita' moment, even as a girl in Nazi Germany, and the very first diary entry I translated (27 December 1938) began by observing that the 'future looks quite black' and ended with:

Most of the girls I meet make me sick. They are envious, jealous and cheap – all of them. Behind their nice words they are terribly stupid.

She evidently once had friends, as several pre-war photographs suggest: she can be seen picnicking in fields with them in 1935, or perching with two others on the back of a bench in the grounds of Victoria College, Prague, in 1938. In that one preserved picture from her 'beautiful Prague time' Gerda, wearing a long black coat with wide fur collar, holds her head coyly to one side and smiles brightly, aware that the camera is more interested in her than in her two unsmiling and rather plain-looking companions. Fast-forward to 1943 and the start of her two years in the 'ATS' ('Auxiliary Territorial Service', the women's branch of the British Army) and she is describing the 'girls' there as 'a very rough crowd' who 'poke their noses into other people's business' and 'don't like the Jews and unfortunately I am one'.

Unlike the 'Class of 1886', who looked back to Smith College and 'Composita' as a happy reminder and celebration of themselves and their lasting friendship, and who would have never described their fellow Smithies as 'boring and catty', the Gerda of the diaries viewed herself as isolated and apart. She wasn't 'Smithie' material, if 'Composita' is the test of a lifelong identification with others of a similar breed. In later years, she saw other women as common, rude, rejecting, and they frightened her. She was on her own. The only group to which she belonged, by birth and blood, heredity and history, was a shameful secret.

CHAPTER NINE:

ALL LOVE

Today my beloved Sandy died. We had him destroyed. He was unhappy and in pain and it might have gone on like that for a long time. I couldn't bear to see him suffer so. He did not appreciate my help in the end, but snapped at me when I touched him. I could not have nursed him back to health. He would not let me carry him. He didn't eat in the end and would not take his pill. So, I thought it would be best for all if he goes, but I did love him so. He was my best pal, my best companion, and I do miss him so very much. We had 8 perfect years together. He could be a bit naughty and I smacked him hard at times as I got a temper and I hate destructiveness, but on the whole, he was a happy contented dog with the love of us all and the company of Dinky which he loved. God bless him and thank You very much for having given him to me. 8 years is quite a good long life for a dog and I think he would have hated old age. Dear God forgive me if I've done wrong. I always try to do my best but I go wrong sometimes. Give me strength to carry on and forgive me all my sins. Bless Sandy for me. I miss him so. I miss his love. He never shouted at me and nagged at me. He was all love. Oh, Sandy, I miss you so.

(Gerda's Diary, 23 November 1964)

Peter Thornthwaite

Following its first airing in *Remember Who You Used to Be*, this eulogy to a beloved dachshund deserves further commentary. In that first account of Gerda's life and family history this entry was overtaken by the chronology of events impatiently awaiting their narrative turn. Though Sandy had an entire page and entry to himself, as befits his importance, there is more to consider here than her sadness at the passing of a favourite pet. His prime place in her life is becoming as clear to me as it was to her after his death, so he is back and this time straddling his own chapter with his little legs.

Did she love Sandy more than us? Though I understand its source (jealousy), it is probably the wrong question. They are different kinds of love, and what Sandy meant to her, which she got from no one else, was uncomplicated, unconditional love. He never 'shouted' or 'nagged' at her, and if she sometimes had to tell him off and smack him, he was soon licking the hand that hit him. The worst he could do was bark incessantly and seek out olfactory sources of pleasure and interest wherever they collected. Even in the eulogy above, my mother was well aware of the more animal side of dogs, and I remember her reprimanding Sandy for sniffing out dogshit in the park and 'rolling in dirt', as she put it, for which he had a particular propensity. Surprisingly, for a woman whose pet phrase was, 'Don't touch me, you know I don't like being touched', it was his unashamed tactility that attracted her and to which she responded in kind. Sandy was allowed on her lap when she sat in her wing armchair to watch TV (he never interrupted her programmes) while she absently stroked his sleek, short-haired, sand-coloured body. Afterwards, all the times they were together, just the two of them, body against body, returned like a deep regret, for only with Sandy could she be herself and once he was gone so too was that opportunity. His company uncomplicated her life. For a woman who didn't think she deserved to be loved, and who found herself unlovable, a fat, short-haired dachshund called Sandy could go where family feared to tread.

Dinky (a miniature dachshund, long-haired and dark) survived him by several years, but could not fill the absence left behind. As my father, Jack, could never be a Joe, so one pet dog could never take the place of another. When I go through her last deeply affecting words in memory of him, what strikes me this time round is how she identified with a dog, and I wonder if this struck her too that dark November day and for the remainder of her life. He was unhappy and in pain and it might have gone on like that for a long time. She was speaking of herself of course. *I think he would have hated old age.* Ditto Gerda. *He was all love.* And that was something we (being human) could never be. If even Jack sometimes fell short of the high standards set by a low-slung, stubby-legged dachshund, then what hope had her children, who measured a mother not by what they could do for her but by what she could do for them?

Coincidentally, while revisiting my mother's diaries and old photographs, I read a newspaper article about the entertainer Paul O'Grady, who died recently, and his great love of dogs. Such 'genuine love', the article suggested, is a sign of selflessness and consideration for others. For the Paul O' Gradys and Gerdas of the world, the death of a much-loved dog creates a lasting absence in their lives and a longing for what has been lost. This insight changed my view of her. She was, I realised, a woman who wanted to love, though one who could only show that side of herself with dogs, especially floppy-eared ones like Sandy. All her life she had sought companionship, friendship, love, acceptance, and in him she found them all rolled into one.

Gerda's love of dachshunds was probably a German thing. A dachshund like Sandy is the focal point of a pre-war photograph identified only by 'Balkon' (balcony) and the year, '1936', in the 'Gerda Gallery' on my phone. Apart from a broad-faced, white-shirted, grinning Gunther stretching almost horizontally across the foreground, they are a foreign-looking family of that era; rather serious, obediently eyeing the camera. Only Gerda, sitting next to a pale-suited Tatta at the back, looks down, almost dreamily, eyes half-closed, her left hand lightly touching the shoulder of the woman in front. Aunt Bertha? The Aunt Bertha who wrote to her niece in 1939 and hesitantly asked for help to leave Germany? Three years earlier, safe inside the photograph of 1936, the woman I identify (possibly mistakenly) as Aunt Bertha gently but firmly holds a dachshund, a Sandy lookalike, in her arms, while fifteen-year-old Gerda looks fondly down at the dog. And (a previously unnoticed detail), I see that the shape of the large white collar of Gerda's blouse matches the large drooping ear of the dachshund. Other fresh details then emerge, such as the Slavic facial appearance of the three older women with their greying, scraped-back hair. If the woman holding the upright dachshund is the Aunt Bertha who was deported and killed in November 1941, who then are the other two? Not Gerda's mother, who died in

1927. Other unnamed aunts, perhaps. As for the balcony itself, I didn't really take it in before with its dark potted plants. The dachshund, when I first examined this photograph two to three years ago, naturally drew my attention, as her lifelong love of this breed of dog was well known, but scrutinising the picture again, its self-satisfied central positioning in the formal family group portraiture is striking. And I notice something else too, another previously missed detail: the woman sitting to the right of Aunt Bertha attracts the dachshund's attention with the stiff admonishing finger she holds up to make it behave as becomes a member of that family, and his jaw is open with a silent bark.

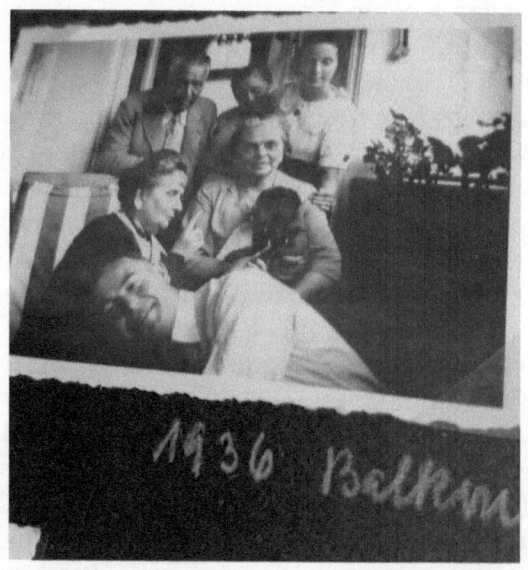

The apparent word, Balkon, and the date, 1936, appear under this photograph. I have translated 'Balkon' as balcony, and there are plants in the room, but it doesn't look much like a balcony.

Peter Thornthwaite

The first half of my mother's scrawled suicide note instructed the reader (my father presumably) to 'Look after the dogs'. If Sandy had swallowed his pills in November 1964 like a good boy and survived, I wonder if Gerda would have swallowed hers that December night seven years later. 'I never want to leave Sandy, I love him too much', she had written in an earlier diary entry (4 January 1960) when leaving everything seemed necessary again, so her own departure was out of the question until he died. I wonder too if his last pathetic performance for the family, as he slid his slug-like sagging stomach across the kitchen lino, came back to my mother at the end of her life, and if she believed she was joining him.

Sandy would have died anyway, well before December 1971, because (as she herself acknowledged), '8 years is quite a good long life for a dog' and long-bodied dachshunds are relatively short-lived. A replacement 'second' Sandy in her life, loving her as much as she loved him, might have averted or at least delayed her suicide, but there was only the one.

My mother left two dogs for us to look after: Dinky, the black long-haired dachshund, who seemed not to notice Sandy's absence and enjoyed the extra attention (standing erect on his hind legs like a circus dog for our approval and applause) and Teddy, a corgi, a dog fit for a queen but with no great love for my mother, who wrote him off as a 'nasty, bitey thing' owing to his predilection for dark hideaways behind sofas and armchairs. Teddy had once snapped at her, and that was the end of their relationship. When it was her turn to go, Dinky and Teddy needed looking after but not by her.

The 23 November 1964 diary entry, when I first read it,

aroused some retrospective jealousy, I admit. How could she love a dog more than us? Very easily, apparently. Sandy was never 'rude' to her, never turned on her, showed his affection with his tongue, licked the hand that fed him and took him for walkies, and was a warm deadweight on her lap as she absently stroked him while watching television. Examining it again, but taking the family and my feelings out of the equation, I understand that my mother felt what Sandy was going through because his suffering was hers – so unbearable at the end that he even turned against her helping hand and 'snapped' when she stroked him. It was a measure of her love that she had him put down, destroyed. And I understand something else: that her diary entry marking his demise is the first and last time she disclosed such depths of love. There was one previous occasion, twenty-five years earlier, shortly after arriving in London from Germany, when her diary entry is unusually effusive, unlike the mother I remember. Dated 24 June 1939, it stands out in a lifetime of diaries: her sudden outpouring of refugee love for Joe, her first lover, Jewish like herself.

Ich liebe Joe ich liebe Joe ich liebe Joe, ich liebe ihn so sehr.

Leaving Nazi Germany and its persecutions behind for a new life in London, Gerda was ready for love and Joe just happened to be there at the right moment.

Joe, Joe, Joe.

Marking a crucial juncture in Gerda's life, Joe entered her diary two days before she turned eighteen and just as her future was taking shape. Unfortunately (though not for me), her 'Big Love' didn't last.

Peter Thornthwaite

Joe was not the right one. He was until recently still very much the big love; he was extremely in love with me and I also liked him . . .
(Gerda's Diary 11 December 1939).

Joe couldn't last eight months, let alone her 'eight perfect years' with Sandy.

That later love was a measure of her social isolation in the 1960s. She had no friends and her diaries include people only if they are 'downright rude', 'ever so nasty', 'ignore' and look past her, or (in one memorable instance) accuse her of theft. As for her place in the family, she remained the intersection through which the everyday traffic of family matters passed, yet at that crisis of Sandy's passing I missed its impact on her, being too absorbed in my own misery. It was only when I finally read her diaries that I felt it and realised that with his death she moved one step closer to her own.

That Sandy was not just her 'best pal', her 'best companion', but her only one, occurred to me recently when, thinking about 1971, the year of Gerda's release from the role of wife and mother, and other memorable events from that time, I overheard myself crooning lyrics from a Carole King song, *You've Got a Friend*, from her album, *Tapestry*, released earlier that year. If my mother heard it on the radio, I don't suppose she noticed that it was a song written with her especially in mind. She is the one the song is about, although by 1971 she had no friends. If she silently called out (which I doubt), she expected not to be heard, and by then it was too late. For my mother, it had been too late for a long time. Her sky had permanently clouded over and darkened, things had gone too far, and a friend was the last comfort she wanted. No distress calls, as she was about to go under, were afterwards reported by the family.

Now I am the one to close my eyes and think of her, and she's got a friend in me whether she wants one or not. More a friend now than a son, it can only represent an improvement in our relationship, for as a son I could never be much of a friend. In that sense, a song from the year of suicide, about lasting friendship, has brought us closer together. She could hardly have foreseen such an unlikely gesture from the future, but nor could she have foreseen that one day she would open her diaries to me and tell me all, or that I would gladly give her three years (and counting) of my life.

Looking through my research notes for this chapter on the death of Sandy, 23 November 1964, and the irreplaceable loss to my mother of everything he represented to her, I came across a note of something that occurred exactly twenty-five years earlier. On 23 November 1939, one of the makers of Nazi Germany, Hans Frank, then Governor-General of occupied Poland, decreed that Jews wear a white armband with a blue Star of David in public. The Star as a mark of identity had been proposed by Goebbels as early as May 1938 – about the time that Gerda, returning to Germany after her year away at college in Prague, was thinking of emigrating to Palestine. She did not pursue that plan; nor did the Nazis implement theirs, so she was spared the Star during her last year in Germany. Secret Police Chief Reinhard Heydrich (of Wannsee Conference and 'Final Solution' fame) picked up the proposal after the November 1938 pogrom. Had it become law, it would have reminded Gerda (if she needed one) that she was nothing if not Jewish. Again, no immediate action was taken to mark Jews more visibly in public. Following Frank's initiative in Poland, however, from September 1941 the Yellow Star became an obligatory badge for all Jews in the Reich, thanks to Heydrich.

CHAPTER TEN:

'MASK'

My research notes also reminded me that Hans Frank had risen with the Nazi Party, initially as a lawyer. Elevated to personal legal adviser to Hitler, with trusted and discreet access to his past, Frank had been asked in 1930 to investigate his ancestry following a blackmail letter from Hitler's nephew threatening to expose his uncle's part-Jewish origins. The story emerged in Frank's memoirs, *In the Face of the Gallows*, completed while facing execution at Nuremberg Prison in 1946, with the man convicted of war crimes and crimes against humanity claiming to have obtained, during his earlier investigations, correspondence between Hitler's paternal grandmother, Maria Anna Schicklgruber, and a Jewish merchant named Frankenberg. The collection of letters Frank had apparently uncovered touched on the paternity of Fraulein Schicklgruber's illegitimate child and the unnamed father's financial obligations. Hitler's grandmother had become pregnant while employed as a housemaid or cook in a Jewish household, and according to the so-called 'Frankenberger thesis', the unknown father was the nineteen-year-old son of her employer,

Leopold Frankenberger (although it has since been suggested that Frankenberger Senior could have been the Jewish father). The actual identity of the father makes no difference, as the thrust of this sensational allegation, since refuted by most historians, is that he was Jewish. Despite the implausibility of the thesis and absence of supporting evidence, it is interesting to see Hitler's own heredity and blood doubted and darkened by the libel, even if it was dismissed by the investigator himself after confronting Hitler with the findings that he might be a quarter Jewish. I have read that Frank was inclined to believe the allegations. As a vehement and high-profile anti-Semite, with a lot to lose even if only a quarter Jewish, Hitler understandably denied the story, although his own physical appearance was hardly the best advert for Aryan supremacy. If he had something to hide, he acted as if he hadn't. With the unattractive yet mesmerising mask of a man impassioned by his own rhetoric, vehement gestures and drilling declamatory voice, the public face of Hitler never once doubted itself, and if he ever suspected that a quarter of himself had betrayed the rest, it would have surely come out at some point.

Impressed apparently by his employer's denials, Frank dropped the matter until Hitler had been dead for a year and unable to counter any revived allegations and outrageous blood libel. His investigations had not shadowed Frank's illustrious Nazi career. Though apparently disliked by Hitler, he had thrived in the Third Reich. He was put in charge of Legal Affairs in 1933 and the following year was awarded the 'Blood Order' depicting an eagle gripping an oak leaf and on the reverse a swastika superimposed on sunbeams. The lawyer continued his loyal service to the regime following his promotion in 1939 to Governor-General of occupied Poland. The decree of 23 November, introducing the Jewish identity badge, his keenness to 'annihilate the Jews wherever we encounter them', and the mass murder of Poles as an energetic policy under his guidance, marked him out as a man with a mission to get things done.[27]

In post-execution photographs of a dark-suited, supine Hans Frank, laid out on what looks like a metal bench or shelf and identified by the name tag on his jacket, *H. Frank*, his face is a bloodless white by contrast with the dark receding hair, black eyebrows and the black holes of the nostrils viewed from above, giving it a mask-like appearance. The lips are slightly parted, allowing us a glimpse of his teeth. As might be expected after death by hanging, this was not his usual face. Photographs of Frank in his Third Reich prime depict utter self-assurance: a confident, challenging, even combative, expression, with menacing dark eyes and a penetrating gaze that drills into you. Post-execution, his eyes are shut, and for that reason alone he could never have seen this face in a mirror and might well have blanched at the reflection looking back at him in a prevision of it. When I examine further these internet images of the man dubbed 'the Butcher of Poland', as well as other high-ranking Nazis hanged after Nuremberg, I see that in some photographs the rope remains around the neck of the corpse, but in the *memento*

---

[27] His great mission, 'to annihilate the Jews', was frankly acknowledged in a speech to senior Nazis on 16 December 1941. Frank also said of the Jews: 'The more that die the better'.

mori images of Hans Frank the noose is absent. The black and white details are difficult to make out. He seems to be lying on a metal surface, a grey blanket folded under his head and propping it up, as if to make him more comfortable. His arms have been arranged across his tubby stomach in a suggestion of repose, his hands touching. Evidently, his body was deliberately laid out like this after being taken down, composed in a way at once humane and humiliating, because other Nazi war criminals are similarly displayed. The images are unaccompanied by any explanatory text, so I am left to speculate. In Frank's case, instead of a rope still around his neck, some sort of white cloth like a surgical mask with dangling strings is evident beneath his head.

From what I have read of his trial and conviction at Nuremberg, Frank faced up to his own guilt, declaring that a 'thousand years will pass and the guilt of Germany will not be erased' and acknowledging his own share in it. His post-arrest conversion to Catholicism, and the series of religious experiences he claimed to have experienced, suggest a changed man. With no apparent regret for what he had specifically achieved as chief administrator, he felt a generalised remorse for his share of the 'terrible guilt' and a sense of contrition previously unapparent in the fleshy features of the man who had been Governor-General of occupied lands, which he had ruled from Wawel Castle in Krakow. A witness at the hanging thought the condemned man looked 'relieved' at the prospect of atonement. Frank himself, understandably 'nervous and swallowing frequently' at the end, but 'with a smile on his countenance', asked for God's mercy. On the other hand his son Niklas, only seven at the time of the execution, was not deceived for very long by the face of contrition and grew up to detest and revile Frank with an intensity that his father was fortunate in being spared from witnessing. The son also wrote a memoir, one rather different in detail and tone from his father's, referring to him as 'a slime-hole of a Hitler fanatic'.[28]

Frank's admission of guilt included no acknowledgement of any share in the responsibility for setting up and promoting death camps, of which there were four in occupied Poland, and for which he blamed Himmler and the SS. During his six years as Governor-General, countless Poles – whom he regarded as 'slaves' of the 'Greater German World Empire' – and around three million Jews, were murdered. The man who decimated the population and asked nothing more of the Jews than that 'they should disappear' (which they very nearly did), before handing his captors the thirty-eight volumes of his 'Journal' to be used as evidence against him at his trial, was bound to have difficulty convincing the Nuremberg judges of his 'deep sense of guilt' and remorse, despite speaking from 'the very depths'. Nor did he persuade them of the limits of a Governor-General's responsibility for developments outside his remit, such as the four death camps and the 'horrible atrocities' committed during a six-year Nazi 'reign of terror' within the General Government for the Occupied Polish lands. Possibly, Frank wasn't entirely taken in by himself either and sought to conceal the extent of his complicity behind a mask of contrition.

The photographs of a supine, white-faced, dark-suited Hans Frank laid out for posterity – his usually penetrating

---

[28] From memoir by Niklas Frank: *In the Shadow of the Reich* (1991).

eyes shut, his hands resting comfortably on his tummy and his fingertips touching as on a tomb effigy – brought to mind again that TV documentary about Josef Mengele, which interpreted 'mask' metaphorically to describe how the true identity of the 'doctor of death' had been unexpectedly 'unmasked' in Sao Paulo in 1963 by a Hungarian expatriate, Gitta Stammer, whose family had unknowingly provided cover for him while he was on the run from Nazi hunters. Mengele's first contact (under an alias) with the Stammers was arranged by a friend and Nazi sympathiser, Wolfgang Gerhard (whose name Mengele later adopted as a final alias and cover for his own death in 1979). With a little help from his friend, Mengele resided with the Stammers from 1961 to 1974, the cover and protection they represented continuing long after Gitta Stammer's chance 'unmasking' of the man she thought was someone else.

During her surprise encounter, early in their relationship, with the image of a much younger Mengele (in his thirties) looking back at her from a newspaper, Gitta Stammer had recognised him by the familiar smile and that tell-tale gap between his front teeth. When she showed Mengele the newspaper article on 'the Nazi Executioners' and the picture of himself (then in his prime) and said 'It looks very like you,' he denied it, but then decided to tell her the truth: 'That person is me.' Once 'unmasked', Mengele convinced the Stammers not to give him up. I also learned that his good friend Wolfgang Gerhard visited the Stammers and persuaded them not to report the fugitive's location to the police as this might also get them into trouble. There was a monetary incentive for silence following the 'unmasking', since Mengele (supported financially by his own family) invested substantially in the purchase of several farms during his thirteen years of close connection with the Stammers. There were certainly advantages for both sides in remaining connected and the family keeping mum about their discovery, but I also wonder if Mengele had a soft spot for families, not just for the cover and protection they provided, but for the comfort and security of being part of one.

Hans Frank's 'death-mask', as it appeared in the post-execution picture of him, and the 'unmasking' of Mengele, both had some deep underlying connection with my mother, but it took me a while to find it. Though Frank admitted his share of the 'guilt of Germany', his heartfelt contrition was arguably just another mask behind which he also hid from himself. Mengele admitted no such culpability, doctoring the story of his Auschwitz past to his son, and had he been apprehended and tried, he'd have doubtless maintained that stance to the end. Both, though, had much to hide and continued doing so in their different ways. It never occurred to me until a few years ago that this was also true of my mother. Indeed, when I looked back after her death, she wore a face incapable of deception. Far from 'masking' her true feelings, her face painfully and unsparingly exposed them. There was no excoriating distress or pain she could conceal from us, which is not to say that I always noticed or cared at the time. As I write this, some lines from Sylvia Plath come to mind about how 'terrible' it is to be 'so open'. It was unfortunate for my mother that a woman with so much to hide had so little ability to hide it. All she could do to mask her vulnerability was shut down and withdraw into herself beyond reach.

My initial investigations into her life coincided with the second national Covid lockdown (January 2021). It was a fortuitous coincidence as it drained my days of other diversions and distractions and replaced external with internal events. For months, masks became part of 'normal' life, coming between people in shops and streets and in every conceivable transaction. The continuing Covid pandemic provided an opportunity to concentrate on this new 'project', undistracted by paid employment or social contact. My mother, I reflected, would have taken to wearing a mask. This is not to suggest that she'd have been more at home in a society in which social avoidance is the norm and the socially responsible thing to do. But a woman whose rule in life was 'tell nobody anything' and 'keep it all to yourself' must have felt much safer behind a mask, and as she also avoided tactile contact as she got older (over forty), it would have been a comfort to be able to share with others a healthy avoidance of physical proximity. 'Don't touch me, you know I don't like being touched.' That phrase of hers echoed inside my head throughout lockdown. Self-isolated, home alone, no friends, with only her television for company, shielded from drafts by her thick knitted blankets and the dark wings of her deep armchair, she unwittingly modelled the socially responsible citizen of the not-so-distant future.

It briefly amused me to picture my mother, who considered herself an outsider, as fashionably mainstream in 2021, fifty years after her death. She needed no government edict to understand that socialising, mixing with others, transmits infection – with families among the worst offenders because they still considered bodily contact natural and even essential to intimacy. And she also appreciated the importance of rules (having made enough for herself in the later diaries) so she would have adapted easily to the new directions for social interaction: maintain sufficient distance, discourage close proximity (especially with those close to you who keep forgetting), don't touch anything touched by others, wash and disinfect your hands immediately following suspected contact, don't breathe air exhaled by other mouths. Those were rules she could live by.

An amusing conceit, it didn't survive the first draft of *Remember Who You Used to Be*, because although partly true, it seemed disrespectful to her memory; uncaring, insensitive, and it cast her in a bad light, which was never my intention. Yet I was reluctant to let it go because the ubiquitous facemasks of Covid suggested a link to her past: specifically, to the seminal significance of a missing gas mask in her story.

As she rarely mentioned the war, still less her pre-war years in Germany, that gas mask stands out as one of the few markers of an eventful former life. That she revealed something of such significance to her was extraordinary enough. Evidently it stood out for her too, as a life-changing event, for her in-built censor failed to suppress it, and maybe it was her way of showing that at one time she was more than one of the stay-at-home mothers in a new council estate – that she once hid diamonds inside a gas mask in London.

The story has since gained in significance what it has lost in truth. When she first told it, we believed her because we were young enough not to doubt the word of a mother, but six decades later I dismissed it as one of those apocryphal family stories all the better – all the more revealing – for being almost certainly untrue.

The Second World War, the Home Front, Blackout, Blitz – all of that was a largely unknown part of her life until I read the diaries and letters, and it remains only sparsely mapped in them. Her first 'English' diary (though half in German) covers the period June to December 1939, and the war itself had no more chance of squeaking through her inked script than light through a blackout curtain because Gerda's love affair with Joe Schwarz occupied every page. After 11 December 1939 Joe virtually disappears from her diaries and there are only isolated sightings of Gerda for the next three years, and no connected account of what she was getting up to. Other sources provide occasional tantalising glimpses, as in that unsent letter to her distant brother (1 December 1940), which described the household at SE15 during nightly air raids:

I don't see any Germans at all. I've lost every connection with them. As for me I am very well indeed. Mrs. Stainton passed away recently. So, I am maid to her 28-year-old daughter and her 34-year-old son (who is in love with me and I the same and whom I am going to marry). Please don't laugh, finally I am 19 years old. He is very much like you in his character but that doesn't disturb me. Well perhaps that doesn't interest you very much. We are all sleeping on mattresses on the floor, I haven't been in a real bed for nearly a year because of air raids. I find the war terribly thrilling and exciting, if it wouldn't be for Tatta.

It is worth mentioning again for its rarity. Had she sent it to Gunther, as intended, it would be lost to me. As it is, it allows one of the few glimpses of Gerda's night life during her domestic service phase of the war. As to her reasons for not posting it – whether it seemed an intimacy too far to describe for her brother's amusement such lax sleeping arrangements, or she thought better of mentioning Tatta's situation in contrast to her own 'thrilling and exciting' time – I can only speculate. On reflection, the contrast to her own 'thrilling and exciting' time might have appeared insensitive and uncaring, and she was learning to censor herself.

Unique among her wartime experiences, the story of the gas mask somehow remained uncensored, possibly because it concerned money – a lot of money – enough to have changed everything. Even her children knew that 'diamonds' meant money and were a girl's best friend. They were the lovelier for having been lost, and as for linking them to a gas mask, that surprising connection between disparate things made it more credible, for who could make up a story like that?

Though it has stayed with me all my life, I didn't visualise a Second World War gas mask until recently – that is, I had no special reason to examine one (online) until I began investigating my mother. As ever, the internet subsequently filled in gaps in Gerda's diaries. When she first told the story, she didn't describe the actual mask, and I don't recall being especially curious about it at the time. But I suppose I must have had a sense even then of the incongruity of diamonds being concealed inside such a thing. My initial research in 2021, when I first looked into her story, seemed to connect us, for I was finally following up on something which had mattered to her so much that she had to tell us about it.

Peter Thornthwaite

So, by way of checking her story and finally getting to the bottom of it, I found out all I could (online) about the manufacture (commencing 1938) in Blackburn of enough civilian respirators to mask the entire population, and their widespread dissemination two months before war with Germany. By July 1939, 38 million gas masks had been issued to the entire population, including babies and children. The German bombing campaign known as the Blitz (from 'Blitzkrieg', German for 'lightning war') wouldn't reach them until a year later, September 1940, but they didn't know that then. The possibility of poison gas dropping from the sky at any moment appeared good enough for everyone to carry a gas mask and learn how to strap it on in an emergency. Gerda, like everyone else, would have read the official instructions, but perhaps with a different sort of foreboding, since she herself was also from Germany, the source of the deadly gas:

Your mask should be kept carefully. Never hang it up by the straps which fasten it over the head. This will pull the rubber face out of shape. It should be kept in the special box provided. Keep the box in a cool place away from strong light. It should never be held close to a fire or hot water pipes or left out in the sun. To put it on: hold the mask by each of the side straps with the thumbs underneath and the inside of the window facing you. Then lift the mask to your face, push the chin forward into it and draw the straps over the top of your head as far as they will go. Run finger round face piece taking care head straps are not twisted. If out of doors turn jacket collar up to stop gas drifting down neck, and put on gloves or put hands in pockets. Put up umbrella if you have one. Putting your mask away: After the mask has been used you will find that it is wet on the inside with moisture from the breath. This should be wiped off with a soft dry cloth and the mask allowed to dry before it is put away in its box. Do not try to dry by applying heat.[29]

Though the prospect of gas pouring from the sky worried eight or nine million Londoners, there were unintended comic touches in the official instructions – the jacket collar turned up to stop gas drifting down the neck, people putting up umbrellas against the poisonous downpour from Germany. Whether people saw anything funny in such things or not, the 'Mickey Mouse' masks for children lightened the mood. Made of red rubber, with bright white-rimmed eyes, a black and blue snout and big round black ears, these cartoon masks were designed to be fun to wear. A young Gerda, walking the London streets (which she did with and then without Joe) in search of diversion and entertainment, might have noticed children with 'Mickey Mouse' masks and babies wearing gas helmets in prams, but gas masks for dogs would have certainly got her attention as more endearing than comical. And she would have paused to admire the gas-masked dummies in department store windows. No such period features of street life on the Home Front entered her story of the gas mask and the diamonds. My mother was never one for telling stories, and though she lived and loved in London for much of the war, she left little evident trace of her presence there.

As far as I can tell, Gerda was unafraid of the Nazis and

---

[29] Government information, July 1939, on use, storage and maintenance of gas masks. A Ministry of Home Security, issuing official instructions, was established in 1939.

their poison gas and had no fear of it reaching her in London; or if she did, there were worse things to consider. Why waste a lovely young face in a gas mask when it is your best asset and every second counts? Why look like an alien? But the gas mask retained one special function for her: as a hiding-place for the only inheritance she possessed of any value.

For all the Civil Defence precautions, warnings and drills, poison gas never fell from the sky during six years of war, but her gas mask came in handy as an unlikely and therefore good hiding place for her diamonds. Given this important function, it deserved a place in her diary when the rest of her life was denied access, yet there is not a single entry concerning it, either when the loss was first discovered or later. That gas mask would have no special place in her life or memory of the war if not for the lost diamonds, but they made all the difference, and in consequence I know as much about wartime gas masks as she did, probably much more, since she had no particular reason to research them, and lacked the peculiar interest I have in her life. For Gerda, I imagine, a gas mask clamped to her face (perhaps as she practised putting it on in the mirror), felt hot and smelly and made her gag and look ugly. Back then, she loved her appearance and would have disliked watching the best part of it disappearing inside a magnified insect mask with flattened black rubber skull, goggling eyes, and a proboscis with a perforated tin snout smelling of disinfectant and asbestos. High-stepping London Chorus Girls in short white satin skirts might wear them and still look attractive, at least from the neck or the waist down, and masks might enable the 'telephone girls' seated at London switchboards to 'carry on regardless and keep connecting'; and in some posters loving couples could be seen kissing snout to snout. As she saw things, Gerda had only her looks to recommend her, and they needed to be seen at all times. Behind the face that could turn the heads of policemen in the street a German Jew looked out, a little anxiously, though that was probably less obvious to others than to her. My guess is that she wouldn't be seen dead in a gas mask. For all the official hype, it was unlikely to attract admiring glances in public or become a must-have fashion accessory, even if smartly-dressed women and elegant shop dummies wore them in West End department stores, and it could be discreetly hidden inside a handbag with a special compartment. Other inconvenient aspects of civilian war in the city, like the 'Blackout', sometimes prompted a more effective sales pitch, for example with the range of luminous accessories like buttons that glowed in the dark and made the wearer outwardly more visible, and I can imagine Gerda wearing those if she could afford them.

'Do You Carry Your Gas Mask?' asked a 1940 British Pathé newsreel, knowing the answer. 'Some of us have been inclined to forget it.' This, I believe, is what she did all the time. One of the hundreds of images featuring gas masks (very popular on the internet) shows two men with austerity wartime haircuts and brown cotton coverall work coats in Baker Street Lost Property Office stacking floor-to-ceiling shelves of masks in numbered cardboard boxes. My mother's gas mask might have ended up unclaimed on a shelf. Although I lack evidence for this, I assume that by spring of 1940 she wasn't among the 1% of Londoners who could still be seen carrying their gas masks in public. How she lost hers, where it ended up, was never made clear. One version of the story involved the ARP (Air Raid Precautions) wardens responsible for warning people of suspected gas attacks with wooden football rattles and carrying out monthly inspections of gas masks. Apparently one such official visited Gerda's address while she was out and collected her gas mask. I recently came across a photograph of an ARP warden, in cap, suit, tie and wellington boots, handing something to a woman in a flowered dress in an English cottage doorway – both frozen in time as he delivered one of the '300 new filter pieces for the village gas-masks'. If replacement filters were delivered door to door in villages as well as towns and cities, why would the warden in Gerda's story take her mask away to have a new filter fitted? Her diamonds were apparently concealed inside 'the lining of the gas mask', yet my internet research identifies no such 'lining' in the typical black rubber mask with its round non-flammable eyes and a perforated snout containing an asbestos filter more harmful to the wearer than the German gas that never dropped from the sky. For her story to remain credible, it required detail and explanation, and I now know that she had more than diamonds to hide.

CHAPTER ELEVEN:

THE DIAMONDS

In view of environmental breakdown, rising sea levels, deforestation, loss of species, I am aware that the world is coming to an end faster than people would have liked for the sake of their families and humanity. Apparently, we are approaching a 'tipping point', and in less than fifty years a third of the world's population will be living in Sahara-like deserts. In this global context, recovering the lost life of an unknown and unremembered woman who killed herself fifty-odd years ago at the age of fifty, might seem a waste of time and effort. Against those larger and looming losses, the loss of a few wartime diamonds seems insignificant, even to me.

This is a story about loss, about how you can lose almost everything and still survive. Gerda 'lost' her diamonds (so she said), but when she told us that story, she doubtless had other losses in mind. For Gerda never forgot father, family, friends, the future she might have had but for Hitler and history. They were part of the everything she had to leave behind when she left Germany. In May 1939 she was young, still seventeen, and losing everything bothered her less then than it did later. The diamonds were just another loss in a series of losses, and by no means the last, and there is no evidence that it troubled her unduly at the time.

Her story about the gas mask and the ARP warden seems unlikely, yet might just turn out to be true. Why invent such a story? She could have simply said she lost or misplaced the diamonds. A straightforward explanation like that would be credible, less likely to be doubted by an overly inquisitive son asking his long-dead mother awkward questions. Possessions – valuables, things you think you can't do without and miss as though they were part of you – they are always getting lost, and it was all the more likely in wartime, with the Luftwaffe overhead dropping bombs on London and the household huddled and cuddled together on the floor. She could have 'lost' the diamonds in the normal way, not knowing how or when or where. It was a nuisance, a bit careless, even irresponsible and a betrayal of Tatta's trust, but worse things happen in war. It would be awkward explaining the loss to her father (if he survived) and Gunther – Gunther could be most unpleasant – but at least he was a world away and the worst he could do was never let her forget it.

The gas mask story might be true if only because it seems so unlikely. Who would think of concealing diamonds inside a gas mask? She might. Her habit of secrecy was already embedding itself by then like a dark sediment deposited under all her later layers, and elaborate concealments came naturally to her despite suspecting nobody in the SE15 household of going through her things. A gas mask is as good a place as any to hide something of value; better actually, for who would think of probing a black mask smelling of rubber, disinfectant and asbestos for priceless gems? In the absence of further evidence, it is impossible to decide one way or another, and at least not knowing for certain what really happened leaves room for speculation, which can be more fun than facts.

The responsibilities of ARP wardens, a final internet search revealed, included sounding the alert with football rattles if poison gas was suspected, policing blackouts, evacuating areas around unexploded bombs, rescuing people from bombed buildings, and checking gas masks. They were also to be informed of any flaws found in a gas mask. Flaws might arise from rising temperatures inside the mask as wartime make-up easily smudged or melted. The hairstyles of the period could also cause problems. Anyone with thick hair, like Gerda, might experience difficulty fitting the mask to her face and ensuring a tight seal. So, perhaps hers was flawed and needed checking, and she might have asked her employers to mention it to the warden if he called round while she was out, forgetting all about the diamonds.

That line of inquiry led me back to the letters. Though there are no 'diamonds' in her wartime diaries, there is a veiled reference to them in two nearly identical unsent letters to Gunther in January and June 1944:

As for the so-called "goods" Tatta managed to give me, there isn't a Brosel left – because I was in need of it and couldn't get one eighth of its real value, so I'm afraid you've had it.

My first interpretation of these letters was that Gerda had decided to brazen it out and inform Gunther that she had sold the diamonds and got very little for them. Her brother was then scraping an expatriate living 'leading a 5-men orchestra' playing 'swings and hot music in the new bounced Boogie-Woogie style' at the Boris-Palace in Quito, Ecuador. Evidently, she thought better of it. That bomb shell of a letter would have exploded in his face. When I considered the matter further in *Remember Who You Used to Be*, I concluded that her bold confession remained unsent because:

Gerda was afraid to face – recoiled from – difficult things. Dreaded them. What happened to the diamonds was one such difficult thing.

That was my view of the matter until recently. The assertion of the confession and especially the bravado of 'so I'm afraid you've had it' are unlike the mother I remember, and it seems she thought better of bluntly admitting what she had done with no attempt at excuse or apology. It evidently weighed on her mind as she redrafted an almost identical letter, apparently with renewed determination to send it, but maybe it was enough to write and retain it as a reminder of her good intentions. She had finally admitted the truth of their inheritance. There was no inheritance. It was all gone. Gerda was strong enough to accept it and get on with her life. Why disillusion and upset Gunther who had come to rely on it, could not believe that all was lost, and would only blame her? It now seems to me that not sending such unwelcome news to her brother shows strength, not weakness.

It occurred to me that she hoped to get his sympathy, placate him, by admitting that circumstances had forced her to sell the diamonds for a fraction of their real worth.

'Actually, I am hardly better off than you', the unsent letters suggest, 'for I too expected more and ended up with next to nothing.' Then I realised that she knew Gunther better than that. There was no point expecting sympathy for the sister who squandered their inheritance. No, he would not forgive her. So, in the end she wrote him the kind of letter she longed to write – confrontational, aggressive, careless of his likely response had he received it. 'Yes, I sold the diamonds, and that's the end of the matter. Like it or lump it.' She knew very well that Gunther would lump it.

This, then, is the definitive version of what happened to the diamonds. It sounds like the truth. Gerda badly needed the money, so she sold the remains of the 'family fortune' for a pittance, or as she later admitted in another unsent letter to her brother, for '£100'. Later still, as a mother, she would say of any sudden windfall of money (florin or half a crown) we got at birthdays or Christmas, 'It's burning a hole in your pocket.' Doubtless, those diamonds were burning holes in hers. For sheer verisimilitude, the real explanation of what happened to their inheritance exposes the 'gas mask' version as a complete fabrication. As a refugee and domestic servant with negligible income and no assets apart from her looks, Gerda needed money for clothes, makeup, going out, having a bit of fun, pictures, etc. Depending on the timing of the sale, Tatta was either still in Nazi Germany and in no position to benefit from diamonds, or dead from abdominal cancer in Quito. As for Gunther, he boasted about leading his own band in the 'Boris-Bar' where 'a multitude is listening to the clever music of Gunther-

Heinz' and their 'bouncy Boogie-Woogie', so he was succeeding in Ecuador without diamonds. Kurt had long since disappeared in Buenos Aires. There was nobody to look after Gerda but Gerda herself.

That's true. She sold the diamonds, just as she described and as she bravely admitted to her brother in two unsent letters. Of this I have no doubt. But this new revisionist interpretation of her life needn't stop there, for in telling us that she 'lost' the diamonds, my mother spoke a deeper truth. 'Lost', 'stolen', 'sold' are conflicting versions of what actually happened, yet all are true. With all her other losses in mind when she told us the story of the gas mask, loss had to come into it too. The diamonds were all that remained of the shops, properties, assets stolen by the state. As they had been 'sold' or 'transferred' to new 'Aryan' owners for a fraction of their 'real value', so the diamonds were 'sold' at a similar loss. The implication of Gerda's 'confession' is that she was robbed, just as their father had been robbed.

Though literally 'sold', the diamonds – far from offsetting past losses – merely perpetuated them. Gerda (who had become my mother in the meantime) always associated them with loss, as can be seen in yet another unsent letter (dated 25 November 1954) to Gunther:

Received your letter today and it put me in rather a bad mood. No. 1: My hair. It has gone very thin in places and I don't fancy to be bald. No. 2: "The Kinderchen". I wish I would never have had them. I haven't had them for 15 years now. I either lost them or they got stolen, I don't know which, during an air-raid in the war.

Already, at the age of thirty-three, she was (she recognised) losing her looks – her only asset – and apparently her once lustrous dark hair was the first to go. Gerda had made the mistake of sending Gunther a photograph of herself looking worn and weary with wind-blown hair in a muddy camp of Nissen huts in Oxfordshire. His letter, to which she refers, had again brought up the subject of the missing diamonds – for which he had yet to receive an adequate explanation – as well as commenting unkindly on her slack and slovenly appearance. My mother drafted an angry, hurt, assertive reply, which he never had an opportunity to read. In Gerda-land, looks were everything, and to lose them was a loss from which a woman could never recover, though no more than a young mother could expect from life in her early thirties under a corrugated-iron roof with three young children and no friends. As regards 'the *Kinderchen*' – 'the little children', as her old family referred to the missing diamonds – Gerda appears here not to remember exactly what happened to them, whether 'lost' or 'stolen', and there is no mention here of having 'sold' them. The truth, which she could hardly explain to her brother, is that all three were true.

I wish I would never have had them.

It is an unsurprising epitaph for diamonds of such provenance and I wonder if she was remembering herself as she used to be – eighteen and in London, her good looks intact, her hair thick and dark, war coming but not yet arrived – and also remembering them, her diamonds, and what they meant to her then. I can just about make her out there, sitting on her narrow bed in her little room in SE15, holding them, admiring the unequalled hardness and brilliance of the starriest stones on earth, forgetting for a moment or two her life as a domestic. She was less ambivalent about diamonds then. As things turned out, she derived more guilt than 'Geld' from them, for all their initial promise. Even diamonds could not deliver. One had not been enough to stop Joe leaving her in the winter of 1939. Well, he was just another loss to add to the others that year, and she was in London and looking better than ever. She had not lost her looks, and they were her real 'diamonds'.

By November 1954, fifteen years older than that domestic with diamonds, she was a mother of three, losing her hair, and drafting a hurt reply to an unkind letter from a brutal brother, and she had definitely come down in the world. She was down there, among 'the proletariat', as she called them, and looking as much a mess as many of the women with her in a camp of corrugated iron-roofed Nissen huts in a field. That year, Kitty Kallen's version of *Little Things Mean a Lot* reached No. 1 in American charts, and she probably heard it on the radio about the time she got Gunther's letter from America. If so, she might have agreed with Kitty about not caring that much for 'diamonds and pearls', for Jack still thought she looked lovely and sometimes touched her hair as he passed her chair and told her how nice she always looked.

There she sits, my young ageing mother, in a draughty Nissen hut repurposed after the war as temporary housing, remembering her diamonds. They were long gone by then, and she would have almost forgotten about them but for Gunther's snide reminders. If she regretted the loss, it was also a relief, for they were always a worry to her and without them and unencumbered there was less to expect from life. Perhaps she was also remembering her last outing to the pictures, for she still managed to go even then, with Jack looking after the children in the playpen. I like to think that the recently seen film was *Gentlemen Prefer Blondes*, which came out in 1953, and that she was remembering Marilyn Monroe in that bright pink strapless gown of hers, singing *Diamonds Are a Girl's Best Friend*. It was just the sort of film Gerda loved, though I don't know if she had actually seen it or could have agreed with Marilyn about diamonds. By then they had lost their sparkle for Gerda and had a distinctly dark underside.

CHAPTER TWELVE:

'ROSEBUD'

Relatively few diamonds survive the journey from the bowels of the earth to the surface. The few diamonds in Gerda's possession as she waved goodbye survived her own journey from Germany to a new life in England, but not for very long. When exactly she and her diamonds parted company is not recorded in her diary or in any unsent letter to her brother, but most likely it was while she was still a domestic in SE15 and needed the money after Joe and the end of her first 'Big Love'. Something had to fill the hole left in her life.

Watching *The Repair Shop* on BBC iPlayer, which I do as an almost daily diversion from my dead mother, I sometimes fantasise about finding her old gas mask and taking it to the barn with a view to broadcasting her story as she would not have wanted. *The Repair Shop* likes an occasional backdrop of war, displacement, diaspora and intergenerational difficulties to darken things up a bit. Because of Gerda, I home in especially on dead mothers. Ageing children think about these mothers all the more once they are no longer there to complicate matters, viewing them as absent rather than dead, 'looking over us from somewhere' and 'keeping an eye on things'. When some artefact intimately associated with a prior generation is brought to the barn for repair and restoration, I naturally think of her, although of course it isn't only absent mothers who are missed. A disintegrating diary, a diamond engagement ring, a refugee's battered suitcase, a sailor's logbook from the *Titanic*, a wedding ring containing ashes – whatever bears a unique imprint and holds special meaning and connection. Such artefacts are doubly touching, for they are the opposite of a memento mori: not 'remember you must die', but 'remember that we live'.

The Repair Shop has its detractors deriding the emotionalism and sentimentality. Families mourn the 'passing' or 'loss' (rarely the 'death') of loved ones in a televised ritual of remembrance and renewal. I love it for those reasons and because in my experience the familial dead really are closer at hand than we realise – closer still if you hold something of theirs in your hand – and hover about so long as something they once held is retrieved for repair. No longer around, unfortunately, to look after the things once so dear to them, they are nonetheless mindful of breakages, damage and neglect, and their likely views of the wonderful repair and restoration are always sought at the end. Invariably they are delighted, as the current custodians of the heirloom will confirm. The familial dead are summoned back to witness this sudden interest in them, which comes as no surprise. Though I could (and probably will) watch *The Repair Shop* until it closes, I have reservations about my mother, who had no wish to be summoned back and nothing she wanted repaired. There is little likelihood of her gas mask or diamonds turning up at the barn, or of her looking down from 'somewhere' and 'keeping an eye on me' while (mindful of the TV camera) I speak on her behalf: 'It meant so much to her. She'd be so pleased to see it as it used to be, so happy it's still around.' Parents and grandparents remembered by Repair Shop families deserve everything they get, and it couldn't be otherwise. You don't get invited to the barn to complain bitterly about someone you dislike and would rather forget.

Gerda was missed but not mourned. As I recall, nobody said how much they missed her kindness and love or wanted her back in the sentient world. That she has taken up more or less permanent residence in me is less from an excess of love on my part than from an excess of paper on hers, for it is through the contents of her suitcases that I have finally got to know her. Apart from diaries and photographs and the letters she received over three decades, nothing of Gerda has survived and still holds the essence of her, such as a perfume bottle. But there are the five suitcases, and they count for something. 'They contained my mother and her previous family,' I could say. Actually, a suitcase is not a bad idea. In *The Repair Shop* they speak of the journey of a particular thing, as though it had a separate life and history, a trajectory of its own – the current owners only transient custodians. The five suitcases didn't stop when she did, but continued on their separate journey irrespective of her, and she had no say in the matter.

No single thing brings her close. She comes and goes as I read and try to conjure her up. She sometimes motions me from a distance and I glimpse in passing the ghost of a Gerda. Other ageing children seem to find their dead mothers more easily. A close-up of a woman's dancing shoes from the 1940s reveals the permanent impress of her big toe on the insole, and I am impressed by the pains taken by the repairer to preserve that touching imprint of personal history when the wearer was young; excited; had a future; loved dancing. A Mother of Pearl purse with a red silk lining brings back another mother, and if I held that purse I might think differently about mine, such is the power of suggestion. There are times I close in on her. 'Yes,' I say to myself, 'there is definitely something of my mother here,' and though it is someone else's story, it touches some hidden part of a more intimate history. A manicure set, a twenty-first birthday present, which survived the Blitz, when Gerda was twenty-one. The remembered woman was 'always well turned out' (like my mother before she became one). 'You could hear the bombs dropping, windows out, devastation everywhere.' Gerda also heard it, if differently, from the floor of the house at SE15, afterwards recording her excitement and the thrill of aerial war in that unsent letter to her brother, and for a moment I hear again the Blitz in her voice. A pre-war spice box like a little silver train, filled with cloves, nearly brought her back, though (as far as I know) Gerda practised no Jewish customs, said no special words over wine and candlelight and the sweet aroma of cloves. The woman who brought the spice box in for repair said it was 'supposed to sweeten conversation'. My mother in her later years could have done with one of those.

Watching *The Repair Shop* reaffirms my faith in families. Dead parents and grandparents, sisters and brothers, daughters and sons, are remembered as the artefacts once special to them are proffered for repair. Love holds families together through generations, and guilt provides extra glue as an incentive to finally get restored something that has been left far too long. Nothing is so damaged that it can't be repaired, and always beyond expectation. The outcomes are dependably positive. Visitors can't thank the repairers enough, and the repairers can't thank them enough for another opportunity to repair something more than the cherished artefact. Everything broken gets fixed; families are reunited and go away happy, including the absent ones who approve the repair and are pleased to be home and a focal point once again after years in a drawer or attic or garage or garden shed. Such miraculous repairs – deemed impossible until the cloth is whisked away to reveal the transformation – offset even the damage of death. It is a simple formula, which *The Repair Shop* never tires of repeating, and seems to work well enough for other people. Not so for Gerda. It could be said of my mother that she had hidden fault lines long before she started a family, and though she escaped intact in 1939, the breakage appeared twenty-one years later as hairline cracks and spread through the last decade of her diaries, and she had to stop herself 'going to pieces'. It could be said that in her case the damage was irreparable, way beyond the remit of *The Repair Shop*.

With people, as with the things they loved and by which they are ever afterwards identified and remembered, the compulsion to go back to a time before the damage was done or first became apparent can be irresistible. This reflection put me in mind of what many still regard as the greatest film ever made, *Citizen Kane* (1941). One source indicates a UK release date of January 1942, though the internet appears otherwise uninterested on this point, so Gerda possibly saw it sometime during the war, perhaps encouraged by RKO 'erroneously' promoting it as a 'love story'. As months and even years of her wartime diaries are missing, I can't go back to them as a source of information and, despite being a frequent movie-goer, Gerda rarely referred to films in her diaries, and never to how they affected her. The reverse flow of the story in *Citizen Kane* as the investigative reporter goes back through his life to the source put off audiences and the film was considered 'bad box office'. If she ever saw *Kane*, it must have disappointed her; there is no real love interest and she would have had no identification with a bloated old man who dies before shedding years and flesh and looking his charming best as an ambitious young man with all the money and future he needs to get there. For me, though, seeking the real Gerda as the reporter seeks the real Kane, this film is the key.

At the end of his life and the beginning of the film, Kane whispers one enigmatic word, 'Rosebud'. The newspaper reporters never find out what it means. Only cinema audiences (or in my case solitary DVD viewers) discover that 'Rosebud' is the name of the little sled Charles Foster Kane remembers as he dies. If the boyhood sled had not been incinerated, along with all the other 'junk' littering Kane's cluttered 'pleasure palace', Xanadu, it is just the sort of thing often brought to *The Repair Shop*.

Early in the film, Kane's estranged first wife, who is also 'the President's niece', and their son Kane Junior, are reported to have died in a motor accident in 1918, their deaths mentioned briefly in passing in a newsreel reconstruction of his life. But supposing Junior hadn't died. Supposing he visited his old Dad one last time in that vast, echoing mausoleum of a mansion Kane called home and retrieved 'Rosebud' before it was burned in the basement incinerator. Junior would be well over a hundred by 2017 when *The Repair Shop* first opened on TV, but his son or grandson, remembering the importance of the sled to the family, could have gone. No, let's imagine a girl instead. Kane, a dominant alpha male, controlled women like Susan, the 'opera singer', and nearly drove her to suicide. So, it's fitting that his hypothetical representative at *The Repair Shop* should be a granddaughter, who fondly recalls visiting Granddad at Xanadu during her early years and seeing the sled there. Her grandfather sometimes called her 'Rosebud' too, a pretty name, and when she was old enough to see the film, she thought of Granddad Charlie as a little boy playing with his sled in the snow. That little boy was the real Charlie Kane, she always thought, underneath the later outer layers. It was handed down to her, the little sled with the burn marks from the incinerator but with its name, 'Rosebud', still legible. There had been a little globe, too, with a miniature enclosed snow scene and when you shook it, snowflakes fell from a glass sky, but unfortunately Granddad had dropped it and it broke.

What this hypothetical granddaughter didn't mention (and perhaps didn't know) during her imaginary visit to the thatched Sussex barn was that 'Rosebud' was also a nickname for a favourite clitoris. There are other theories. For Orson Welles it apparently signified the love of a lost mother, little Charlie Kane having been plucked as a boy from his mother and that snowy idyll of childhood.

Perhaps what 'Rosebud' meant to an old man aloof and alone in his mausoleum of a home was that, for all the wealth and power of a newspaper tycoon and media mogul, the only thing that really mattered at the end of his life was the memory of an unviolated childhood as he played with his sled in the snow. During my most recent viewing of the film, I noticed something new. After the boy is plucked from his innocent past, another sled appears, a birthday present at his new 'home'. Though its name is half hidden from view, it surely couldn't be 'Rosebud'. After multiple replays, I still couldn't make out the name. What does this signify? That the original 'Rosebud' can never be replaced? That childhood happiness, once lost, can never be duplicated?

Asked if he discovered what the name means, the investigative journalist tasked with unlocking the mystery – the enigma of the word itself and of the man who whispered it before dropping the glass globe on the floor – wonders if 'Rosebud' was something Kane 'couldn't get or lost'. It remains, he admits, 'the missing piece of a jigsaw', though 'it wouldn't have explained anything'.

I have often replayed the end of the film, scrutinising the vast 'collection of nearly everything' crated up in Xanadu for disposal. I have noticed how the little sled is picked out separately, as if it has some special status, only to join the rest of the 'junk' in the furnace. The final shot of black smoke from the incinerator chimney seems especially significant. These days, I am oddly reminded of my mother, whose similarity to Charles Foster Kane is not obvious. Disparate things sometimes disclose the closest connections. Like Kane, Gerda 'liked to collect things', couldn't 'throw anything away'. Lacking the interior space of a Xanadu, she made do with an old redbrick semi in Cowley, Oxford, but she too had a zeal for collecting things unwanted and junked after her death. And there is a deeper connection. As a public figure, Kane was the most publicised person on the planet; private Kane the most unknown and unknowable. My mother had no public profile and disappeared from view without anyone noticing outside the family, and yet for the last few years I have sought her more assiduously than the dogged reporter tries to hunt down Kane and still feel no closer to my quarry.

Though *Citizen Kane* wasn't her kind of Hollywood, I wonder if looking at my mother's life through the lens of such a film might yet reveal something new. 'Kane's world is now history' ran the headline. Ditto Gerda's world. Kane was a collector – the vast interior vistas of his 'pleasure palace' crammed with his 'collections' from across the world. Ditto my mother, if mostly of discarded clothes from the backstreets of Oxford. She even catalogued them, with labels detailing each item – which Kane never got round to doing – though to compare her hundred-odd suitcases of cast-offs with the sheeted collections cluttering up the vastness of Xanadu is stretching the comparison. 1871 was the year that Kane, still just a boy with a sled and mother and father, 'came into some money'. My mother came into 'some money' (the long-awaited compensation from Germany) exactly a century later, in 1971. It is the losses, however, that really connect them. 'Mr Kane', we are told, 'was a man who lost almost everything he had.' It would take too long to list Gerda's losses, and Kane would be hard pressed to come up with anything to match them.

And then the question of love. According to Kane's best friend, all Charlie 'ever really wanted out of life was love' but he 'didn't have any love to give'. Was that true of Gerda too? She loved her dogs, Sandy especially. If an anguished concern for the welfare of ill-treated animals is the measure, then my mother loved. Her heart went out to suffering things – even to us, her children, at times – not so much because we suffered, but in anticipation of the suffering to come. From January 1960, with Nazism on the rise again, she observed in her diaries how young and vulnerable we were, how unaware in our childish innocence of the great harm about to befall us. For a month or so, we were the '*Kinderchen*', the little children, and she had to get us out of harm's way, but when her fear of what the future would bring abated, she went back to herself and her everyday anxieties.

So, Kane had no love to give? 'Yes, and my mother too,' I could suggest. Yet it would be no truer of her than of Kane, for having read and reread her diaries, I know more about the woman behind the words. Those January 1960 entries were a revelation: she really did love her children, I realised, at least while we were still young enough to be loved, and hoped only to spare us a second Holocaust. It was her way of showing that she cared, by writing it in her private diary. She had once loved her Tatta unequivocally, too, until he got on her nerves with his expectations and demands. She loved Joe until the 'Big Love' turned out to be an 'arsehole'. She loved Jack, who called her his 'Angel' and 'Dream Girl' in wartime love letters, and in her idiosyncratic way she still loved the Jack who pressed steel night after night for wife and family. Like Kane, though, my mother found it difficult to love, or to show it.

Peter Thornthwaite

The newspaper men looking for the real Kane after his death want to find out 'who he was'. Thompson, the reporter investigating Kane's life, has his leads to follow, as I have mine. The diaries and letters available to me are more reliable as witnesses, for they can be read and re-read and I can return to them whenever I like. They amount to a body of evidence for and against my mother. But no one who knew Kane could help Thompson uncover the secret of 'Rosebud' because no one, his 'best friend' included, really knew him.

For me too, the 'Rosebud moment' is yet to come, thanks to her, and I still wonder if she packed suitcases with evidence of a past life and put them away for posterity because she really wanted them to be found and their contents read. Meanwhile she remains as elusive as Kane, and there might never be a 'Rosebud moment', though I live in hope.

As for her last words, they lack the mysterious appeal of 'Rosebud'. As a one-word epitaph, Kane's definitely has the edge on hers, although I formerly considered her suicide note a model of brevity at eight unequivocal words. *Rosebud*. That word echoes down the film, as unattached as the man who whispered it with his last breath, and a singularly enigmatic one at that. My mother's last words, which (as I recall, the note having disappeared with her) sloped and slurred down the torn-off sheet of paper, are more moving with the passage of time. They lack the echoing resonance of 'Rosebud', yet I frequently hear their dying fall and, for all their plainness they are the equal of her best lines from earlier years. She was capable of epitaphs. In early summer of 1938, after returning to the Reich from her year abroad at Victoria

College, and with *Kristallnacht* several months and a mindset away, Gerda inscribed in her diary: 'The beautiful Prague time is over.' There is some faint echo of that in the last words she scrawled one December night in 1971 on a lost scrap of paper.

CHAPTER THIRTEEN: HAPPY DAYS

1 May 1945 in the S.O. Book 135 Supplied for the Public Service (used as a diary): 'Jack and I are married.' This statement prompted one of her notes to self: 'Must try to slim' as 'nobody will like a fat Jew girl'. Luckily, Jack did. His love letters, as revealed in *Remember Who You Used to Be*, refer to her as 'my Dream Girl', 'such an Angel'. Her 'foreignness' and awareness of being 'different', which underlay her sense of separation and exclusion, were for Jack her great attraction. She had 'grown' on him, he supposed, 'because you are so very different from other girls'. She appreciated the compliment and probably winced at it. His letters touch me again with their surprising eloquence. Jack, aware of his epistolary limitations, found it 'hard work writing letters', but a love such as he had never felt before brought out something I never descried in him until much later, after she died. On first reading his letters, I found a different man to the factory father I remembered. The unexpected eloquence, combined with the unintended pathos of many lines, touched me as deeply as anything my mother ever wrote, maybe more, because (unlike my pre-parents in 1945) I

know what happened later. 'How I love you. It hurts.' It would hurt much more later, Dad. 'To make you happy is my one ambition in life.' It seems unfair to mention her suicide. 'I know I am very lucky and certainly don't think I really deserve such happiness.' You did, Dad, but you weren't very lucky. 'Can't you feel my love for you even though we are so far apart?'

He was thinking of geographical distance then, being stationed elsewhere, yet he could have sensed another distance too. Gerda had her own absences to live with, and so did Jack. Sunderland, where he came from, and the North East had to go after they married; for although 'Jacky's people' were 'ever so nice and kind', when she met them on the 'best leave I ever had in my life', what was 'home' for him was soon repellent to her pampered middle-class upbringing. Sunderland was 'a rather dirty town because of all the shipping business' and it only got worse when they were wondering where to live after the war: 'I don't want to go to Sunderland, I hate it there. It's dirty and awful and all dirty proletariat there.' That was one of the absences he lived with for the remainder of their marriage. But in May 1945, at the end of war and the start of married life together, Jack had, I am sure (and I write this without irony) 'happy days' to come with his 'Dream Girl' and 'Angel'.

His love letters, set out in full in *Remember Who You Used to Be*, were nearly left out. That book concerned Gerda and her foreign family, tracing a more eventful history (as I saw it) than Jack could offer, and as it had to make room for the Third Reich, World War and the Holocaust, it allowed little space for her English family, including Jack. We'd have been a distraction, a digression, and if Gerda and her first family took precedence over us, it was a necessary excision and rather a relief to cut us out. As for Jack's love letters, I eventually relented, including them in the final draft because they were as much part of her story as his. Aside from his love letters though, Jack hardly got a look in.

So, now I'm making up for my father's previous absence from the story. Gerda still takes up most of the space, of course, and it is essentially her story I'm re-telling (or telling differently), but Jack now has a place in it and this time won't be omitted. His inclusion in this present book is for her sake too, because his love shows her in a different light. It was on my father's behalf that I blamed her (as I have only just realised) not just for killing herself but for omitting him from her suicide note. After all his sacrifices, everything he had done for her (such was my line of reasoning), his absence from her last written words ('Look after the dogs, I've had my chips') seemed at best an unintended insult, as if he meant so little to her that she simply forgot to mention him at the end. He loved her and never criticised or blamed her for anything, so far as I know, so I did it for him after he died.

Jack was the kind of father who gets remembered in *The Repair Shop*. A caring man, he left behind when he died the sort of vintage tools occasionally taken to the thatched West Sussex barn for repair. His father, a ship's carpenter on the Sunderland docks early in the twentieth century and a big man at six foot four (a trait not passed down to me, unfortunately), left Jack his old woodworking tools with the initials W.T. (William Thornthwaite) inscribed on the worn beechwood handles, and he in turn left them to me. Gerda got diamonds from her father, I got tools from mine, but like her I also lost or sold them.

I was recently reminded of him by an eighty-year-old 'Jack in the box', as featured in *The Repair Shop*. If still alive, my father would be 108, but they were not unalike in appearance. That boxed Jack was in a sorry state. 'We definitely have to get the spring back in him,' the repairer said with a smile. To do that, Jack was taken out of his box, and a start made on his face, which after a good clean looked much brighter and the eyes bluer – just as I remember my father's eyes. His clothes were then turned back-to-front to restore the original brighter colours. Finally, the head was re-attached to the spring, the lever pressed, and Jack got his bounce back.

What Jack Thornthwaite, widower, ex-sheet-metal-worker in Cowley, Oxford, would have made of *The Repair Shop* (which 'opened' twenty years too late for him), I'm not sure, but knowing a few things about him, I could safely say that he always shunned sentimentality, nostalgia, looking back. Once in a pub, having selected on the jukebox (this was the 1970s) the famous Vera Lynn song, *We'll Meet Again*, I looked at him expectantly. After a silence I asked if it reminded him of the war, meeting Mum, etc. 'I don't want to think about any of that now,' he said, 'it's all gone.'

'Dad was a lovely, lovely man,' a daughter said on *The Repair Shop*. As I type this, I see my own dad cushioned in his coffin, face strangely shrunken, cheeks pinched and rouged, hands crossed, my kind and caring father supine and smart and stiff as a dummy in his best suit, and I push the image away. My mother invited no such epitaph. He was much nicer than her, less complicated, easier to love and remember, and the slab of marble commemorating him is still visited regularly and cleared of weeds and soil. While she was alive, it was less easy getting to know a man who wasn't there by day. Working nights for twenty-five years, up for another shift as we were getting ready for bed, my father was more noticeable as an absence than as a presence – a dependable absence who was always there and for whom we could do important things like taking it in turns to roll his ciggies for the night. That would be something for *The Repair Shop* if I still had it – his old Rizla rolling machine – and a way of connecting with him again: remembering how we packed the moist tobacco into it, licked along the gummed edge of the paper, rolled the cylinder and manufactured as if by magic perfect cigarettes, a log-pile of them for his long night at the 'Press'.

With his health and her future in mind, plus the money she could save on cigarettes, my mother replaced them with polo mints; instead of dragging on fags to get him through the clash and heat of the night, he sucked on cool mints with holes. 'I don't want you dying on me,' she used to say. She even appeared in a TV advert for polo mints. I don't recall seeing her one and only television appearance (and seeing your mum on TV is something you would remember), but I can imagine her words when interviewed outside Woolworths in Cornmarket Street in the early 1960s: *My husband goes through packets of Polo mints every night and swears by them.* Or perhaps, facing the cameras and the whole country like a proper housewife with as much right to be there (and interviewed in front of TV cameras) as anyone else, for once the right words came: *My husband never believed he could ever give up smoking until I gave him Polo mints, and now he never looks back*. Whatever she actually said, it put her on national TV for a few seconds, and I have no reason to doubt that it happened as Gunther also acknowledged it in a letter.

As with ciggies, so with Saturday afternoon wrestling. She had her jumble sales (*my only excitement in life*), he his television wrestling. It was his only opportunity to deliver forearm smashes or lever a muscled arm high up behind his opponent's back. 'You're getting over-excited, Jacky, I don't want you kicking the bucket on me, so no more Saturday afternoon wrestling for you.' And that was the end of that. She was genuinely frightened that he might drop down dead if he got too worked up and leave her with three children and not enough money. They both had to make sacrifices in life.

If anything brings my dad back, it is the wrestling, which became popular when ITV began showing it in the mid-1950s. At the peak of its popularity in the mid-1960s (around the time Gerda banned it) it made household names out of men like Mick McManus and Jackie Pallo, wrestling rivals for eleven years. With this internet information at my fingertip, Jack jerks back to life. This is definitely something we shared, father and son, two of the twenty million viewers watching the 1963 bout between Jackie Pallo and Mick McManus. 'Mr TV' Pallo, fair-haired, smooth-chested, pallid-skinned next to swarthy, hairy-chested McManus, 'the Man You Love to Hate', with his cropped black hair and black trunks and short forearm jabs. The internet retrieves something else from my past, unremembered for sixty years. 'Not the ears, not the ears', McManus pleads as his opponent cauliflowers them again. And I can see Jack give it and take it with all the moves – the sit-on back breaker, arm lever, aeroplane spin, cross-shoulder back breaker – more alive than she liked to see because such spasmodic moves from a husband frightened her. Exactly when the ban began, I can't remember, but it had something to do with another iconic gladiator of the TV wrestling ring and my favourite, Billy Two-Rivers, a Canadian Indian, whose Mohawk name was Kaientaronkwen. Billy wore a feathered headdress, had a Mohawk hairstyle, and sometimes did a war dance, which was beyond excitement. What the internet didn't disclose, but which I recall with sharper clarity than anything else from that period, is that Billy Two-Rivers, when sufficiently maddened and worked up by his war dance, chopped at his opponent's neck and felled him. That chop was Jack's downfall.

No more wrestling for you, Jacky boy. It's not good for you. You get too over-excited.

Jackie Pallo and Mick McManus were both about five-foot-six (I'm five-foot-eight) but seemed much bigger then, like my father. Jackie Pallo once played a gravedigger in an episode of *The Avengers* and was accidentally knocked unconscious in a fight with the judo champion character played by Honor Blackman, striking his head as he fell into the grave. Retrieving that from an internet search also reminded me of the last (and unfortunately lasting) image of my father in his coffin, which in turn brought back his final appearance while still alive, in a hospital bed, his eyes tight shut and his hand in mine – or rather mine in his; for although the dementia was rubbing him out, his core vitality was concentrated in that big veined hand clutching mine in its vice-like grip. When it was time to leave, Dad wouldn't let go, but held on as if drowning, and eventually I had to prise his fingers away as gently as his iron grip allowed. It was an uncomfortable parting.

After Gerda's suicide, my father came into his own, assuming in her absence a more solid presence than before. Alive, she had taken up the domestic space – not deliberately, but by virtue of her role, which with his night job nudged him into the margins of family life. With Gerda gone, and nights at the Pressed Steel also behind him, this was now his house. The things by which we knew her remained in situ for a while – the hundred suitcases of second-hand clothes for the family, the patchwork quilts she knitted and stitched, even the coats and skirts, cardigans and blouses hanging in her big mahogany wardrobe with the curtained glass doors. When I visited – Jack was living alone then, the three of us having left (four including his wife) – her absence was a palpable presence in the house. It collected in the enclosed spaces she had made her own – attic, pantry, under beds, on tops of wardrobes – but actually it could be felt anywhere. If Jack sensed it, I couldn't tell, and he was hardly going to mention it; perhaps he noticed it less as it became more familiar if not more comforting. Also, she had her parts of the house, he had his, and that continued after her death. During my visits we generally stopped in the big front room with its wide bay window overlooking the busy road connecting factory with city. My mother's sitting room was at the back, where long after she died I could imagine her watching a flickering television from her winged armchair. We could pass through it if we wished, via French windows, to the mostly sunless conservatory he had built for her shortly after we moved in, and which was never used for its intended purpose. As I recall, from my many visits home after her death, we sat in the dark, but that was probably because I mostly remember the evenings, winter evenings especially, and our predilection for a degree of darkness conducive to desultory conversation.

It was during our evenings at home that he came into his own. Dad missed her, of course. It probably wasn't what she intended, but by killing herself she had torn pages out of his life too, but that wasn't a topic for conversation. Even after several glasses of his whiskey there was no going back to that December morning when, returning from work and ready for his own bed, he found her inert in hers. What he thought about her suicide, how it affected him, I was careful not to ask. He wasn't a private person like her, and during her extended absence from the house he told me about his own half-hidden life and the 'happy days' (as he referred to them) before they met. For a long while suicidal Gerda remained a no-go area, with the exception of his repeated refrain whenever an ambulance blue-flashed past. 'There's trouble for someone.' That allusion to the unmentionable was as close as he ever got to it, though it was close enough. As I recall, the blue light and the siren interrupted those evenings of reminiscence at regular intervals, and his response was as predictable: 'A horrible noise. It gives me a bellyache.' It was the sort of raw, visceral thing he said when something really got to him.

That flashing blue light still flashes as it did fifty years ago, but I might have misremembered its frequency and even its colour. Were emergency vehicle lights blue in the 1970s? As usual the internet tells me more than I asked of it, revealing that the use of the blue emergency light actually originated in Germany during World War Two.

Not Drowning but Waving

As a result of blackout measures for aerial defence from 1935 (the *Verdankelung*), cobalt blue came to replace the red used by emergency vehicles. So, it seems I have Nazi Germany to thank for yet another colourful memory concerning my mother.

Those evenings with my father are my equivalent of the 'magical times', the 'special moments of connection' remembered by visitors to the Repair Shop, for he told me everything he had kept back while she was alive and we were still a proper family. Looking back at them now, I even feel sentimental about the blue light and siren of an ambulance as it flashed and wailed past. Those remembered evenings remain as evocative for me as old sunlight in a leaded stained-glass window must be for someone recalling its pictures of painted birds and butterflies and the father who hung it in his garden shed.

His face is a bit blurred for me now, half-erased by the subsequent dementia. His voice remains audible, though distant, as if on a phone with a poor connection. Although I thought of him as a 'Geordie', he was actually a native of another tribe called 'the Makems and Takems'. Twenty-five post-war years had half disguised his origins, yet his pre-war accent and dialect were still there underneath, breaking through after his wife's death as though he had never left the Tyne and Wear.

This is my father, still audible, speaking in his original voice across a widening gap of years, and these are some of the things he told me:

Wilfie Raynes [his best friend] was killed in France: a direct hit in the turret of his tank. Just before they left, Mrs Raynes had said, 'Look after him, Jack,' and he said, 'I've got enough to do to look after meself, Missis.' Later he didn't dare tell her the news, 'But blow me down if I didn't meet her in Sunderland High Street.'

'You'd have loved it when I was young.' Recalling the markets, buskers with accordions and violins, pigs' heads at the butchers, penny dips, a sweet shop where they raffled a monster Easter Egg for Doctor Barnardo's, a terrific big toy shop, a fight in Johnson Street, a man gripping another man's head by the ears and banging it on the cobbles.

The old Empire music hall, Miss Vesta Tilley on its green dome, and the time the circus came and a monkey escaped and climbed up 'to be with Vesta'.

And the old Victoria Hall, where children pressing against the doors that opened inwards were killed in a fire.

Fragments of a pre-war, pre-Gerda time were coming back as she made room for them. The family had never asked him about his past and he seldom had occasion to speak of it, but prompted by my genuine interest he told me more in one evening than in the previous twenty years. Such reminiscences soon became a normal feature of conversations with my father in my mother's absence. I took no notes – unfortunately, for they would have come in handy now – and if his remembered past appears fragmentary it's down to my unreliable memory, not his. Though I didn't know then what I know now from her diaries – that she hated Sunderland and made him promise that they would never live there – I was half-aware at the time that she was giving him permission to speak. One of the compensations of her suicide was that it returned his past to him. I wouldn't have put it like that, in those words, but I was already thinking along those lines.

And I was happy for my father; it was something I could do for him. This was no stream of recollections pouring out of him now that he finally had a chance to speak. There were long silences, and it was often when he said nothing that he had the most to say, and so I prompted him when necessary. I needed to hear the words as much as he needed to speak them.

'My life's been a shocking waste.'

He often said such things, without rancour or regret, as if at the end of a long conversation with himself, and the conclusion he had come to was obvious enough. It was no sudden realisation illuminating his entire life with the flashing blue emergency light of truth, merely something to be acknowledged. Things could not have turned out differently, even in different circumstances, and I didn't contradict him. Unhappy reflections, I soon learned, were easily bypassed by a sympathetic pause followed by a prompt such as: 'I was really interested, Dad, in what you were telling me the other evening about work on the farms.' Back in the flow, he would remember cutting and stacking the hay at Houghton le Spring: 'You had to stop if it rained. One wet bundle in a haystack and you could have a fire. I've seen many a stack burn.'

And the milk round, the long dark mornings clattering into Sunderland. And when it was too cold for the ponies, they used the farmer's car, a Rhode. 'I loved to ride in it, it was a real treat.'

If I asked him then about that make of car, I've forgotten what he said, but with access to the internet if no longer to a father, I find it was a British car made by Mead & Deakin Ltd from 1921 to 1930, its name taken from Cecil Rhodes, a great imperialist who gained almost total domination of the world's diamonds and founded the great diamond company, De Beers, in 1888, which was still monopolising diamond distribution into the 21st century. That old Rhode bulks in Jack's memory, a big square car built to last, as does the two-ton yellow Ford truck he drove around the mining villages, delivering pickles and sweets and bottled beer to the working men's clubs. 'Of course, the traffic was nowhere near what it is today.' He got thirty bob a week working for Robinson's, Guinness for breakfast – 'the Guinness wasn't like it is now, it was thick and creamy' – and his ciggies wholesale in cartons of 200.

'Ah, happy days.'

Going to Nan's and seeing huge snowballs in the street.

Nan all in black – cap, shawl, skirt – taking him to the pictures Friday night and getting him a pennyworth of oranges and a packet of peanuts.

His other granny, 'like Queen Victoria', in Bolton; they once visited, his first and only holiday as a child, taking a horse and cab to the station, and it was grand, everyone staring: 'They must have thought we'd come into a fortune.' That didn't happen again until 1927 and a horse-drawn hearse to Sunderland cemetery.

'Poor Mam.'

Working. Washing clothes all week. The old copper in the outhouse, the ritual: lighting the fire, boiling the water, stirring the washing with the poss-stick, lifting it out onto the pine table against the wall, scrubbing with soda and soap, back into the tub, hitting it '200 times' with the poss-stick, rinsing, putting the 'blue' in. When she wasn't washing, she was baking bread, cakes, toffee to sell to the neighbours.

Age twelve, working at the farm, polishing the harnesses, his father coming to tell him, 'Mam's dead.'

Knowing the signs – the 'Dear me, I don't know', the long sigh, the 'Poor Mam', the shake of the head, the absent look – it was then up to me to divert Dad back to the safety of a more distant past where misfortune and death were recalled more with a casual acceptance of *that's how it was in those days*.

'What was that were you telling me the other day, Dad, about Seaham Harbour?'

Picking coal at Seaham Harbour, the black waves on the beach. Going with Father Bob to the slag heaps. 'A real character, he was,' big and broad, 'a well-dressed man' with a waxed moustache, dark suit, fob watch, gold chain, the chain worn where it rubbed against the waistcoat pocket. Father Bob at the bar, one foot on the brass footrail, his boots specially made because of his misshapen big toes. Chewing a great wad of tobacco, teeth black with it, spitting brownly into the spittoon. 'A devil sometimes.' When Nan wouldn't sew a button on his trousers, he 'sat on the doorstep with his flies open and sewed it on himself'. A champion at quoits, always drew a big crowd, flinging a quoit through a glass chandelier without breaking it.

Father Bob didn't break that chandelier about a century ago. A memorable feat by a memorable grandfather. That so much of his pre-war, pre-Gerda past has survived is thanks to him more than my prompts, because (unlike Gerda) Jack liked to remember. No matter where they took him, or on whom they next alighted in their zigzag way, his memories were a pleasure long denied. He was back there, free to roam, revisiting his own past, delighted by the sights. One minute he was remembering a man without legs. 'They cut them off right up here–' indicating the top of his thighs – 'and put him in a leather harness and he went scuttling through Sunderland.' The next, it was kites on Tunstall Hill, sledging on Strawberry Hill, two boys colliding with a beer-wagon at the bottom and dying.

While he speaks, I can just make out his shape in the bay window. He is telling me again about the 'lousy blooming night' he had with his bad back. 'Oh, dear me, I thought that was the end, I couldn't turn over in bed, I was poleaxed.' It tickles him again to envisage 'dropping down blooming dead, but with exercises, walks, fresh air, sun, and vitamin pills, the old man should last a few more years'. Dad liked to refer to himself as the 'old man', as if to forestall others thinking it. 'Better have a wash and shave, or you'll be thinking I smell. The old man smells.'

Around the time of Gerda's death and the first miners' strike, when blackouts in London reportedly brought out the friendly Blitz spirit in people, I photographed my father washing up in the scullery. It's one of the few pictures of him on his own. As the man with the camera, his absence from most of the family photographs of the 1950s and 60s only struck me when I looked for him in them. The 'scullery window photograph' stayed outside the albums and lay forgotten in a drawer under a pile of papers until it came to light during a recent clear-out. Straightaway it took me back to spring 1972 and the old house as it looked then. Apparently unaware of being photographed as he stands at the Belfast sink, rinsing something under a tap – a cup or mug but his hand covers it – he looks absently out of the scullery window. There wasn't much to see through the textured glass – a smudge of half-light and the red brick of the next house – but he looks intently at something. This being a few months after his wife's death, he was probably thinking of her, although it could have been something else entirely. There were many occasions when I wasn't there to see him looking through that pebbled glass, alone with his thoughts and with no camera to observe him; but this being my only photograph of my father in the scullery in that early spring light, I probably read more into it than was there.

The little scullery, adjoining the breakfast room with its cream-painted pine shelves and black cast-iron cooking range, has become the room he mostly occupies when I now try to bring into focus not just the outline and shape of my father as he was back then but the detail – the thinning grey hair, the light edging his face, the old suit jacket, his hands at the taps, the way he looks through the window. It's where he seems most at home. He was often there, in the scullery, when I visited, wearing an old jacket over his jumper, peeling vegetables or washing up and looking absently out of the semi-opaque window while his hands carried on independently of him. That photograph has come to typify him. Framed, it has a permanent place on the narrow shelf above the desk where I am typing. It functions as a permanent reminder of his appearance then and, less tangibly, of his state of mind.

Fortunately, remembering him there – especially in the scullery with its Belfast sink and quarry-tiled floor, where he spent so much of his time – doesn't have to be left to chance because I had the presence of mind (and a camera handy) to take this one iconic photograph of him washing up some months after her death. If his features ever leave his face (which they sometimes do), I'll always have the 'scullery window photograph' as a reminder of what he looked like.

He must have been thinking of her, I have decided, while he gazed at the redbrick wall opposite, but his mind was also wandering back to the interwar years before they met: her still recent death pulling the thread of connection, his father unexpectedly coming to the farm to tell him something, and Jack looking up from polishing the harnesses and wondering what was up. Searching the framed photograph for further clues, I wonder what type of glass the scullery window framed, and checking the internet I learn about 'textured glass' of 'different levels of opacity'. There is 'pebbled glass' too, described as clear glass with 'a soft, hammered grain that mimes a surf-beaten pebbled beach'.

Studying a dark-jacketed Jack (shaded further by the dim light), his face half-lit in profile, I see this impromptu photograph of my old dad as the embodiment of absence – absence defined as inattention due to thinking about other things, absence of mind. Assuming that my mother flitted in and out of his vision, was it as she first appeared in the ATS cookhouse, an 'Angel' of the khaki kitchen? Or, when stationed elsewhere, he felt 'hopelessly lost' without her? Or on their wedding day when he could hardly doubt her happiness?

Only so much can be drawn from a photograph, and if not for its likely date and the absent look of a man caught unawares, this would seem an unremarkable and rather out of focus photo of my father in the old scullery doing the washing up. All kitchen sink and no drama. For me, though, his remaining life is contained in that caught moment.

The Scullery Window Photograph

Peter Thornthwaite

Hardly a day passes when he doesn't catch my eye, his absent expression showing me that he still misses her and how she is more of a presence than ever for not being there. He loved her, maybe more so after she died because he could then see Gerda at her best without what she had become obstructing his view. It was her face he saw in that semi-opaque glass, not its ghostly lineaments but as it appeared when she looked back at him as he was leaving and took him in again when he returned to the cookhouse and her. That was his Gerda.

He loved her all right. The recurring question is whether she loved him. Looking at him looking out of the scullery window, I wonder if her suicidal intentions interposed a more noticeable distance between them towards the end. He picked up on moods, far more than I acknowledged while she was alive, and might have sensed a change in her – a deeper shade of distance. Whether he did, or she was better at dissimulating than anyone realised, I never discovered, but it must have been difficult to detect anything unusual in her appearance as she usually kept things to herself. It must have taken something extraordinary – I'm not sure what exactly – for her to say goodbye to him when he left the house for another night at Pressed Steel, knowing he would find her dead by morning. Did she have to steel herself to do it? I doubt it. She had already said her goodbyes, to herself.

Did she love him? All the evidence is weighted on his side. Read his wartime love letters, and you can't miss it from the first awkward yet eloquent words. He even tried wooing her in German: *'Ich liebe Dich'*, and I wonder if that later emboldened him to say it to her face.

On her side, there is one piece of historical evidence –

an undated diary entry from the days of their wartime courtship:

Jack is really one of the best fellows in the world and don't you ever forget this, Gerda.

This shows appreciation, certainly, and acknowledges his love and her luck in finding a man who (as he also wrote) would 'do anything on earth' to make her happy. Unfortunately, I have only Jack's love letters to Gerda to go by and not hers to him – if she wrote any. While stationed elsewhere, he missed her to the extent that, unused to and uncomfortable with putting pen to paper ('I really do feel such a stranger to it,' he confided), he 'looked forward all day' to writing to her and wished he could tell her to her face the 'pleasure' he derived from doing so. He imagined himself there, watching her as she read his letters, and seeing 'those lovely dimples' when she smiled and that 'twinkle' in her eyes. A stranger to 'this letter writing', this Jack is also a stranger to me, and when I re-read lines like, 'You must love me with the burning passion I feel for you,' he sounds more movie star than tank driving instructor from Sunderland.

Those were his 'happy days', I suppose, when he was away from her and wrote his first and last love letters, and I am grateful to Gerda for that – for bringing out in him something he didn't know was there until she arrived, and which might never have emerged but for her. It would be presumptuous to look further into their love life and question if it lasted and for how long. Maybe she liked him being stationed elsewhere, for it meant receiving such letters and being loved passionately but from a distance, which is less demanding and something she was used to by then. As I recall, my mother got used to her husband's absence during twenty-five years of nights after the war and perhaps even welcomed it because nightwork meant better pay and she had her bed and (eventually) her bedroom to herself.

In those wartime letters, which she kept in a dusty green silk-lined writing-case, Jack might have sounded momentarily more cinematic as he expressed a love foreign to his fingertips and lips, but he wasn't the 'RAF pilot' Gunther saw in the photograph she sent him of her new husband, and (as my mother later stated in her diary) he would never amount to more than a factory worker.

Unfortunately, the evidence is stacked against her. Jack's postwar place in her life and ours was defined by absence. I remember the photograph albums from two decades of family life, with Dad (the unseen photographer) an absence so taken for granted that I didn't notice it until recently. He was there, of course, just out of sight on the other side of the camera. His final absence was from her suicide note. She had written no letters to him during their end-of-war courtship, so not writing that last note to him was at least consistent with their previous one-sided correspondence. It was unfair of me to compare it (as I felt obliged to do in *Remember Who You Used to Be*) to Virginia Woolf's wartime (1941) suicide note.

Dearest one, you are my whole life. Without you I just don't exist.

Three decades of sporadic diaries evidence the scope and depth of Gerda's writing, and it is no criticism to compare her suicide note unfavourably with the final written words of one of the finest writers in the English language. I expected no more of my mother. She was no Virginia Woolf, and Dad was no Leonard.

Unwilling to forego a last look at his love letters, I emptied Gerda's green silk-lined writing-case onto the bed and flicked through them, looking for the stand-out lines. So passionate when he penned them eighty years ago, so poignant now:

You have given me, my Darling, the hope and longing to live of which I never dreamed.

If the 'past is another country', so too is love – at least, this love by this man for this woman in these circumstances – so I reflect as I re-read his thankful letters to her. They do things differently there, he discovered, and although by his own admission it was all foreign to him at first, he quickly picked it up. If nothing else, it was worth reminding myself of his once overwhelming love for Gerda. Then, returning his letters to the dingy green writing-case marked 'PRIVAT', I glimpsed a few last words of one of them, which I must have read repeatedly before but failed to mark.

Perhaps I shall have a letter from you tomorrow.

It reminded me of Aunt Bertha (letter dated *den 17. Juli 1939*) mildly chiding eighteen-year-old Gerda for not writing to Tatta who 'is long missing a message from you' – until I wondered if the tone of Jack's ending was not one of plaintive hope, as I assumed, but of expectation. He looked forward to a letter from Gerda, which could be imminent. Lines from other letters confirmed it:

Thank you so very much for your two very charming letters.

You are such an Angel to write me such a charming letter.

So, she did write to him after all, and I had somehow overlooked it, but as I am only too happy these days to rehabilitate my mother, I felt a shadow lifting. She wrote love letters too – and to him, my father-to-be, and not just some Joe Schwarz from Berlin or H.D who earlier wanted to marry Gerda (according to her diary) and whom I know only by his initials. The question now is: Where are her love letters to Jack?

My working assumption has always been that she kept all the paper evidence of her life and history. Her stash of old family correspondence, including letters (mostly Gunther's) critical of her and hurtful. She kept everything, good and bad. She kept Jack's love letters – of course she did – but what about hers? If it had been up to my father, they would be there now, on one side of that green silk-lined writing case marked 'PRIVAT', as he'd have treasured them while she lived and still more after she died. But Jack was not the keeper of the letters.

She had wanted the diaries destroyed. Perhaps in the weeks preceding her death she had started culling them – hence the missing months and stubs of torn-out pages – and for some reason her love letters to Jack had not escaped the cull. It is certainly an intriguing possibility.

Finding evidence that she wrote them is not the same as actually finding her missing letters but is the next best thing and means that a further drastic revision of my mother is called for. As a protective and sheltering father figure in her life, Jack's function was not unlike Tatta's, and it was this sudden throwback to the other man in her life that led me to the truth of the matter. Gerda had loved her Tatta. There is not much evidence of this love in her diaries; indeed, most of the evidence points in the opposite direction. But his absence from her diaries is not evidence of absence from her thoughts. If anything, it proves she thought too deeply about him.

And surely the same goes for Jack. She could not bring herself to summon him at the end, let alone write a 'Dear Jack' suicide note. Too difficult. Too painful. She needed to let go. Just naming him would bring back from the night factory the loving husband who (as he had once written) wouldn't 'exist' without her. What she was about to do would hurt him terribly, as she had hurt Tatta when she left him, although in time he would realise he was better off without her and could leave work for good with her long overdue compensation money from Germany. Like Tatta, he was the one who would do 'anything on this earth' to make her happy, and now she was doing what little she could still do for him by dying.

CHAPTER FOURTEEN:

CARDIGAN BUTTONS

I used to drop girls like hot cakes before I met your mum. When I saw her in the cookhouse, I thought: That's my girl.

With those retrieved words it all came back – how often she came up in conversation during those visits home after her suicide. The family had closed protectively around him, her manner of death unmentioned as a distressing and shameful subject to be avoided and thus spare him further pain – our unspoken assumption that he must be more hurt than us, having given his life to her, whereas we had merely taken. But as the subject was never broached, this is only conjecture. It occurs to me that I am still protecting him – sparing his feelings, misremembering our closest and most connected conversations, blanking her out – although my father has been dead for twenty-five years. Her suicide, I have long assumed, was too difficult a subject to raise with him, and when a kindly dementia rubbed out the rest of her too, that was the end of the matter.

How much of Gerda survived in his memories and for

how long, who knows? I never tracked her there. But it now appears that, not only did she frequently come up in conversation in the early years following her death but she did so spontaneously and without any prompts from me. He wanted to talk about her. Long before a dormant and hungry dementia awoke in him and fed, maybe Dad was doing his own selective erasing. The most recent Gerda probably got less of a look in. The body in the bed that December morning succumbed to earlier and happier memories of girls dropped 'like hot cakes' and her first appearance 'in the cookhouse'. He never spoke of her as an 'Angel' or 'Dream Girl', but something of her mystique as a good-looking foreigner came through his kitchen memories as he relived his incredulity that she could be interested in a working-class man like him from Sunderland. Above all it was her 'difference' from other, English, girls that made him want her.

The diamonds sometimes came up in conversation – how she smuggled them out of Germany and later concealed them in her gas mask during the war, and how the mask was taken away by an ARP warden while she was out. That was the story she told, and he appeared to know nothing more about the case of the disappearing diamonds. Now, having read through my paper inheritance, I probably know much more than Dad ever did. For instance, I know that it was the first thing Tatta inquired about in his first letter (20 January 1942) to his daughter after the hiatus of more than two years in their correspondence, referring to them as 'the goods' and asking her if she had sold them or was 'still in possession'. I know that Gunther was also keen to know what had become of the diamonds and never received a clear answer. I know that the family referred to the missing diamonds as the '*Kinderchen*', the 'children'. My father probably knew none of this – or if he did, he never said – although he once casually mentioned in passing that Gerda had left Germany in 1939 with the family diamonds sewn into her cardigan buttons.

That I could have mislaid this crucial detail and remembered it more than fifty years later is curious considering its far-reaching significance, and its sudden re-emergence halfway through writing this second book about my mother suggests something just as important: finally things were starting to come together; connect.

When it came back to me, this long-lost essential link in the story of how Gerda had got away with diamonds changed everything. What possibly triggered the memory was a story in *The Repair Shop* about an engagement ring passed down through three generations and kept safe until lost. In time a missing diamond was found somewhere, then a blue sapphire. The eighteen-carat gold band turned up later, missing a section. It was many more years before diamond, sapphire and gold band were reunited as one ring. As told, there was something mysterious and magical about how the pieces eventually came together, as if willing the inheritors to find and reunite them.

Gerda's cardigan buttons were a lost and found piece of vital information as valuable (to me) as the diamonds they once concealed, and I had Dad to thank for it. If I had forgotten the buttons, what else might be strewn on the seabed, waiting to be found?

Soon after they met in the cookhouse and she told a dazzled Jack things about herself, Gerda must have got round to the diamonds and how she smuggled them out of Germany. No wonder she seemed so wonderfully 'different' from other girls. In love from the start, Jack would not have questioned her story, accepting it as yet another side of her multifaceted non-Sunderland exoticism. It was the kind of backstory only an 'Angel' or 'Dream Girl' from abroad could come up with. She might have told him a lot more than he remembered or mentioned to me – such as what it felt like sneaking diamonds past Nazi security. Important practical details were also missing from his memories. Was she wearing the cardigan at the time or had she packed it in her suitcase? Maybe he told me and I have forgotten, and I have to ask myself: was I as excited then by the revelation of the cardigan buttons as I am now? Did I ask the probing questions I would put to him if he were alive and still had a memory? Was I merely pleased with myself, getting him to talk about the fascinating young foreigner he met in the camp cookhouse, who wasn't just another hot cake to be dropped? Thinking back to those conversations with my father in a darkening room in a house empty of her, it occurs to me that, if he remembered nothing else from her stories, that detail alone of the cardigan buttons has become an inheritance to cherish, handed down from father to son, neither of us grasping its significance at the time. Or maybe he did get it, while it's taken me a further fifty years to catch on.

If I could revisit those desultory conversations, listen in on them, they might give up more of their secrets. With my curiosity about her during this second search intensifying rather than abating as I half expected, my antennae are more than ever on the alert and twitching for the blood heat of exciting new information, especially if it brings her closer. That moment of revelation concerning cardigan buttons passed, not unnoticed at the time but not especially marked out. It was enough then just to connect with him, and of course I don't regret the many evenings I gave to my father when he most needed company. Attentive, interested, curious to know more, I listened and let him speak, the flow and momentum of reminiscence uninterrupted by a nosy son with a magpie's attention to shiny things. Dad had found a place for her among his 'happy days', and I censored questions that might remind him of the unhappy ones. She came up often enough but in passing, alongside older memories of picking coal at Seaham Harbour where the waves were black; street entertainers like sword swallowers; early morning deliveries of milk churns by horse and cart to Sunderland; whatever bobbed up in the flow.

As for the revelation itself, turning it over in my mind, examining it from every angle, I see her in a new and brilliant light. She must have talked it over with her Tatta, planned it months before leaving Nazi Germany. Gunther had left the previous November, a week before *Kristallnacht*, but he must have been in on it too – subsequently broaching the subject in his coded way in letters home because Tatta was doubtless under surveillance as one of the remaining Jews in Breslau failing in their civic duty by not leaving. It led to further investigation, yet another painstaking search of the five suitcases and another long evening of my life given up to Gerda and her first family. Gunther's letters, jumbled up and no longer in the date order in which I had definitely left them, finally gave up one piece of apparently overlooked evidence – a letter from New York, dated 20 January 1939, with this interesting question for his sister:

Have you the chance to take with you some garments and outfit in case of emigration?

Obviously, then, Gunther was involved in the diamonds plan. Why otherwise make such a point of asking his fashionable clothes-conscious sister if she intended taking 'some garments' with her 'in case of emigration'? It is a perfectly redundant question. Of course she would be taking clothes with her. Further examination of Gunther's correspondence from that time, checking it for any reference to a cardigan as an item of clothing essential to the success of Gerda's emigration, yielded nothing. Yet that in itself suggested he was almost certainly in on it, for he would surely take pains to avoid too specific a reference to anything (such as a cardigan) that might arouse suspicion if his letters home were intercepted and examined by the Reich authorities.

Then there is the question of Aunt Bertha's possible role in all this. She too must have known about the cardigan buttons. Bertha was looking after her brother when Gerda left, making his coffee each morning and keeping the two rooms of his new reduced accommodation clean and tidy. Now I think of it, I always wondered why Tante Bertha had asked her niece (letter of 17 July 1939) about the 'two dresses' she had ordered before leaving Breslau. They needed altering and the invoice was sent to Tatta after Gerda left. Assuming that Bertha was simply checking the details of the order and costs, and that as a woman she rather than Elkan would look into such matters, I had thought no more about it other than noting Gerda's last-minute attention to new dresses and adding to her wardrobe while there was still a father to pay for them. Re-reading the letter, but with cardigan buttons in mind, I wondered if Aunt Bertha's apparently innocent queries were also code. Was she really asking: *And your cardigan, dear Gerda, the buttons? Can you please let us know what has happened. Are they secret? Are they safe?* She must have been good at sewing, given the domestic accomplishments of women in the 1930s, so would have easily and expertly disguised the diamonds as pretty cardigan buttons for her only niece. Aunt Bertha probably proposed the ruse in the first place.

Whether Gerda wore the cardigan when passing through security, or had it packed neatly away in her case, is unknown. Most likely she wore it. The alternative was too risky, with official fingers going through her layers. A Jewish girl, seventeen years old, emigrating, would have been questioned closely about her luggage, ordered to open the suitcase, explain its contents. It would be like opening up herself to their fingers. I could see her brazening it out, waiting innocently as suspicious uniformed officials slowly sifted her silken things, inspecting each item. She wouldn't be the first Jew to smuggle valuables out of the Reich, and those officials were no doubt wise to diamonds being concealed or disguised as something else. The penalty, if found out, was unthinkable. So, Gerda would have worn the cardigan, nervously fingering the sewn buttons while her suitcase was being searched, her diamonds meanwhile hiding in plain sight. A brilliant ruse. If that is what really happened, I admire her nerve and bravado. The woman I read about in the later diaries was full of suspicion and fear. That seventeen-year-old girl, if the above supposition is true, was not fearless – nobody could be unafraid in those circumstances – but she successfully disguised it. And she got away with it, too.

There is another possibility: that her father sent on the cardigan alongside other clothes and necessities following her arrival in London. That would have been the safer option. He adored, and doted on, his daughter. Would he have really put her at such risk by encouraging her to smuggle diamonds under the noses of Nazis? The diamonds were all that was left of the family fortune, and Gerda's emigration was the last chance to give the widely dispersed family a financial future, so Tatta must have been tempted. But could he really have put his 'child', as he thought of her then, in danger of arrest, incarceration and worse? And if found, the diamonds would lead the authorities back to himself and Bertha in Breslau, and that would be the end of them too. No, a distressed Tatta could not have made such a decision.

It then occurred to me that she made it. The diamonds disguised as cardigan buttons was her plan, and she was sure she could carry it off. The alternative – sending them on later with all the other things – was too risky. As it happened, an expensive typewriter did get lost in transit – as Tatta rather bitterly complained in his letter of 30 June 1939. If he could get so upset about the loss of a typewriter, imagine his distress and despair at the loss of the family diamonds.

There is no written evidence that the plan was hers, but then there is no evidence that the diamonds existed until her diary entry for 25 September 1939, when her secret marriage plan for the new love in her life, Joe, was that he 'should buy an engagement ring and take with him one of my diamonds'. Evidently, Gerda was the sort of girl who made things happen. She took control of her own 'emigration plan', apparently with no help from family; Gunther had praised her great 'skill' in doing so. She got out, which took some doing. Gerda was obviously more resourceful than I realised, and I now believe that she was the one to 'sew' the cardigan buttons plan seamlessly into her own scheme of escape. Tatta was a broken man in 1939, and she couldn't rely on him. Gerda had to think and act for herself.

The truth can't be known but (all things considered) she got the diamonds and herself out of Nazi Germany. She would have actually enjoyed the danger, I think, as she later found Luftwaffe air raids over London 'thrilling and exciting'. As for it being her idea, Gerda's subsequent references to 'my diamonds', which at first sounded possessive and selfish since they surely belonged to the whole family, simply reflected the fact that she had come up with the cardigan buttons plan in the first place and that the diamonds were her responsibility (and reward) for carrying it out so brazenly.

The man who would be my father saw Gerda and knew he had never seen any girl like her. There were no Gerdas in Sunderland between the wars, at least none likely to come his way. The war made such improbable connections possible. After they met in the ATS cookhouse in 1944, and he got to know her and heard her story, Jack knew she was the one for him. With limited experience of girls who escaped the Nazis with diamonds sewn into their cardigan buttons, he knew when he was onto a good thing.

CHAPTER FIFTEEN:

MANY NICE CLOTHES

I have many nice clothes to cram in.
(Gerda's Diary, 20 May 1939)

Anne Frank lacked the luxury of a suitcase when leaving home in a hurry. As recorded in her diary, 8 July 1942, she took only the clothes she could wear. Gerda, still relatively free to leave three years earlier, had diamonds in her cardigan buttons. Anne concealed vests and pants and stockings – the basics a girl in hiding will need – beneath her outer layers. Rereading the entry, I think of my mother who also wore sedimentary layers of clothing, more so in her later years when she felt the cold. Anne Frank's situation in Amsterdam in July 1942 was more dangerous than Gerda's in Breslau in May 1939, yet she described the sudden frantic flight from the authorities with a sense of humour irrepressible even in such circumstances.

The Diary has little to say on the subject of clothes. Apart from leaving home for a new life in hiding, when Anne layers them out of frantic necessity, there is only one further entry especially concerning clothing. On 7 October 1942, she imagines living in Switzerland with enough money from her father to meet all her clothing needs. The list begins with underwear – basic clothing, nothing fancy or fashionable. Though 'imagined', it is a list of things a sensible girl in hiding would compile with an eye to the future to see her through a few more years of world war. For over two Diary pages she can have what she wants. Though basic, with no fineries or frills, there are more than enough clothes available to an imaginative girl, so that merely listing them is almost as good as actually having them and momentarily displaced the privations behind her and still to come. And there is another luxury associated with Anne's dream shopping list – getting out, the freedom of outdoors, the remembered fresh air.

It was different for Gerda, who had a practical rather than imaginary task ahead once she got the permit and visa to leave. She might well have dreamed of all the nice clothes she could have packed if allowed, but of necessity seventeen-year-old Gerda travelled light. There are no recorded details of her luggage, but Kindertransport children were allowed a single suitcase and I assume the same restriction applied to her. The reference to 'cramming in' her 'many nice clothes' also suggests a limited suitcase space. The excited diary entry, three days before departure, indicates a strong interest in fashion. Unfortunately, the 'nice clothes' are not detailed or described anywhere. Judging by the clothing she accumulated during the 1950s and 60s (enough by 1965 to fill more than a hundred suitcases), the mother I remember retained a passion for clothes, if not noticeably for fashion, because they were mostly from jumble sales and charity shops (less fashionable then than now) and packed and put away with mothballs for the future. Gerda's post-war circumstances – having to 'scrape and save' and 'make ends meet' – differed markedly from her pre-war circumstances as the spoilt daughter of a wealthy businessman in Breslau. Of course, her financial circumstances changed during the last few years in Germany. Well-established Jews like her father were punished with 'penalty taxes' and relieved of their businesses, property, and other assets. In spite of the repeated depredations, her old German photographs suggest that for many years – indeed right up to the end of her time there – Gerda had 'many nice clothes' and looked lovely despite the upheavals happening around her. If the pre-war photographs had survived as my only guide to her German years, there would be no visible sign in the black and white images of increasingly adverse and divisive political and social circumstances or intimation of worse things to come. As the decade darkened for Gerda and her family, she merely looked lovelier, brighter, apparently untroubled by external events, unperturbed even as her world collapsed. As for her clothes, other than researching female fashions in the Third Reich for general context, I just have her German photographs for evidence.

In Part Two of *Camera Lucida*, Roland Barthes recounts how, shortly after his mother died, he looked for her in old photographs. Seeing her as she appeared before he was born, he read his 'non-existence' in the clothes of the period such as a hat with a feather, gloves, linen. If his absence troubled him, he doesn't say. Seeing Gerda in fashions from the 1920s and 30s (not wearing a stylish hat with a feather, but still looking like someone likely to look right through me) is pleasant enough and actually rather a relief. These early appearances of hers had one immensely reassuring message for me: that I didn't exist and therefore couldn't be implicated in her life or in any way responsible for what was happening to her then. Lacking any future family obligations, she herself appears lighter and airier for it. She could hardly anticipate that a future son in his early seventies would end up browsing through her old German photographs on his mobile phone, delighted to read his non-existence in them.

Here are some pictures in my 'Gerda Gallery':
- Gerda with headphones, sitting sideways on a chair and holding open a big picture book, her short flowery dress revealing girlish white knickerbockers and pale stockings.
- Gerda with black bobbed hair, ruler-straight fringe, little white frock with dark belt.
- Gerda with same straight dark fringe and white frock, sitting on bedroom floor with her curly-haired doll, Pierrot clown, and black and white building bricks. She is just about to place another brick on the precarious pile. The Pierrot she clutches in her left hand would surely assume an expression of consternation if his slick, plastered, black-haired head wasn't at that moment flopping backwards in Gerda's grip and his white ruffed neck seemingly broken.
- Gerda still wearing white frock, perched on the arm of a carved oak chair and looking sideways at the large father who occupies the rest of the seat and looks sideways and seriously at her.

- A decadent 1920s Gerda with amused eyes, looking up saucily at the camera from the chaise-longue where she reclines, an unlit cigarette angled from her lips, the long neck of an uncorked champagne bottle in a silver bucket at her side.
- Gerda in a light-coloured swimsuit holding a rubber ring and reclining on the roof of a striped canvas shelter on the beach; a stout and stern-faced Tatta in high-waisted contoured trunks leaning against the shelter and also holding a rubber ring in his right hand.
- Gerda posing formally in a garden with older boy (brother?), both in sailor suits.
- Gerda in striped dressing-gown, showing a bareness of leg on the balcony.
- Gerda, age twelve, at her desk (if that is her in the front row on the left) in her classroom; what appears to be a pearl necklace, whitely defined against a dark top with three pearlescent buttons, distinguishes her from the other girls.
- Gerda, about fourteen (the photograph is dated 1935) wearing a pale sleeveless linen top and culottes in bright garden sunshine.
- Gerda, age fifteen, at a ski resort in 1937, wearing a dark beret and long black double-breasted coat with wide astrakhan collar; one of a happy group of family and friends in the snow with toboggans; even her father in tweed jacket and plus fours is caught in hearty mid-laugh.
- Gerda, same year, same place. Wearing a light-coloured beret, striped rollneck sweater and

baggy black trousers and projecting herself towards me with such energy that I could imagine her skating out of the photograph. Those Turkish-style trousers are also a surprise, widening below the narrow, belted waist and gathering in at the ankles. They seem to act like black sails propelling her across the sheet of ice. You can almost hear the hiss of her skates. A dark pine-wooded slope rises steeply behind her. High above is the insect smudge of a ski-lift. Some distance behind the skating figure, too distant to make out her face, the small padded figure of a young woman has stopped to watch Gerda skate away. Looking more closely, what I took for movement is the opposite. Her skates are pinched together as she poses, and it is only the outthrust arm and clenched fist that simulate motion. She has paused for this picture, but still the turn of the head towards the camera, the sun in her face, that assertive gesture, suggest a young woman full of energy and the sheer pleasure of being there.

- Gerda aged sixteen with two friends, in front of Victoria College ('Ladies Finishing School'), Prague, 1938, perching on the back of a white bench with painted black serpentine legs. Bright sun (lighting up the grand stone front of the college) but still early in the year, as signified by the long coats. In her black coat with wide astrakhan collar and her dark beret, Gerda angles her head away from the others to give the camera a better view, but holds her hands together on her lap like her companions. The girl at the opposite end of the bench wears her double-breasted herringbone coat unbuttoned, showing her skirt. The friend in the middle wears a dark jacket and matching long skirt. Gerda smiles and shows her dimples and (this is speculation outside the picture) her delight at being away from Germany and with friends. Unusually, the shadow head and cap of the photographer appears in the bottom left-hand corner.

Gerda with headphones and picture book

Peter Thornthwaite

After repeat visits to the 'Gerda Gallery', these images seem more essentially her than the 'English' photographs of the mother I half-remember. Unselfconsciously photogenic, at home in photographs, her face and pose showed none of my mother's fraught relationship with the camera. As Barthes observed, the photograph is evidence of past existence, undeniable proof that the person in the picture was once there. I don't doubt that Gerda was there in the German photographs, whereas I am not so sure of it in the English albums from the later 1950s and through the 60s. Maybe this explains why I feel so uncomfortable with them and return with relief to my mother as a child and young woman again, where I see something forming but not yet defined in her face. As nothing appears to trouble her in those mostly unspecified foreign places, it doesn't trouble me either, and I am happy for her and almost as pleased as she seems with her youthful appearance and pleasant surroundings. Undoubtedly, too, she is more endearing from a distance: unfamiliar, foreign, doubly foreign since that world is gone. She had a future then, which marks her off from the mother I remember. The photographs point to a better future than the one she ended up with. As evidence of her pre-existence, those old black and white pictures don't tell the whole story or even a fraction of it, of course, but they show something of her life before and after 1933. One classroom photograph (I go back to check) was taken in 1933 (the date is written underneath). Hitler also became Chancellor that year, but I can detect no anxiety or uncertainty in Gerda's classroom face. She doesn't know what is about to happen.

You wouldn't know it from her German photographs, but Hitler shadowed her early years from the beginning:

as leader of the Nazi Party in 1921, the year she was born, and then as Chancellor when she was twelve. It didn't seem to bother her. While Nazism transformed Germany, a seemingly oblivious Gerda posed on sunny balconies, in gardens, picnicked with friends in flowery fields, and later wore a long dark coat with astrakhan collar and wide lapels and big buttons at mountain resorts where toboggans and skis and ice-skates signify the excitement and fun to be had in cold, high places. Her albums span the ascendant Third Reich. Crowds and banners and swastikas and public notices to keep Jews out are so reliably absent that it seems another country, and I could almost wish myself there, unnoticed, slyly observing her as she used to be.

Looking at a house with a 'shadowy porch', Barthes wished he was there too, in that house in the photograph. Looking at Gerda's German pictures, I feel a different attraction. They don't include anything remotely like the almost abandoned place Barthes wished to inhabit. She is there, and though I am (as usual) on the outside looking in, I am content to see her safe inside a photograph long before my time. No harm can come to her there. With photographs like these still possible, surely things couldn't have been that bad for her? The sunny beaches (which I would like to share with her, if invisibly) end in 1933. The year marking the beginning of a new Germany also marked Gerda's last seaside appearances with her Tatta. That was the end of childhood, bobbed hair, straight fringe; the last of the little girl straddling his shoulders or crouching on sandy hands and knees within the arch of his legs. The beaches have gone but other idylls remained, if only photographically. When the Nuremberg

Race Laws of 1935 excluded fourteen-year-old Gerda from Reich citizenship and rights and prohibited sexual relations with Volk of the right 'German blood', she seemed unaffected and unconcerned in front of the camera. Despite hundreds of further legal restrictions, Gerda flourished in photographs, appearing blithely unaware that she had ceased to exist.

To 'emigrate or not to emigrate', that was the question after 1933, and the eldest of the three siblings, Kurt, who trained as a lawyer, did go that year – to Switzerland, then France -- so Gerda must have been aware then that history was turning against them. As late as September 1938, the Jews of Breslau were still proprietors of many enterprises, but I don't know exactly when her father lost everything. The decree of 27 April 1938 ordered all Jews with assets of at least five thousand marks to provide detailed lists of them; later that year, the Breslau authorities compiled a list of properties owned by Jews. Tatta could protect Gerda from harm, but not from history. Yet her photographed face bears no impression of the world outside her own skin. History was happening so fast it was hard for the family to keep up. Even the diaries and letters reflect nothing much amiss in the year before *Kristallnacht*, other than Tatta drinking too much 'liquor' (October 1937). Gunther twice visited his sister during her college year in Prague (1937-38), flirted with one of her college friends, and carried on writing his amusing letters. Seizure of Jewish assets meanwhile progressed. Life was daily becoming more unliveable for German Jews. Gerda was emerging as a lovely young woman.

Lovely but not obviously fashionable. Despite the later reference to her 'many nice clothes', the evidence of the

German photographs is that her outfits seldom varied and were rather unremarkable; if she hadn't become my mother, I wouldn't look twice at them. White blouse with large black buttons and outsize collar, short black jacket and long skirt, polka-dot blouse and dark pinafore dress with large white buttons, ankle-length winter coat with astrakhan collar, beret. Though they give her that period look, I look in vain for tight-fitting black velvet suits, sleek dresses, satin jackets with leaf designs in greens, yellows and reds, chiffon, frills, daring décolleté. She wore 'good' clothes, of course. As the daughter of a successful purveyor of gentlemen's attire, she had money for new outfits when she wanted them, and her father understood the importance of appearances. Tatta could look presentable on the beach in genital-sculping trunks, well-dressed even in the flesh, if also formal and a little stiff. Away from the beach (and sometimes on it) he appears in light-coloured suits (linen in summer) and wide, striped tie. As a portly proprietor of gentlemen's clothing shops in Breslau, he knew how to wear clothes, filling the white shirts, capacious jackets with broad lapels, and wide, high-waisted trousers like a man comfortably at home in them and ready for business anytime, anywhere.

Gerda wore the clothes befitting the daughter of a respected Breslau businessman, but perhaps she chose less ostentatious or glamorous outfits, not wishing to draw undue attention to herself, though well aware of her attractions and the need to make good use of them. Also, being negated by the Nazis didn't mean she was unaffected by their attitude to fashion. I have discovered that the increasing demand for 'German' fashion and fabrics, and the organisations established from 1933 to control the industry, had greater impact on women. As to whether her father's gentlemen's attire business was also affected by such developments, the internet doesn't say, though his livelihood would be affected soon enough by the enforced transfer of Jewish-owned businesses to eager Aryan hands. From my limited internet research, it is clear that Paris-led female fashion, or 'Jewified' fashion as it was known, and the close-up female face of Hollywood, were particularly reviled. Even Gunther, after he left Nazi Germany in November 1938, revealed the continuing influence of official German attitudes in his disapproval, disgust (and suppressed lust) at the sight of young American women roller-skating down the streets of New York with their powdered faces, rouged cheeks, coloured sports hats 'with feathers of an altitude of about one foot', and 'poignant' lipstick. Apparently lipstick, being composed of animal waste, was especially nauseating to Hitler's lips and perfume sickened him, but being the kind of man he was, the Fuhrer made an exception for Eva Braun who also promised cosy 'domesticity' and stuck with him through her two suicide attempts.

Hitler's abhorrence (if she was aware of it) did not inhibit Gerda from trimming her eyebrows so as to resemble the pencilled arcs of a Claudette Colbert, or applying the faintest trace of lipstick. Her outfits, modestly stylish, not inexpensive, are as far from high Parisian fashion as she was from Paris, yet a sense of style was starting to show through the black and white images, a suggestion of sophistication. Nothing satiny or sleek, but sometimes almost chic. As I type this, I seem to be describing somebody other than my mother, and of course I am.

Among her 'many nice clothes' one outfit stands out not because of its stylishness or glamour, but because I can't see her wearing it. The identity of the fair-haired girl in Gerda's old photograph album is unknown, as is her connection with Gerda: no name, date, place. She looks up, smiling shyly, from the high grass where she sits holding her ankles, the apron skirt of the flowered dirndl dress demurely covering her knees. With her prettily embroidered neckline, puffed and gathered sleeves, and endearing smile, in the bucolic setting of grass and flowers she is the idealised female type of the Third Reich. Wholesome, healthy and looking forward to mothering more Aryans. A smiling Eva Braun wore the same traditional folk costume – flowered dirndl dress with apron skirt over a white blouse – to please Hitler as she served him and his circle on the sunlit terrace of the Bavarian Berghof. For a place in Gerda's album, the 'dirndl girl' had to be a friend (but not for very much longer, judging by her appearance). Though just as fresh-faced and appealing (more so in my view), Gerda could never be anything other than Jewish, which cancelled all other identifiers. Yet she was equally an open-air girl in the photographs, especially in those winter resorts with her toboggans, skis and ice-skates. If young female outdoor energy and good looks were all it took, Gerda could have been a Nazi pin-up – but for the wrong hair, heritage, history, blood. However, it was not a look she favoured, and she could no more wear a dirndl than turn Aryan.

For me she was at her most attractive in the Gerda 17 years old photograph. Taken on or after her birthday on 26 June 1938, it is the portrait of a young woman: black hair brushed back, eyebrows a shade too thick to be pencilled, eyes shining, smooth skin, white teeth, wool jacket with wide astrakhan collar. 1938 is remembered as the year of *Kristallnacht*, the Night of Crystals, the Night of Broken Glass of 9–10 November, but if the picture of Gerda 17 years old was taken on or soon after her birthday, the nationwide state-sponsored pogrom (when shop windows like those belonging to her father were smashed, over a thousand synagogues burned, Jewish homes and schools, hospitals and cemeteries vandalised, and around 30,000 Jewish males arrested) was still over four months away. Gerda 17 years old doesn't seem anxious or pensive. She smiles, shows her dimples and looks directly at the camera, as though the best is yet to come, and I am reminded of how Sylvia Plath felt at the same age: 'Now, now is the perfect time of life.'[30]

As an ageing son visiting his mother's life thirty-three years before she ended it, I am favourably inclined towards the young and hopeful woman I never knew. Her exceptional good looks at the age of seventeen make the task of measuring out her life with old photos a pleasure but a poignant one. Let me say this once and for all: she was lovely, my pre-mother. That doesn't make what happened to her any worse than if she had been unprepossessing. What touches me is her awareness of her attractions and their power to protect her. Notwithstanding Nazi Germany and the persecutions present and to come, she appears untouched by them. It was not until years later that the pain shows through the photographs like a stain. No trace of it appears on her 17th birthday.

---

[30] From a Diary Supplement dated 13 November 1949. Sylvia Plath expresses 'the rapture of being seventeen'. *Letters Home* (as above).

Another photographic portrait was taken at the end of the year, December 1938. The dark hair waved at the back, dead-straight fringe, more of a pencil line for eyebrows, lips parting in a smile, marked dimples and cheekbones, portray Gerda at seventeen-and-a-half and as lovely as before – but different, reminding me of someone I have recently seen. Making the most of the camera (knowing the camera makes the most of her) she looks radiant as ever, though this is now the month after *Kristallnacht* and not the best time for a young Jewish woman to look radiant in the Third Reich. Then I see it. The hair, the eyebrows, the face, the smile, the jacket with its zebra-like black and white design and exaggerated padded shoulders are Claudette Colbert to a T in *It Happened One Night* (1934). I recently watched it on DVD. The Hollywood star also had short dark hair, waved at the back, straight-cut fringe, arched pencilled eyebrows, big eyes, prominent cheekbones, smile, white blouse, black and white striped top belted at the waist. In the December 1938 portrait, Gerda is missing Claudette Colbert's dark beret, but I know she often wore berets and similar close-fitting narrow-brimmed hats at a jaunty angle, since they reappear in photographs of that period. As I recall, my mother liked Claudette Colbert, though I hadn't realised until this photograph that she modelled herself on her. This, then, is Gerda's 'Claudette Colbert Photograph'.

Peter Thornthwaite

The 'Claudette Colbert' Photograph

CHAPTER SIXTEEN:

MEMENTO MORI

'Cameras go with family life,' Susan Sontag observed in *On Photography*. This was as true for Gerda's first family in pre-war Germany as for her second in post-war Britain. The German albums, which her father presumably sent on to her in London in 1939 just before the outbreak of war, 'chronicle' her life from early childhood to young woman, but without her diaries and family correspondence as cross-reference, I couldn't construct a coherent 'story' from the pictures alone as dates and the names of people and places are mostly missing. She is always there, among family and friends, but apart from instantly recognisable images of Tatta and Gunther, when and where they were photographed is either unspecified or indecipherable. And there is nothing to identify them (to my eyes) as Jewish, and no sign of Nazism in sight.

Those early black and white photographs 'chronicle' my pre-mother's life between the wars, and it is clear that she was loved and that the camera loved her. The 'Gerda Gallery' on my phone is mostly pre-war; there are two pictures of her and Joe in London streets in late summer

1939, but I have to expand and blur them for more detail; one of her in ATS uniform in 1943; then almost nothing until the English 'Nissen hut years' of the late 40s and early 50s. More 'recent' photographs (from the mid-1950s to the end of her life) are absent from the 'Gallery', and I realised with this second book that I could no longer avoid examining Gerda and family during the final photographed fifteen years of her life. Looking through the 'English' albums and reading my past existence in her clothes would be duty, not pleasure.

On the face of it, they more than the 'German' albums present a more 'readable' and legible 'chronicle' of family life, because at least I was there and could see younger versions of myself in most of them and half-remember the places. Sontag's observations on the intimate connection between cameras and families suggest (to me) that such a 'chronicle' became too common and ubiquitous to attract the interest of anyone outside the photographs. Every family was doing it, year after year, for no better reason than holding up a mirror to their changing familial lives. As Sontag put it, it was a 'rite of family life'. Evidently, mine like millions of others needed a long series of pictures to prove we existed at different times and places, that we changed and yet were still connected.[31]

They are a 'chronicle' of my early life too, which I had no desire to revisit, so it was more with nausea than nostalgia that I dragged out the large suitcase of albums from under the bed, clicked it open and spread across the floor in my attic study a glut of family photos from those half-forgotten decades. Had we really valued ourselves so

---

[31] Susan Sontag, *On Photography* (Penguin 2019, p. 7).

much as a post-war family that we needed so many dated reminders?

Dorothy Bohm, a 'pioneering photographer' and, like Gerda, a refugee from Nazism, recently died at the age of nearly a hundred (twice my mother's age), and I had read in one obituary that photographs satisfied for her 'a deep need to stop things from disappearing' and 'made transience less painful'.[32] Looking at fifteen years of photos on the floor, I felt the opposite – a deep need to stop things from reappearing.

Still, it had to be done, and having more or less exhausted other primary sources of information, I had to look elsewhere for her. Unfortunately, the photograph albums covering the period of my childhood were an obvious and unexplored place to look.

Although 'recent' compared to the German photographs, they are old enough to have acquired a patina, a faint film of otherness and distance, and I started to study them with more interest than expected and a renewed sense of purpose, for this initially unwelcome task was developing into a serious investigation. Research. What I needed to find was not how we appeared at various stages and evolved as a family, and certainly not to view earlier versions of myself, but to trace her place and presence in the chronicle, see how well she fitted in, if at all.

Sontag described photographs as 'memento mori', stating that the subjects are 'touched with pathos'. They show that those caught on camera are 'irrefutably there',

---

[32] From Dorothy Bohm obituary by Amanada Hopkinson in *The Guardian*, 27 March 2023.

but it is 'just for that moment' and their lives are 'heading towards their own destruction'. [33] Barthes also observed that, no matter how 'alive' people appear in old photographs with 'their whole lives before them', their deaths are not in the future but the past.[34] It was with such comforting insights in mind that I set out.

She was 'heading towards her own destruction' like the rest of us, but naturally we didn't know it then and I doubt if she did either, though by the 1960s she must have had some idea of the direction of travel. Looking at pictures of her, I couldn't help calculating the number of years remaining, and even in earlier photographs found myself looking for ghostly intimations of her future absence. If she smiles in these pictures of family life, I reflected: *She is smiling, yet has only ten or five or three or two years to go to suicide.*

The photographs are mostly undated, but there are clues like the approximate age of the children we used to be and what we were wearing at the time, and sometimes something more specific. Here, for example, the family pauses to pose in an ornamental garden, which I couldn't recall; fortunately, the actual year – 1960 – is prettily picked out in the flower border behind us, as a gift to family photos and perhaps also to celebrate the first year of a hopeful new decade. Gerda in light summer clothes rests both hands on the shoulders of a little boy who has to be me, aged nearly nine, in striped polo shirt, short trousers and sandals, leaning back against his mum. Sandy looks at something interesting beyond the

---

[33] Susan Sontag, *On Photography* (as above), pp. 15 – 16 and 75 – 76.

[34] Roland Barthes, *Camera Lucida* (as above), p. 96.

photograph. The letters HOLS can be just made out in the flower beds behind us, and further back are two steep-roofed cottages with tall chimneys. This must be our usual holiday destination on the South coast, and the brief shock of connection – seeing her there standing behind me, her hands on my shoulders, touching – made me wince. Looking more closely, I noticed a white-shirted, open-collared man standing behind her with his arm around her shoulder. Another surprise: my father for once inside and not outside the family photo.

It was less obvious up to 1960, when she was still (just) in her thirties, but once my mother turned forty on 26 June 1961 she changed in photographs. As I know from her diaries, Gerda set great store by her looks and regarded herself as '*schrecklich alt*' (terribly old) at the age of twenty-two. As she approached forty, antisemitism was on the rise, Eichmann on trial in Jerusalem, and my menopausal mother was 'going out' of her mind, losing her looks, gaining weight, and generally 'looking a proper mess'. By then too, a kindly dentist had removed all her teeth. The face in the mirror 'looked very old' to her. It is not just her clothes that tell the story. She wore the same short-sleeved white cotton blouse, buttoned cardigan, full patterned skirt, red slip-on shoes – her Mum clothes, as I see them – during summers of the 60s. But there is also something slumped about her appearance, which is much more noticeable now than at the time. She cared less about her appearance, she confided in herself, and even wished she could be 'grey haired soon'. And something else has become more apparent: an absence of expression, her mind on other things. She is not really with us. That my mother saw herself as a 'foreigner, very out of things, still very much the outsider', is evident from the surviving English diaries of the 1940s and early 50s, when she worried if she would ever fit in. It hadn't been clear to me until I studied these more recent photos that her sense of exclusion also applied to family. Evidently, she felt 'very much the outsider' with us too.

The change can be seen in the two nearly identical wooden horse photos. Though of the same scene and subject, they are in separate albums for an obvious reason: several years also separate them, and though the same family sit on the same horse in the same playground, they are different. The red wooden horse I half-recognise, but I couldn't locate the playground or place, and after sixty years or more that horse must be long gone. At first glance they seemed innocuous enough: mother and children astride a rust-red wooden horse. But when I took them out of their albums and placed them side by side, I saw only the differences. In the earlier black and white picture, my mother in a sleeveless white summer dress sits at the front, not holding the red horse's reins (it has none) but instead her favourite dachshund, Sandy. In the later colour photograph, wearing a white cardigan buttoned to her throat, full red-patterned skirt, and familiar red slip-on shoes, she sits at the back behind the children. The wooden horse has aged in the meantime: years of shoes have scratched and scraped the red paint, the girls are teenagers, Gerda drapes her arms around a daughter rather than a dog. She looks older, more worried, with that tightness of mouth I have come to expect behind her smile. This is doubtless more a subjective impression than impartial description, but that maternal embrace doesn't seem natural; it is the sort of gesture a photograph like this expects as a signifier of familial affection and connection. The change of position from the front to the back is significant too. Gerda was still at the head of the family in the later 1950s, but just a few years have reversed that. And her clothes – another notable change – from a summer mother in a sleeveless white dress, to a buttoned-up cardigan and full skirt. Yes, it could be just the weather, but I think it's more. And finally, the dog: present and correct in the first photo and right at the front, absent in the second. There is no Sandy in the later picture, no Sandy anywhere.

Family photos are often discomforting. Although these from the 1960s are sixty years old, they are still too close for comfort and give no sense of continuity or connection, just the opposite. There are a few photographs from early to mid-50s of Gerda sans family; we exist but fortunately not there; so with myself and the others completely out of the picture, I turn to these earlier photos for what I miss in the later ones. The first and probably my favourite is the striped deckchair photograph, where thankfully no children are present and Jack, who must have taken the picture, is no more than a partial shadow.

Gerda relaxes in the classic striped deckchair of the period with its attached sunshade and footrest, her loose dress light and airy and belted at the waist. Alone and having a quiet moment to herself in the sun. Her husband must be there too, since the shadow head and shoulders in the foreground cover her outstretched feet. This is the back garden of 27 Chillingworth Crescent, a council house on the new estate, down the road from the car factory, and it looks like she has recently moved in because, in the window behind her, what looks like an upright striped mattress still leans against the wardrobe. The year can be estimated by the short-haired dachshund held upright by his front paws on the canvas foot-rest while she looks down at him, not dotingly but with the expression she reserved for pets. He is young Sandy. As Gerda reclines there, bare-armed and summer-dressed in council estate sunshine, I am touched by this slimmer, younger version with that dark helmet of hair and summeriness of dress and her bare arms and feet. She is and isn't my mother. The real giveaway is the dachshund and how she holds him upright by the paws and, looking more closely, I see his shadow on the white council house wall: Sandy erectus. What makes this such a peaceful, restful, quiet moment in the sun is the absence of family apart from the dog. She can now relax.

Its charm and appeal intrigue me. Is it that she seems self-contained, more herself without us? We could enter the picture any minute and make our demands, but for the moment she is safe from us and at peace and I wish she could stay that way. Our new council house, from which she would eventually long to escape, is in full sun, and no estate children invade her privacy. The old oaks of Brasenose Wood thicken behind the grey concrete garages down the road, and beyond them are the woods and grassy hilltops, the heaths and bracken of Shotover Hill. It could be the mid-1950s, when she was in her midthirties and still slim and wore light and airy summer dresses. The second Holocaust she could see coming for herself and the children is still out of sight, five years away. She has all her teeth, her black helmet of hair is not noticeably thinning; just the opposite, in fact. She certainly doesn't look like she needs to lose weight, and she is not yet going out of her mind with the menopause. Long after she aged and thickened and her life became so burdensome that she had to lighten it by dying, this photograph is one of the few to grant her the happier afterlife she deserves.

At the top of Shotover, where she often walked the dogs, an old stone bench with an inscription was her resting-place, and there I found her in 1958 with the same sandy short-haired dachshund on her lap, and she is smiling almost like she used to in the pre-war photographs, though with a slight tightening around the mouth. Wearing a cardigan and a lighter-coloured skirt covering her knees, Gerda sits on her own shadow, obscuring all but a fragment of the inscription behind her back: THE LOVED HILL-SIDE. There is another personal connection, for this stone bench is where I also sat, though not with her in this photograph. Looking at the youngish (still in her thirties) mother enjoying the stillness of that moment in time, I remembered its place in our walks but not the whole inscription. So, I had to go back – to the actual stone seat (if still there) and read the words behind her. This was her 'loved hill-side' too, and seeing her sitting there alone with only her dog for company and at peace with herself in old woodland sunshine, I wanted to approach her.

Opportunities to enter old photographs don't come very often. They show either the back gardens of houses vacated years ago, or forgotten places – parks, ponds, promenades, beaches – now mostly unlocatable on any memory map. The stone bench where she sat in 1958 and enjoyed the sun was still there, no doubt, near the sandy level top where we parked the 1954 black Rover 90. Advance research revealed that Shotover was once part of a Royal Forest and its oldest oak (since fallen) dated back to Elizabeth I. I was going back only fifty, sixty years and had never knowingly visited that ancient tree or looked up through its gnarly, twisted branches.

The stone bench photograph merited a return visit, with no expectation of glimpsing a ghost Gerda in the woods or sensing her mute adjacent absence. Not wishing to disturb her peace and quietude or share her moment in the sun, I just wanted to find out how it felt (if more or less connected) sitting next to where she sat sixty-five years ago. For the past three years I have, of course, visited her almost daily in pre-war photographs, but there she was always Gerda as girl and young woman, daughter and sister, never as a mother. It would be a new experience to get close to the woman I half-remember.

The Stone Bench Photograph intended for this space unfortunately went missing during a recent house move. As it is one of the few photos of my still young mother relaxing in the sun, apparently untroubled, I can only hope it turns up.

Reaching the bench, I found it thankfully empty, though there were lots of walkers with their dogs about the place. The scrolled armrests were green with lichen and moss, the stone cold against my sweaty back after the long climb up Shotover Hill, and my body had retained no memory of it. Being stone, it couldn't have changed very much in the short span of a lifetime but unfortunately I had left the photograph behind, so couldn't check for differences. Presumably she saw a similar scene – the sandy, leafy soil, twisted oaks, dense bushes and bracken beyond – though her trees were sixty-five years younger then, with a different configuration of branches.

The inscription on the back of the bench – the last line, as I have since discovered, of a poem by Matthew Arnold[35] – refers to Joseph Burtt Davy, and as I had no palpable sense of a maternal absence next to me on the cold stone, I searched my phone for something to do. An internet image circa 1899 showed a dark-haired man with a dark, pointed beard. Mr Burtt Davy – unknown to me in 1958 (when I was seven) and likely to have remained so but for this photograph of a mother with dog on a stone bench – was a botanist and farmer in the Transvaal from 1903, where he studied the flora and collected thousands of plants before returning to England and working at Kew. As for the local connection, he lectured in tropical forest botany at the 'Imperial Forests Institute' at Oxford and worked on 'Forest Trees and Timbers of the British Empire' – hence his 'LOVED HILL-SIDE' and its ancient oak woodland and

---

[35] *Thyrsis*, 1865, Matthew Arnold's elegy on the death of his friend, Arthur Hugh Clough, whose absence haunts 'the loved hill-side' and echoes through the lines – 'Thou art gone, Yes, thou art gone'.

other species of trees. Apart from Wood Farm Council Estate being roughly equidistant from the stone bench and the car factory down the bypass, I could find no conceivable connection with my mother who, though she also loved this hillside, knew less than me about a learned botanist who returned to England and eventually to Oxford from the Transvaal. Googling 'Transvaal', I came up with gold and diamonds, uranium and platinum; then suddenly, as I was about to abandon the search, it lit up with the history of 'British concentration camps' in the South African Republic, Orange Free State, Transvaal and the Cape Colony. Burtt Davy reached the Transvaal the year after the Second Boer War ended, and by then the tented camps for Boer internees (with separate ones for Black Africans) had vanished, leaving only the flora to attract his scholarly interest. Within minutes on that stone bench, I learned everything I had never known about Kitchener's 'scorched earth' strategy, children dying 'at the rate of 50 a day' from starvation and contagious diseases in the camps, and an alleged government 'policy of extermination' against the civilian population. Though such a policy was disputed, the welfare and survival of the internees (mainly women and children) was considered 'an abysmally low priority'. In an internet photograph of one such victim – a little seven-year-old Boer girl called Lizzie Van Zyl – she resembles, in her shrunken, skeletal appearance, weighing only 15lbs, an image from Auschwitz. Lizzie called for her mother before dying from typhoid fever and starvation in 1901.[36]

---

[36] The plight of Lizzie Van Zyl was publicised by Emily Hobhouse, a welfare campaigner and pacifist, who visited the British concentration

In mid-Google, I looked up. A man walking a dog had stopped in front of the stone bench to ask:

'Are you a scholar?'

'No', I said, explaining that I was just searching the internet for information about the subject of the inscription on the stone bench and shifting to one side so he could read the whole of it:

OUR SCHOLAR TRAVELS YET THE LOVED HILL-SIDE.

Joseph Burtt Davy was a Quaker botanist, I told the man with the dog. As he wished to know more, I recounted everything I had just learned about the tree-loving travelling scholar. After several years as a botanist in California, in 1903 after the Second Boer War, Burtt Davy moved to South Africa, where he studied the flora of the Transvaal and farmed before returning to England in 1919 and working at Kew. At Oxford he lectured on tropical forest botany and trees of the British Empire. As the inscription suggests, I continued, Burtt Davey liked walking this 'loved hill-side' and no doubt made scholarly notes concerning its numerous ancient and unusual trees, and it was from this stone bench (I added on a more personal note) that I went on family walks from the mid-1950s to the end of the 60s. I thought better of mentioning the photograph of my mother sitting here in 1958.

'You are a scholar,' he said. 'You've told me something I didn't know.'

---

camps and brought the conditions of internees like Lizzie to the attention of the British public.

CHAPTER SEVENTEEN:

IT HAPPENED ONE NIGHT

After his mother died, searching for her in old photographs, Roland Barthes lost her 'among images partially true, and therefore totally false'. I had much the same difficulty finding mine. The photographs of Gerda as a mother seemed the falsest of all, yet these were presumably how I remembered her, facsimiles of the actual woman. In 1898 (a year before the start of the Second Boer War) Barthes discovered a sepia print of his mother aged five, posing with her older brother under the palms of a late nineteenth-century 'glassed-in conservatory' known as 'the Winter Garden', and there he finally found her.[37] I did not have to go so far back to find mine and when I did I realised that 1958 (the year of the Stone Bench Photograph) and even 1955 or '56 (the likely years of the Striped Deckchair Photograph) were still too recent. Those of her in the 1950s were preferable, of course, to representations of her in the years nearer her suicide; for as I went back, she gradually shed years and became more herself. But she wasn't far enough away, and I had

---

[37] Roland Barthes, *Camera Lucida* (as previous), pp. 67 – 68.

to go back to before I was born, before she became a mother, a wife, because any association with her 'English' family changed her for the worse. Once we were entirely out of the picture and inconceivable and couldn't edge in even as a shadow, then I could again regard her with the detachment of historical distance.

No, there was no need to go back to Gerda age five. Seventeen would do; a significant year, her last in Germany.

The two photographic portraits of Gerda aged seventeen and seventeen-and-a-half from June and December 1938 are classic Hollywood close-ups. You see it in the bright eyes and smooth skin from which the slightest blemish (if one existed) is airbrushed out, and in a smile close to laughter. Within six months of the 'Claudette Colbert Photograph', Gerda was boarding a ship to leave her country, and (rather serendipitously) the onboard entertainment featured 'a cute film with Claudette Colbert'. I know this from her 'Journey Note' dated 23 May 1939 at 'a quarter to midnight'.

The film is not otherwise specified and her ecstatic 'Journey Note', recorded for posterity as the ship prepared to depart, gives no clue. 'Unfortunately', she 'couldn't understand most of it as they spoke in American slang'. That is her only comment on the film other than it being 'cute' and starring Claudette Colbert; so, as usual, I am left to speculate. One of the highest paid female film stars of the period and evidently the movie model for the photographic portrait of Gerda taken six months before she boarded the *SS President Harding* at Hamburg docks, the Claudette Colbert of *It Happened One Night* seems closer and more relatable than other stars like Marlene

Dietrich and Greta Garbo. As the winner of the 'big five' Academy Awards in 1934 and a 'major box office hit', the film about a young woman running away to follow her own desires would have been an obvious movie choice on a ship full of escapees from Europe. Many of the passengers were, like Gerda, refugees from Nazi persecution and ready for a risqué romantic comedy and preview of what life might be like beyond the Third Reich. Maybe I want this to be the film Gerda watched as she left Germany, for the plot has parallels with her own life. Claudette Colbert plays a socialite, a spoilt heiress on the run from a wealthy and controlling father, and although that wasn't quite Gerda's situation at the time, she was also 'on the run'. She still loved Tatta, of course, but after a year of coping with a deflated father and shrinking future, having to share the last few months in much reduced accommodation, Gerda was only too happy to leave.

It was serendipitous too that I found, with remarkable prescience, a DVD of the film in a local charity shop, just as I was planning this chapter. For several compelling reasons, *It Happened One Night* had to be Gerda's onboard 'cute film with Claudette Colbert'. There is the title for a start. An earlier decisive event had 'happened one night' the previous November, leading directly to her own seminal night aboard an American ocean-liner. 9-10 November, 1938, the 'Night of Broken Glass', marked a breaking moment for the Jews still in Germany, Gerda included, whose determination to get away culminated six months later in an onboard cinema with Claudette Colbert on the run with Clark Gable. Everything was again happening one night.

Not Drowning but Waving

After the months of composing careful letters in English to refugee and au pair agencies and middle-class Englishwomen willing to take on desperate and grateful girls like Gerda for household duties; after dealings with the Gestapo and doing things she had never anticipated, like looking after the father who used to look after her; after doubting she would really get away; after all she had gone through, young Gerda deserved *It Happened One Night*. It was exactly the sort of Hollywood movie a runaway needed to feel good about herself. In the new Germany, all the eligible young men had already left or were leaving, and romantic opportunities were going with them. Gerda had earned this unexpected opportunity to see Clark Gable string a blanket (the so-called 'Walls of Jericho') as a makeshift screen between his and Claudette's bed and begin to undress in full view of the audience, fiddling with his trousers before thinking better of it and taking off his shoes instead. She deserved to see her screen lookalike take Gable's place at the roadside and do what he could never do – hitch a dark skirt high up a stockinged thigh and show a length of leg seldom seen (by Gerda) on a cinema screen. She deserved the brief trumpet blast at the end as the 'Walls of Jericho' fall down. It probably didn't matter that Gerda couldn't understand most of the film because of 'the American slang'. Film is a visual medium, and she could see what was happening between the stars. Also, being allowed to see a film at all, let alone this film, was more delightful for having been illegal, a forbidden pleasure, until this moment. After *Kristallnacht*, the authorities had decided that German Jews were insufficiently excluded from German life and barred them from cinemas, theatres, etc;

so to sit in front of a cinema screen and watch a movie star who looked rather like herself was wonderful enough but to see Claudette Colbert, with her straight fringe and pencilled eyebrows, on a night like this augured well for the voyage and the future. Like everything else happening that night aboard the ship, it was a new and thrilling experience. No wonder Gerda was deliriously happy.

Maybe I read too much into that film and its parallels with her situation at the time, especially as I can't be sure that it was the 'cute film with Claudette Colbert' she saw that night. There is little enough to connect them. Gerda's situation – escaping Nazi Germany just in time, leaving a father and a past behind for an unknown future – was no romantic 'screwball' comedy. The film was light relief from the difficult, dangerous situation Gerda had escaped but which still confined her father and aunt and other unnamed family. Yet as I scrutinised the film she had most probably watched that first night aboard the American ship, while it prepared to depart for New York (though she would disembark long before then), I saw only connections. The Claudette Colbert character, Ellie Andrews, has abandoned her sheltered upbringing to elope with an aviator playboy. Gerda had also left a once sheltered and monied life and a doting but controlling father to venture out on her own, though she was no spoilt heiress – except for the diamonds sewn into her cardigan buttons, which she later sold for next to nothing. Ellie meets Clark Gable's out-of-work reporter, Peter Warne, and falls in with him. Aboard the *SS President Harding*, Gerda met a slick, good-looking Jewish refugee from Berlin called Joe and fell in love with him and though it led to no 'Walls of Jericho' moment for her, and was all over within months, her first (and possibly last) great romance included a surprisingly risqué seduction scene.[38]

That interesting scene in Gerda's life, when she seduces Joe against an unseen background of world war, reminds me that she once viewed her life as cinematic – for instance referring to 'the film of Joe and me' which 'must have a happy ending' (Gerda's Diary, 28 September 1939). Such entries suggest that for a young woman in unusual circumstances, the rapid montage of life-changing events inclined her to look up and see what was happening to her as a 'film', as if imagining herself projected there on the big screen accommodated the outsize dimensions and dramatic impact of the new experiences coming her way daily. Her first great romantic love in London with a good-looking refugee called Joe, then the outbreak of war with what was once her country, were pure motion-picture, as were the later Luftwaffe air raids of the Blitz when night after 'thrilling' night she abandoned her own bed to huddle on the floor with the rest of the household. With such things going on internally and externally, no wonder she viewed her new life through her favourite films.

And so, as *It Happened One Night* was screened for her on the first night of a new future, it was inevitable that (even without understanding most of the dialogue) seventeen-year-old Gerda first saw herself onscreen as a Claudette Colbert lookalike hitching a lift by showing

---

[38] Just how risqué was gradually revealed to me by the English translation of her German account of her interaction with Joe in her 1939 diary. What also surprised me was the active role Gerda played in the scene.

Peter Thornthwaite

Clark Gable what a thigh-high length of leg can do to get things done. The film star she most resembled showed her what was possible away from the Third Reich.

Triangulating the most memorable nights in Gerda's life, the first was *Kristallnacht*, when windows broke throughout Germany and could be heard breaking for years to come. She wrote nothing about it in her diary – or if she did, she later excised it, which was not unusual as her later diaries show. I am now inclined to think of it as a deliberate omission. Her father owned shops in Breslau, and even if his windows weren't shattered that night, others were – in Breslau and beyond. Hearing them break in her diary, each time she went back to that night, would bring what was happening too close to home. 'The Night of Broken Glass' was the first of the three nights when Gerda's life changed forever.

The second happened after she had crossed the fault line of the turning year and made it to 23 May 1939, and just as the first had marked the end of everything, so the second night marked the beginning. It must have been wonderful, realising that her life would never be the same, certainly more wonderful than frightening once she was really leaving.

And the third? The night of December 1971 (exact date unknown) when she left again, this time leaving her English family with a suicide note to remember her by.

I am just beginning to see the connections.

CHAPTER EIGHTEEN:

OZ

Nothing appears to connect the filming of *The Wizard of Oz* (from October 1938) with Gerda's post-pogrom plans to escape further persecution, and at first there seems little to link Dorothy's Kansas with Gerda's Third Reich. But the similarities in their situations soon emerge. As things turn bad at home, both girls dream of getting away. Both find themselves transported to another world. Dorothy Gale (a twelve-year-old girl in the film though Judy Garland was already sixteen) leaves home and family, seeking a place 'way up high' where she can leave 'trouble and clouds far behind'. Gerda, too.

The film reached American cinemas on 25 August 1939, just over a week before Chamberlain's announcement of war. British audiences had to wait until 12 November for the technicolour gardens and great glistening leaves and petals of Oz to take them away from world war and gas masks for a few hours. *The Wizard of Oz* was also released in Germany in 1939 (I was surprised to learn) until another internet site informed me that it didn't get there until the 1950s. Was it banned in the Third Reich? As far as I can ascertain, the only German to see it was Goebbels.

This film features in an earlier chapter, specifically concerning Josef Mengele of Auschwitz-Birkenau infamy, but I make no apology for going back to it. On closer inspection, its parallels with Gerda's situation in 1939 are too obvious not to be noted. Also, having previously suggested connections between the great and powerful Wizard and men like Hitler and Mengele who also assumed mega powers within their vast spheres of influence, I am keen to find pleasanter and more life-affirming associations as befits a film loved by millions including my mother (and me).

If the technicolour spectacle of life over the rainbow had appeared to German cinemagoers, the idealised image of a country girl, her hair tied with pale blue bows, singing and dancing along a 'Yellow Brick Road' in her checked blue and white gingham pinafore and white blouse, would have been a familiar and pleasing one. In her rustic appearance, Dorothy is not unlike the demure 'Dirndl Girl' pictured in the pre-war 'Gerda gallery' on my phone. The fact that Judy Garland was actually seventeen by the date of the film's release, and wore under her country costume a light-fitting corset and additional sewn-in panel to suppress her breasts, might have enhanced her appeal to German audiences imbued with Nazi ideology and the ideal of women as young budding mothers – especially as the shape of Dorothy's breasts, tucked away inside an innocent girl's pinafore and blouse, is unmistakable despite attempts by the costume department to disguise it.

When Gerda first saw *The Wizard of Oz* remains unknown, but it was probably when the movie reached

London, a few months following the outbreak of war. She lived half her life in cinemas. As Gerda projected her life into films, and films into her life, the story of a girl wanting to get away was her story too, only magnified. Both girls are separated from their families. For Dorothy, the farmhouse window blown against her head marks the moment of transition from one place to another. For Gerda, the breaking windows of *Kristallnacht* marked hers. The thick black swaying rope of the Kansas twister lifting and spinning a farmhouse high up in a dark and tumultuous sky doubtless brought to mind the racial 'tornado' Gerda herself had only just escaped. As with Dorothy, the 'twister' uprooted and landed her in another life. After the storm, Dorothy opens the farmhouse door, not to the sepia dust and dirt of rural Kansas but to sudden technicolour and the blooms and birdsong of Oz. Ditto Gerda, when she left the Nazi past far behind and looked to a brighter-coloured future.

A little bridge spans the bluest of streams, a symbolic bridge for Dorothy to cross from Kansas to Oz, and the Yellow Brick Road offers the only direction of travel. With little 'Munchkins' singing and dancing to see her off (Judy Garland at 4'11" dwarfs them), her adventures begin. For Dorothy, there is 'no place like home', and having got as far away from it as possible and left monochrome home for a place where there is only technicolour, she spends most of the film trying to get back. Yet after arriving in Oz, she leaves the fallen farmhouse without so much as a backward glance. I have replayed this scene repeatedly, pausing it, going back and forwards, and can confirm that Dorothy doesn't look back. With her eyes full of Oz, the farmhouse is forgotten, and she cheerfully walks away from it. With most of the film and wonderful adventures still ahead of her, there is no return to sepia just yet. And that too must have resonated with Gerda, who also left home and Tatta without a backward glance.

Both girls were only too glad to get away. As Gerda's 'Journey Note' of 23 May 1939 reveals, she was having her 'Oz' moment and making the most of it as another such time might never come. Safely aboard the American ship, with fatherland and father diminishing, she has already 'experienced so much' she 'can hardly grasp it'. 'The fabulous food. Wine as if it was bleeding. It was like a fairy tale.' She wonders if she is 'dreaming'. As 'Oz' moments go, it equalled and even surpassed Dorothy's, un-shadowed as it was by thoughts of 'home'. Having only just left, Gerda had no wish ever to return.

Later in my mother's life, she nearly had another 'Oz' moment. Alarmed by the rise of antisemitism in Germany and Britain, she determined that the family should immediately 'emigrate to Australia' (Gerda's Diary, 4 and 6 January 1960). She had previously decided against us becoming 'Ten Pound Poms', but the return of the past changed her mind. How close we came to escaping 'to Oz' I never knew, but the thought of leaving behind her beloved dachshund or quarantining him stopped her before she started: 'I never want to leave Sandy. I love him too much.' She left her Tatta in Nazi Germany more easily than she could leave Sandy twenty-one years later. So, we never got to 'Oz' after all.

Here again, though, she shows her similarity to Dorothy. Both were dog-lovers. Sandy was to Gerda what Toto was to Dorothy. Dorothy loves her Aunt Em – and Uncle Henry too, of course, and Scarecrow, Cowardly Lion, Tin

Man and their human counterparts in Kansas – but Toto is her constant companion. About to leave Oz, she tells the Tin Man, 'I think I'll miss you most of all', but Toto is her 'Big Love'. It is Toto she hugs after singing *Somewhere Over the Rainbow*, pressing his hairy little head against hers at the end of the song.

My mother had Sandy 'destroyed' on 23 November 1964, because she 'could not bear to see him suffer so', and (as mentioned earlier, but it does no harm to repeat it) eulogised him in her diary as 'all love', her 'best pal', her 'best companion'. It sometimes seems to me that there was no greater tragedy in her life than losing that dog. Dorothy nearly loses Toto twice. Had the film also let her leave her girlhood behind, there would have been losses enough to come – Toto included. In fact, the real Toto lasted until the end of the war, dying aged eleven in Hollywood on 1 September 1945. But in the film as it is, the idea of Dorothy losing Toto forever is inconceivable. As she watches him escape the 'Wicked Witch of the West' with her peaked hat and copper-green face and pointed nose and chin, Dorothy cries out, 'He got away! He got away!' That is what audiences wanted to hear. It was certainly what Gerda heard, and it echoed throughout her life.

She was happy for Toto and Dorothy, of course, but the girl's desperation also touched another nerve in Gerda. Judy Garland was almost a woman when she played Dorothy, and already the 'hurt' and 'pain' in her voice can be heard. Perhaps Judy/Dorothy and Gerda too divined in the little dog's plight and scampering escape from the long-fingered grip of the green-faced witch the real dangers confronting others equally desperate to get away from impossible situations and not as lucky as Toto. The 'hurt' and 'pain' are still inaudible in Gerda's diaries at this time, but the fear and relief in Dorothy's voice as Toto 'got away' reached her, I'm sure, because the getting away was what mattered above all, then and later.

For a German-Jewish refugee, a new life as a domestic in a country soon to be at war with her own wasn't an obvious 'over the rainbow' situation, but compared to Nazi Germany it was. In an online Guardian article about *The Wizard of Oz* (17 June 2019), Luiza Sauma recalls her mother's Jewish parents finding 'their own Oz' in Rio de Janeiro, just before the start of World War Two, but remaining 'homesick' for the Poland they had left behind.[39] If Gerda experienced '*Heimweh*' for Germany, she left no trace of such sickness in her diaries or in my memories of her. There were reasons enough for a young Jewish woman not to miss overmuch a country overrun by Nazis, and from the start of her great adventure she naturally (in view of her youth and circumstances) looked forward, not back. And there was another pressing reason for not thinking of 'home'. Aboard the *President Harding*, Gerda found love – not the little love she had toyed with in the past, but an outsize 'Oz'-style love with capital letters: the 'Big Love' as she identified it in her diary. Joe seemed 'perfect, really', and tailor-made for the part. After she arrived in London, the excesses of 'Oz' came out as never before: *Ich liebe Joe ich liebe Joe ich liebe ihn so sehr that soon I cannot endure it any longer*' (Gerda's Diary 24 June 1939).

---

[39] In an article in *The Guardian* (17 June, 2011), Luiza Sauma recalled that just before the outbreak of the Second World War her mother's Jewish parents made a new life in Rio de Janeiro – 'their own Oz, far away from Poland'. But they were homesick, unsettled and, unlike Dorothy, 'couldn't click their heels together' and go back.

Dorothy also found love, a different sort of love – involving a sparsely-stuffed scarecrow, rusty tin man and cowardly lion – as befits a twelve-year-old Kansas girl in blue and white gingham whose first love is a little terrier called Toto. Not for Dorothy the few days in Paris *'ganz allein with Joe'* that Gerda slotted into her itinerary between leaving Hamburg on 24 May and arriving in London on 12 June. Gerda was still girl enough to record that 'nothing happened on the way'. And maybe they were not so unalike after all concerning love. Dorothy's companions in Oz, combining straw, tin and a tawny hide, were an amalgam of a heart, a brain, the nerve – the very qualities she might one day seek (but probably not find) in a man. Meanwhile, Gerda was finding and losing hers. By December 1939, the 'Big Love' was over and she was left 'drinking tea' in her little room and 'waiting for Joe to call'. He didn't.

Judy Garland plays a girl in the film but was in fact only a year younger than Gerda. Her girlish appearance (notwithstanding those suppressed breasts) explains why she wants to go 'home' all the time. She is still a child. No sooner does she reach the rainbow wonders of Oz than she longs to return to Kansas and the homely bosom of Aunt Em, and in this respect she and Gerda could hardly be more different. As she ventures into a hitherto unknown world of great glossy leaves and blooms and streams and pools with giant lily pads, she tells Toto (her confidante throughout) that they must be 'over the rainbow' and 'not in Kansas anymore'. I have often wondered about this for Oz, though wonderful in appearance, is also negatively defined from Dorothy's arrival. It lacks something essential to her happiness. It is 'not Kansas'. This is where she seems to part company with Gerda.

Dorothy learns that only by being exiled from home can she appreciate the true value of her own 'backyard'. When she taps her ruby slippers together three times and transports herself back, she happily drains her world of colour and adventure and ends where she began. There is no need to leave home 'ever again' to seek her 'heart's desire'. A good lesson for a girl to learn then.

Gerda's experience of the Third Reich taught her something different. During her last months in Nazi Germany, she and Tatta moved to reduced accommodation for Jews and after she left her father had further shrinkages of living space and life ahead. For Tatta, there was literally 'no place' he could call 'home' in an expanding Reich with no room for people like him. If, when his daughter left him, she thought she might one day return, subsequent developments in Germany and throughout Europe soon changed her mind; but I don't suppose Gerda ever dreamed of going back.

Dorothy has to leave home before Miss Gulch has Toto 'destroyed' and the farm taken away, and Aunt Em and Uncle Henry are powerless to prevent her because they 'can't go against the law'. When she returns, she seems to forget all about Miss Gulch and her power to dispossess the family and destroy Toto. Nothing disturbs Dorothy's delight at being home again. For Gerda, of course, it was the opposite. Nothing delighted her as much as not being home.

What she saw in the film she never said, and her diaries are typically blank on a subject so close to her heart. A movie from 'the Golden Age of Hollywood', released when she was still enjoying the 'Phoney War' delights of London and the 'Big Love', in later years it would take her back to her own brief Oz. This is supposition, but then most of what I know about Gerda can only ever be that. I am guessing too that Judy Garland remained for her, as for millions of others, 'one of the greatest film legends of classic Hollywood'. Her long association with the star was extended by television with the revival of Garland's career in the 1950s and 60s in *Sunday Night at the London Palladium* and *The Judy Garland Show*. There is no diary record of Judy Garland's death on 22 June 1969 at the age of forty-seven. Gerda was also forty-seven on that date (at least for another four days) and by another odd coincidence it was also the age of Hitler's beloved mother, Klara, when she died. The omission of Judy Garland's death from Gerda's 1969 diary is no surprise, as the outside world rarely gets a look-in anyway, but in fact there are no entries between April that year and the last on 30 September when, complaining that the pills prescribed by her doctor made her 'sicker than ever', she arrived at a fitting finale.

Judy Garland was found dead in the bathroom of her rented house in Cadogan Lane, Belgravia; the cause of death 'an incautious self-overdosage of barbiturates'. Unlike Gerda's overdose a few years later, Judy's was 'unintentional', her death 'accidental', with no indication that she had tried to kill herself. Barbiturates belong to the sedative-hypnotic class of medicines and are occasionally prescribed as sleeping pills. Gerda was possibly also prescribed barbiturates to help her sleep. If so, they soon made her drowsy, as evidenced by the slurred words of her suicide note sliding down the page. Maybe she intended writing more but was too sleepy. There was a lot of Judy Garland in Gerda, who was probably going through an undiagnosed depression at the time. I wasn't there to see it and wouldn't have noticed anyway because it was difficult to distinguish undiagnosed depression from my mother's normal mood. She had a predisposition to suicide, which I could date from the last line of the entry for 4 January 1960: 'If things get really bad, I might try and commit suicide, but only if there is really no other way open'. Coinciding with her alarm at the resurgence of antisemitism, that is her first known recorded reference to suicide. Though Judy Garland's death drew a blank in my mother's last diary, Gerda had followed the star's revived career and was no doubt aware of her history of ECT and earlier failed suicide attempt and what Judy had said about it at the time: that she saw only 'confusion' ahead and wanted to 'blank out the future as well as the past'.

Audiences called out after every concert, 'We love you, Judy!' There was a last vast audience: an estimated 20,000 people queuing outside the funeral chapel in Manhattan on 26 June, which happened to be Gerda's birthday. Her co-star in *A Star is Born*, James Mason, said you could always hear the 'hurt' and 'pain' in her voice. My mother's diaries brought out the 'hurt' and 'pain' in her voice too. Since I first opened them three years ago, they have become essential reading as an audible aide-mémoire, and I am now so sensitised to her modes of expression that the words and silences I half-remembered her by can be heard distinctly again from all those years ago. Behind the entries of the later 1960s I hear her murmuring to herself, and long after I have returned the diary to its suitcase to muffle the sound, the hurt and pain in Gerda's voice ghosts the airwaves between us. She talks about me sometimes, usually in response to hurtful things I said, like calling her 'a witch': 'All I ever get out of him is rudeness and shouting and insults like: you look like a witch etc. etc' (Gerda's Diary 29 April 1968). Rereading that entry inevitably brings to mind the 'Wicked Witch of the West' in The Wizard of Oz, with her peaked hat and copper-green face and pointed nose and chin, and reveals that my mother saw herself through my sixteen-year-old eyes and reflected that if her own son could say such unforgiveable things to her, others could say much worse.

As befits a screen legend of petite Judy Garland's stature, in January 2017 her remains were re-interred in the 'Hollywood Forever Cemetery' in Los Angeles. I am writing this in January 2024, doing what I can to disregard my mother's last wishes and lengthen her posthumous longevity. Gerda was cremated in January 1972, and I can no longer locate the spot where (as I vaguely recall) a potted plant marked the place where her ashes were interred. She got what she wanted in the end: nothing to remember her by.

When the farmhouse window blows in with the tornado and knocks Dorothy out, the ensuing scene (as the twister twirls the farmhouse high in a blackening and tumultuous sky) was entitled 'Dorothy's Delirium' in the production notes. Unconscious, Dorothy then remained in a 'dream state' (Oz being an extended 'dream') until she woke up in her own bed in her own room in her own house in Kansas. During earlier viewings, her loss of consciousness often brought my mother' suicide to mind, but Gerda's post-overdose coma was less temporary than

Dorothy's and probably less colourful and eventful. The cool cloth pressed gently against Dorothy's forehead signifies her passing invalid state, though Uncle Henry feared for a moment they had 'lost her' after that blow to the head from the window. Otherwise, there is nothing really to connect Dorothy waking up to her 'family' and Gerda not waking up at all to us. Even my father's promise to buy her a new portable TV for her sole use failed to rouse my mother from that deep sleep.

What I realised after my last viewing of the film is that Dorothy is an orphan. That had previously escaped my attention. Aunt Em and Uncle Henry are with her at the end, indulgently attentive and concerned as the excitable and imaginative girl recounts her strange and wonderful adventures in 'Oz'. The others at the sickbed make up an unusual family: Professor Marvel at the window and the three anxious farmhands who oddly resemble a straw man, a tin man and a cowardly lion. Then I realised that Gerda was an 'orphan' too. She had no mother from the age of six. She abandoned her father in Breslau and never saw him again. Tatta survived only as a guilty memory. What remained of the family also remained widely dispersed. The last of them – her brother, Gunther – died in April 1971, the year of her suicide, thereby putting an end to any possibility of the sentimental reunion he had in mind.

Maybe I should stop looking for connections, which has become an automatic habit. I look at Dorothy's hair and think: Gerda's was shorter and darker. Dorothy's hair hangs in thick twisted braids tied with pale blue ribbons and is a reddish brown. An internet search reveals that the top was Judy Garland's natural hair (she was 'a natural redhead') and the braids extensions. Halfway through *The Wizard of Oz*, I noticed, the braids are no longer tied with pale blue ribbons and Dorothy suddenly seems less girlish; her red lipstick is noticeable too, and I was reminded of a similar shade worn by my mother. To see it again, so vividly, fifty-odd years after she last wiped it from her lips, is unnerving. As for the ruby slippers, Gerda often wore red slip-on shoes. While looking through the family photo albums of the 1950s and 60s, I noticed the same or similar red slip-on shoes and realised, with a twist of excitement, that I had discovered something new. Gerda's shoes were red but otherwise unlike the six identical pairs at Judy Garland's disposal during the filming. For all her mental vagaries, my mother's size-five feet evidently felt at home in those red slip-on shoes. 'Those slippers will never come off so long as you're alive,' the Wicked Witch of the West tells Dorothy. Ditto Gerda, although her lookalike slip-ons were plainer and flatter and lacked the butterfly-bows and heels deemed necessary for a petite 'twelve-year-old' girl with a bosom; also unlike the ruby slippers, my mother's red slip-ons were not stolen and recovered many years later and put up for auction.

Glinda, the 'good witch' (so like Gerda in name) tells Dorothy she always had the power to go back to Kansas. All she had to do was tap the heels of her ruby slippers together three times and say, 'There's no place like home, there's no place like home.' In her last scene, Dorothy wakes up in her own room with those that love her at the invalid's bedside, and a wise face at the open window looking in to ask after the little girl. It was all just a dream, Dorothy is told, but she insists that she was there and tells them about Oz and how beautiful it was, though she always wanted to go home. The grownups listen but know what really happened. Dorothy got a nasty bump on the head when the window blew in with the twister, and for a minute they feared she wouldn't be coming back, but anyway she's home now and this is her room and she's never going to leave again.

For my mother there was no place like home for killing herself in comfort. She had often threatened a gas oven death, but when it came to it an overdose in the warmth of her own big old mahogany bed was a pleasanter way to go. What was on her mind that night before she gulped down her pills remains unknown, but (and this is only speculation) it might have been the gabled, balconied family home of the pre-war German years. For Gerda, as for Dorothy, there was 'no place like home' at the end of the journey. The house where she died was more of a home than any before it in post-war England. Gerda had gone from rented room to Nissen hut to council house and ultimately to her own semi-detached and neighbours who kept a distance. When the prospect of compensation from Germany for Nazi depredations first appeared in 1958, she had envisaged a further progression to a large detached in North Oxford, but by 1971 even that wasn't reason enough to live. No, she had decided to make do with the house where Sandy last lived and where she was surrounded by her suitcases. There would be no onward journey for them.

Thinking of 'home' and what it meant to her reminds me of another favourite Judy Garland film, *Meet Me in St. Louis*. Whether Gerda saw it in 1945, after it reached the UK, or later, I don't know as it was just another transformative cinematic experience she never mentioned. Some of its appeal to her as a film about the importance of family and home is undeniable. The awful prospect of upheaval confronting an upper middle-class family in 1903 in St. Louis, Missouri moving home because Mr. Alonzo Smith's promotion necessitates relocation to New York, is hardly comparable to the upheavals faced several decades later by Jewish families in Nazi Germany, and yet success American-style almost equally convulses the comfortable Smiths, and their upset at having to move must have resonated as deeply with Gerda. Though no doubt she loved seeing Judy Garland change from girl in gingham to exuberant young woman with rich auburn hair and full fringe, by December 1971 my mother remembered the movie for other reasons. Maybe she was remembering the Christmas scene in which little 'Tootie' in just a nightgown dashes downstairs to decapitate the snow figures grouped on the white lawn because she can't take them with her to New York, while Esther, bare-armed in a red dress, follows her out into the winter garden to comfort her inconsolable little sister. It is a comfort to me to think that such moving scenes from *Meet Me in St. Louis* lit up the dark of my mother's last moments at home as she sat up in bed with her bottles of pills, and as she killed herself just before Christmas I like to think that uplifting lines from *Have Yourself a Merry Little Christmas* came back to her – not the original lyrics (though appropriate enough in the circumstances) but the more hopeful version as desired by Judy Garland.[40]

---

[40] Judy Garland objected to the darkness of some of the original lyrics of 'Have Yourself a Merry Little Christmas', considering them too

Peter Thornthwaite

Imagining what was going through my mother's mind that last night in Cowley, Oxford seems a little insensitive even to me, but if you want to get to know someone, you have to go where they go. Suicide is the ultimate privacy and a no-go area. The attraction for me, though, is that hers inevitably reminds me of other liminal 'in-between' times in her life, and as I have lingered there out of curiosity, so I naturally do the same here at the end of the series. *Meet Me in St. Louis* casts some light on my mother's terminal state of mind, though I'm really not sure if home and family occupied her thoughts as she took the first palmful of pills. More likely, she was back in Oz, and that takes me back to that euphoric 'Journey Note' of 23 May 1939 and her first night aboard the *President Harding*. It was her 'Oz moment', as I suggested earlier, when, like Dorothy Gale, she found herself between two worlds. For the girl in gingham the antithetical places were Kansas and Oz. For Gerda: Germany and England, and also past and future. It was the best of times, for by the age of seventeen (nearly eighteen) Gerda needed the break and a good long rest from daily dread. And to mark the occasion, her passage from one place to another was lit up first by the 'Big Love' (and the transference from Tatta to lover) and then by the looming big war. Liminal felt good to her. For a limited period only, it seemed to stretch far into the unknown and unknowable future, and in the meantime all she had to do was make the best of it.

Like Dorothy, Gerda thought of home – how could she

---

depressive. The lines, 'Have yourself a merry little Christmas/ It may be your last/Next year we may all be living in the past' were changed to: 'Have yourself a merry little Christmas/ Let your heart be light/ From now on our troubles will be out of sight'.

not at that juncture? She missed it, but in the circumstances her attitude could only be ambivalent, so maybe she gave it less thought than might be expected. And there again she is like Dorothy, who thinks occasionally of Kansas and home, but mostly gets on with having a wonderful time in Oz. If (when she thought of them) Dorothy missed Aunt Em and Uncle Henry and the rest, Gerda had less reason to miss Nazi Germany, and it was reassuring to know how much she was missed by Tatta, how his life turned dark when she left.

Looking back (as I know from her later diaries that she did), for all the gathering guilt and regrets, she also remembered it as the time when she was most loved. She felt her father's love from afar and more keenly still as slim, dark-haired Joe Schwarz eclipsed him. Gerda readily accepted the love of men – whether father, brothers, or would-be lovers, as no more than her due. As Glinda reminds Dorothy, it is not a question of 'how much you love', but of 'how much you are loved by others.'

CHAPTER NINETEEN:

HOUDINI

That she felt a special affinity with stars from the 'Golden Age of Hollywood' is only surmise, as there is no tangible evidence, but restating it convinces me of its truth. Like mother, like son, since I also look for her there. She was hardly alone in viewing Hollywood as an 'escape' from daily and (to quote from her later diaries) 'utterly dull and boring' life, but to me in my early role as her cinema associate it was one of her most attractive qualities. Gerda's lifelong passion for classic movies indicates a deeper source of information than even the diaries. The centrality of those highly personal written records has been overstated. Yes, she is to be found there, but over the past three years I have made too much of them as a unique primary biographical source, and the essential truth about my mother would be missing from an account that left out the movies she loved and the Hollywood stars who projected some aspect of her onto the big screen. They were not just idealised celluloid; they were also her.

Going to the cinema meant leaving her days behind, if just for a few hours, and getting away was what her life was essentially about. Leaving Germany in 1939 was the defining moment, although it wasn't until that other defining moment in her life (her death) that the pattern began to emerge. It took me a while to see it. Escape was the recurring motif of my mother's life. From 2 January 1939 when (as her diary shows) she started planning her escape, until her death exactly thirty-three years later in Oxford, it was all about getting out of enclosing situations, getting away. It was what Dorothy did when things got bad in Kansas, and it is tempting to see *The Wizard of Oz* as the defining film of Gerda's life, but there are others. Now that I think of it, *Houdini* (1953), featuring Tony Curtis, could be the key to unlocking her life.

Admittedly, its prime significance for me has something to do with the special mother-son bond, which was apparently just as strong in reality as in the film. Not that the frozen river stunt as depicted was entirely accurate, and the film makes much of a telepathic communication between Houdini and his mother – as when, handcuffed and shackled inside a locked iron box and dropped into an icy river, he rises up from the riverbed to a white roof and would have drowned but for hearing his dying mother's voice calling him back to the hole in the ice and so to life. I make no claim to such telepathic communication with my dead mother, but it interested me that Houdini apparently believed that such a bond was strong enough to escape death. It seems that he continued searching for a dead but still audible mother long after she died, for he disappeared from public view for a few years to look for her amid the scents and candles of seances. In reality (and not just the film) Houdini could not let her go, and I have read on the internet that his friendship with Arthur Conan Doyle, who believed in spiritualism, led Houdini in June 1922 to a séance in a suite at the Ambassador Hotel in Atlantic City. There, after seating her guests around a table, Lady Doyle (a practising medium) rapped on it several times and made contact with Houdini's mother, Cecilia Steiner Weiss, who spoke to her in English, though she had evidently learnt to do so only after she died.[41]

I mention such details not to draw any spurious comparisons. Unlike Harry Houdini (in this and other respects) I don't consider my mother an 'angel in human form', and there was no extrasensory telepathic communication between us then and there is none now. But as I vaguely recall the 1953 film version of Houdini's life, which I remember we watched together, just the two of us, I sense a more than momentary connection with her. It takes me back to a time when we were much closer, my mother and I, so I recall the film with that in mind. There is one scene in particular, early on, when Houdini becomes aware of his uncanny ability to escape seemingly impossible restraints, and I recall her expression – utterly transfixed. Tony Curtis (I have since learnt) was an amateur magician from a Hungarian Jewish family. His sense of kinship with Houdini must have enhanced his performance and its mesmerising effect on us during the early 'straitjacket' scene.

Sweat beading his face, a young Houdini just stands

---

[41] Conan Doyle had faith in Houdini's supernatural powers. I'm not sure if the denouncer of fake seances made contact on this occasion with his mother, who had been dead for nine years, but it appears that she had learnt English in her absence and wrote out fifteen pages of messages in a language foreign to her when alive.

there, tensed, straitjacketed, outwardly motionless, staring up at the glittering chandelier of the Hotel Astor, while the other straitjacketed volunteers struggle and stretch and roll comically about the stage...

And that is where this memory directs me - straight into the film with no scene-setting – and I am so impatient to be there again, watching *Houdini* with her, that I am inclined to overlook the domestic context of one of the handful of special memories I shared with her. The fact is, I don't recall the exact circumstances. Most likely I am recalling a Sunday TV matinee, my mother and I alone in the room, my father in the dank back garden intent on the latest project. Perhaps he was building a retaining wall for the raised rambling lawn which, as I remember, rose halfway up the French windows of the sitting room and seemed about to enter the house when we first moved in. Maybe this was shortly after the move. That overgrown garden needed shoving back, and he was the man to do it. Or by this time, perhaps, he was starting on what turned out to be a solidly constructed but sunless conservatory. Whatever he was doing outside, at home in the cold with his old wood-handled tools, I remember that I meant to help him but was instead indoors, watching Hollywood with her. It was a fortuitous decision. Rather than stand back and observe the oiled teeth of the hungry saw bite into the timber and spit sawdust, or watch him scrape sand and cement and slop it into a bucket, I sat on a pouffe by the coal fire and had a more memorable moment than any he could offer outdoors. Seeing myself there, in the warmth with my mother, sharing the love of movies I most associate with her apart from jumble sales, I realise I have forgotten to mention my two sisters or locate them in the house. They were there somewhere, but at that remembered moment there were just the three of us – my mother, me, and Houdini – and looking sideways at the face in the winged armchair, it showed more than its usual absorption when Hollywood was on. Something unusual was happening.

Without moving a muscle, merely gazing up, intent on the glittering chandelier, while the others fell about on the stage, Houdini shed his straitjacket and was free.

There is no evidence that my mother had any special interest in the man born as Erich Weisz to a Jewish family in Budapest. Yet the reasons for her apparent fascination (at least for the duration of the film) with that ex-Hungarian early twentieth century American escape artist are compelling, though I couldn't have known them then. After emigrating to the US in 1878, the family left many things behind, including their names. Weisz changed to Weiss, and Erich became Erik. Later, as a magician, Erik Weiss changed again to Harry Houdini. None of this, as I recall, came out in the 1953 film. His father, Rabbi Mayer Samuel Weiss, the first Rabbi of the Zion Reform Jewish Congregation in Appleton, Wisconsin, is absent from the film. Houdini's mother, Cecilia Steiner Weiss, is all-important. Surprisingly, given her son's lifelong devotion to her, the internet sites I sourced revealed less than expected about her. A photograph of them together in 1908, in Rochester, New York, shows a woman of not dissimilar height (Houdini was five foot six inches), wearing a large fur hat, fur jacket and long wide skirt, and as they stand there on the pavement, a wagon loaded with sacks on the road just behind them, Houdini appears to be kissing or about to kiss her. Notwithstanding his apparent bond with Bess, who was his wife on and off the stage, his real love was for Cecilia. Houdini wrote passionate letters to his mother, and his happiest moment was at a grand reception when he presented her in a dress once designed for Queen Victoria. Such details are missing from the movie, as is her inability to speak English, but it does show him dancing with his beloved mother in Germany during his European tour.

My mother's interest in the film had (I am sure) nothing to do with Houdini's attachment to his mother and everything to do with his ability to get out, get away, break free, escape against all the odds. Handcuffs, straitjackets, leg-irons, locks, cells, steel and glass cabinets, roped and nailed packing crates lowered into frozen rivers – nothing could hold him for long. Was she thinking of herself? It seems likely. Houdini was an immigrant like her and reinvented himself as she did, and to that extent she identified with him. Possibly, too, her 'interest' in him was confined to a film we watched on television one Sunday afternoon and as usual I am reading too much into it and finding connections that aren't there. Indeed, I could have imagined most of this, and it was more that she was physically attracted to Tony Curtis, who was undoubtedly handsomer than the real illusionist and didn't have Houdini's strangely staring eyes with their disconcerting diamond gleam.

It has been suggested that Houdini's appeal had much to do with the immigrant experience in early twentieth century United States – that, as the world's greatest 'escape' artist, he showed millions of immigrants like himself what could be done, again and again, despite seemingly insuperable odds. If anyone could prove – not once or twice or a hundred times, but repeatedly until death – that a man could be free, it was Houdini. Many like him (but also unlike him, as there could only be one Houdini) had either got away or imagined escaping constraints and confinements of one kind or another, and he seems to have touched some deep desire in them. His most difficult and daring performances proved that it was always possible to break free. I have read somewhere that one thing that attracted his audiences was the possibility that this time – during this repeat upside-down immersion in a glass and steel cabinet filled with water – the great Houdini, human after all, would drown, having defied death once too often. There is something in this, and he must have been aware of this dark side of spectator expectation. But the possibility of the great Houdini dying mid-act, mid-escape, however thrilling to some, proved less attractive than the probability of his getting away with it again and miraculously breaking free. That was what Houdini did. That, I think, was his attraction for my mother.

When he died in 1926, Gerda was five. That year the second volume of *Mein Kampf* was published. For all his accessories from the Dark Ages – shackles, irons, chains, and other ways of trussing up human beings – Houdini could not have anticipated the new Dark Age to come, and it is unlikely that even he, with his supple muscles and power of mind over matter, could have escaped ghettoes, gas chambers and special crematoria, or clawed his way out of a pit he had been made to dig for himself.

I can't know for sure if my mother felt any connection with Houdini and identified with him as someone who got away; but if she did, it was because that film of his life reminded her of her own near-miraculous escape as everything closed in on her. Defining moments in life are not so easily forgotten. Houdini made a career out of his and a legend of his life as a miracle man forever capable of escaping the inescapable, no matter how multi-layered and ingenious the restraints. Gerda, not one for public display or self-promotion, never mentioned her lucky escape, but as she watched that film from her winged armchair by the coal fire, she surely remembered how she also got out. In 1939 she could not have foreseen the extremes to which a civilised society could go when there is a will and a way, but she knew she was getting away just in time and was lucky, and that first night of freedom aboard the *SS President Harding*, as it prepared to leave Hamburg docks, was her Houdini moment. And as it happened, I was lucky too, for I belatedly shared that Houdini moment with her.

Later in life, she again experienced the urge to escape an impossible situation. Though it was hardly comparable to her situation in Nazi Germany during her last year there, she was feeling horribly hemmed in again and with nowhere to turn and increasingly desperate to make a break for it. This time, though, she needed to escape a situation of her own making. 'I am getting too much junk,' she wrote in 1960 and it remained her constant refrain in the diaries of that last decade. Things were enclosing and confining her and she could not see her way through. A repeatedly renewed determination to stop before it's too late breaks out in entry after entry, with decisive breakpoints marked in her diaries by bold exclamation marks: 'Enough of everything!' and 'Enough until death!'

Regarding old clothes and suitcases, she probably had incipient hoarding tendencies, which she half-recognised, but no sooner had she decided to stop ('No more jumbles! Never again!') than she immediately carried on exactly as before. My poor mother tied herself up in knots over this matter and felt unable to extricate herself, no matter how supple her Houdini-like mental contortions.

Am I overdoing the 'Houdini connection'? Probably. The Tony Curtis who gazed up at a chandelier and shed a straitjacket without moving and then went on to perform his death-defying stunts certainly held my attention, and to this day he is the definitive Houdini. Other than a 1953 biopic and what I recall as her marked interest in the man, there is no evidence that he touched something deep in her. Yet his uncanny ability to escape and cheat death and survive against all the odds surely affected a woman with her history. In the 'Chinese Water Torture', which he first performed in Berlin in 1912 and repeated until his death, Houdini was suspended upside-down in a locked glass and steel cabinet full of water. Doubtless such elaborate stunts impressed me more than my mother – and they still do impress me, as I discovered when I looked them up on the internet before writing this chapter – but I can't escape the feeling that this was as much a special and memorable film for her as for me.

Always on the lookout for coincidences, I note that the first year of the 'Chinese Water Torture' act, 1912, was also the year of the sinking of the *Titanic* on its maiden voyage to New York, and I wonder how Houdini (if aboard) would have contrived to escape that unsinkable sinking ship. 1912 was the year too of the International Eugenics Conference at the Imperial Institute in London. Organised by the British Eugenics Education Society to propagate ideas about improving the human race, it was attended by Winston Churchill as First Lord of the Admiralty.

Maybe it was just as well that Houdini died, at the age of fifty-two, in 1926, a key year for Hitler in his continuing Kampf. Two years earlier, the Immigration Act of 1924 all but closed US borders to immigrants from southern and eastern Europe. Given his own Jewish immigrant background and the advance of Eugenics in the US, Houdini missed the worst that was to come. With his wealth and fame, the Immigration Act wouldn't have affected him directly, and as his marriage was childless he could not be accused of adding to the millions of unwelcome immigrants then living in the US. If a student from McGill University had not repeatedly punched him in the stomach to test the strength and durability of a living legend and thereby ruptured his appendix, Houdini might have lived to see the US become an inspiration and model to Nazi Germany.[42] Had he lived to sixty-five, news must have reached him of an ill-fated ship of immigrants leaving Hamburg on 13 May 1939, whose passengers were refused entry first by Cuba, then the US. Gerda left Hamburg eleven days later aboard the *SS President Harding* bound for New York, though America wasn't her destination and no door slammed

---

[42] *The Passing of the Great Race: Or, The Racial Basis of European History* (1916) by the highly influential American eugenicist and conservationist, Madison Grant, would be much praised by Hitler and other leading Nazis for its theory of the superiority of the 'Nordic race' to other 'human races'. After the war, at the Nuremberg Trials, Grant's book was entered as a defence by Nazi war criminals tracing the Holocaust back to America.

shut in her face. Fortunately, Houdini didn't survive to see a time when there was no escaping heredity and history or wriggling free of the skin-tight restraint of 'race'. Not even a Houdini could escape that straitjacket.

I meant to end the chapter there, with that rather apt metaphor, but the thought of people 'escaping' the seemingly inescapable reminded me of that entry in *Anne Frank's Diary* (3 February 1944) when Anne and others envisage the deliberate flooding of Amsterdam by the Germans as a defence against a feared British landing in Holland. For the trapped occupants of the 'Secret Annexe', such widespread immersion offered an opportunity to escape by water – or rather underwater, so 'nobody can see we're Jews'. Houdini's most famous acts involved water, whether being secured inside an iron box and dunked in a frozen river where he would have drowned but for his dying mother calling to him, or suspended upside-down in a glass and steel cabinet filled with water. He tried other elements with less success, having been hung by his ankles from a high building (air) and also buried alive (earth). Earth was his least favourite confinement. In a pit six feet deep underground, without a coffin, Houdini had to be pulled from his own grave when one clawing hand at last emerged, and he later described the earth above him as 'killing'. Water was the natural element for an escape artist of his supple and slippery physicality.

CHAPTER TWENTY:

NOT DROWNING BUT WAVING

The final line of Stevie Smith's last poem, *Come Death (2)*, is 'Come Death. Do not be slow.' As poetry had no known place in my mother's life, I doubt if those words came to mind when it was her turn to let death in; but as a long-awaited moment of release, it was most welcome and she was equally impatient for it to be over and done with. Stevie Smith also died in 1971, and her aunt, the so-called 'Lion Aunt', had 'no patience with Hitler'. Pompey, the heroine of *Novel on Yellow Paper* (1936) visits Nazi Germany and the antisemitism she observes puts her off another German holiday. Death interested Stevie Smith. Her 'gentle friend', it 'probably held less fear for her than most'.[43] This appeared true for Gerda, with her repeated threats to stick her head 'in the gas oven and then you'll

---

[43] 'Come Death (2)' comes at the end of *The Collected Poems of Stevie Smith* (1985), Penguin, and I have also referred to the Preface by James MacGibbon. In *Novel on Yellow Paper* (1982, Virago), Pompey is 'panting to get out' of a Germany overrun by 'uniforms and swastikas', pp 103-104.

be sorry!' That was the kind of histrionic thing she said (I later realised) to impress us with her distress. On further reflection, it was probably her way of familiarising herself with death, flirting with suicide, previewing her absence and its likely effect on the children, as well as a dress rehearsal for the real thing. Her threats weren't taken too seriously at the time, since nothing ever came of them. It was just Mum being her usual self – odd, emotional, oversensitive, making us feel guilty for upsetting her again. Had I unrestricted access to her diaries then, rather than five decades too late, things might have turned out differently, but I doubt it – not with the pleasant prospect of absence always before her, beckoning.

Not Waving but Drowning, Stevie Smith's best-known poem, seems especially pertinent here as I have long had her words in mind for the title of this present book, and when I last looked into them they left me wondering if the plight of the drowned man was also Gerda's. It could not be said of my mother that she 'always loved larking'. She had her moments of fun, but they were genuine and not a disguise, not her way of dissimulating a deeper desperation. If anything, she was too transparent. Possibly she was 'much further out' than I realised. In the poem, the sea isn't mentioned, but the 'poor chap' is (metaphorically) in it while drowning – waving deceptively from a blue distance, 'much too far out' for his waves to be read aright.

The 'Gerda gallery' on my phone includes black and white seaside photographs from 1927, when she was six, to the first year of the Third Reich. All but one are beach scenes, and in these Tatta is nearby. Other family is absent, though an older brother or another relative could be taking the picture. Gerda's mother is also absent, having died in 1927. Whatever space she once occupied in her daughter's early life was more than filled by Tatta, if these seaside photographs can be read that way. To be divested of clothes (though his beach apparel is sometimes white shirt, dark trousers and black bow-tie) is not to be divested of dignity, and even when this big Breslau businessman appears all torso and trunks, his upright, stiff sense of occasion in front of the camera and his unsmiling, even stern, expression assert his position in society and the respect that was only his due. The father and daughter beach photographs enhance his size and status. Aloof on the canvas roof of a striped beach shelter, Gerda is diminutive compared to the big-bellied man in sculptural trunks leaning against it. In others, she is seen on hands and knees in the sucking surf and looking up from within the widely-spaced arch of Tatta's bare legs; or straddling his broad white-shirted shoulders while he perches on the rim of a beached boat and raises his hands to steady her.

Gerda and Tatta on beach with striped beach shelter.

Gerda appears in the sea only once, not alone but among a large group of people unknown to me. I count thirty-five, but others are edging out of the frame. Unusually, Tatta is not there, though he could be taking the picture from the beach, as he seldom missed an opportunity to stay close. His absence makes room for thirty-five mostly smiling others. They can't be very 'far out', as the light-flecked water just covers Gerda's thighs. The sea reaches the chest or neck of some, but they are children or crouching down. The bathing caps of the girls and women (Gerda included), and the one-piece bathing suits of the men, give the picture a period look. The seaside location is specified in German, but indecipherable. The date is 1933. Gerda is twelve as she stands in the sea with her companions, and Hitler is the new Chancellor. So, an important year for both, with their futures still ahead of them.

Her developing body is noticeably contoured by the swimsuit. To me, she stands out from the others, being recognisably my mother even at that age, but her costume is darker and she is near the front, and smiling, which is unusual in my experience of her face. The boy to her right is supported in the water by a woman (his mother probably), her fingers splayed across his narrow chest. The boy to Gerda's left makes a face, fingers widening his eyes so the whites show. Another boy ducks down to his chin – the camera a comic opportunity not to be missed. Their expressions define the moment differently. Boys pull funny faces. Girls and women smile, and because their bathing caps expose more face, their smiles are broader. Two of the five men present (men are in the minority here) look serious, but the one at the back in a bathing cap frames his smiling face with a big rubber ring. It is unusual to see Gerda so relaxed in a social situation, unbothered by the proximity and press of other bodies. They have all assembled there, like a circus troupe, and she is as much part of the performance as the others. It is only because I recognise her that I single her out. Her expression is an acknowledgement of something else. 'I'm here,' it says, 'in the sea with everybody else, having a good time.' Light bathes the group, the shutter clicks, and maybe then she waves to Tatta on the beach.

1933 was the first of the twelve years of Nazi Germany. In this photograph there is no foreshadowing of what was to come, but for Gerda, her family, and this group of thirty-five, the world was about to divide. As to how it changed for Gerda and family, I have some idea, but not for these unknown others. Some, even all, could be friends of the family, or acquaintances. A twelve-year-old girl doesn't just wade into a group of thirty-five complete strangers in the sea and pose for a photograph. Some could be extended family. My inability to identify any faces hardly disqualifies them. As far as I can tell, her brothers, Kurt and Gunther are as absent from this as from the other seaside photographs. The diaries and letters name nobody outside the immediate family except two aunts – one who took up less than a sentence and whose name I forget, and the other, Tante Bertha, achieving only transient presence in a few letters. If it was not for Gerda, this could be a group of thirty-five strangers or a circus troupe in the sea in 1933. Yet here they stand, body against body, safe for that moment inside an old black and white photograph and making the most of it.

Not Drowning but Waving

Group Photograph of Gerda with other Bathers in the sea, 1933.

This is the last of the pre-war seaside photographs. Their cessation reminded me of that German-born British photographer, whose obituary I recently came across and who, like Gerda, was a refugee from Nazism and left for England in 1939. For Dorothy Bohm (as noted in an earlier chapter), photographs stopped things from 'disappearing'. My mother's old photographs stop her from disappearing, which she is liable to do as soon as I look away. If she occasionally got them out to go through them with us, I should remember but don't, and I wonder if she sometimes looked at them in the privacy of her bedroom. Knowing what I now know, it seems unlikely. Unlike Dorothy Bohm, my mother had a deep need for things to disappear, including herself. She left no final instructions regarding the photographs and presumably felt less compromised by them than by the diaries, which bore the deeper impress of her life and so had to go. That others might recognise a deep need to stop her from disappearing probably didn't occur to her at the time.

Her diaries and those old German photographs eventually led me to the Holocaust, which she skirted round in 1939 but returned to later, and I felt I owed it to her to go back and see what I had missed. So, I read Primo Levi for the first time during the centenary year of my mother's birth (and half-centenary of her death), and have her to thank for my getting round to some serious reading at last. I doubt she had read or even heard of Primo Levi. His Auschwitz memoir, *If This Is a Man*, attracted little initial interest when it was first published in 1947, and it wasn't until much later – when my mother started cutting out belated Holocaust headlines and articles on Eichmann and others and storing them in an old brown suitcase – that his writings were translated and reached a wider audience. If they ever reached her, who knows, but I was thinking of her when I pondered his distinction between those ('the best of all') who sank and drowned and the survivors ('the worst'). Referring to Primo Levi in *Remember Who You Used to Be*, I suggested that Gerda was 'one of the saved', insofar as she got away, but added: 'It took me a while to realise that the 'saved' also drown. They just do it more slowly, invisibly.'[44]

---

[44] Primo Levi was specifically referring to the 'Saved' of the 'Lager' (death camp) but I am here using the word in a wider sense to include 'survivors' like Gerda and am not suggesting that Primo Levi included them when distinguishing between

Not Drowning but Waving

Describing my mother as 'drowned' does her an injustice. After repeated visits to the hospital between Christmas and the new year, I still found her unrecognisable. Worse than that – alien. When (fifty years later) I tried to see her again, I kept seeing a body as it might look after long immersion in water, 'its eyes squeezed shut between folds of bruised flesh', as if aware of being looked at and blocking the intrusion, and with a 'drowned appearance beneath the tubes and bottles keeping it alive'. That's how she appeared at the time, or at least as I subsequently remembered her. Actually, I have never seen a drowned body, but it became the abiding image of my mother until very recently. It was the image that floated up when I first read *The Drowned and the Saved* in 2021.

I see her differently now. My mother hadn't 'drowned' in the Primo Levi meaning of the word. She survived, as did other family (Aunt Bertha excepted). Tatta survived. Though 'highly persecuted by the Gestapo and urged to leave without money by pressure of the Nazi-Regime', he also got away – to Ecuador – and in time to write a last letter to his beloved daughter before dying. Kurt, the eldest, the first to get out, disappeared almost without trace after writing to his sister in May 1939. In 1963, nearer death than he knew, Kurt wrote from Buenos Aires, complaining that Gerda had 'told him so very little' about her life and family in England and 'plans' for the future, and asking her to 'make up for this' in her 'next letter'. Kurt's complaint rather amused me. For a quarter of a

---

the 'Drowned' and the 'Saved' (see pp. 62 – 63, *The Drowned and the Saved*, Abacus, 1989, reprinted 2001.

century, he had been entirely unforthcoming about his whereabouts in Argentina and what he referred to as his 'adventurous and raging life', and there he was chiding his little sister for telling him nothing about hers. As it happened, there would be no 'next letter' from my mother because, four months later, Kurt's widow wrote to inform her of his premature ageing and death.

Yet this widely dispersed and disappearing family tried to connect. Diaspora and distance didn't stop them reaching out. Gunther, the most buoyant, salvaged what he could of them. As her diaries reveal, my mother resented his big brotherly efforts to guide and chide her, and she apparently stayed in touch less for sentimental family reasons than for the prospect of inheriting his US dollars. That was my cynical view of the matter until recently, but I now have my doubts. Gunther wrote to her just after the war, observing that after all 'the fun' she had in the army, her life had deteriorated with peace, and instead of 'a better and more comfortable life' she was working long hours, wasting herself 'in a disgracefully hot Nissen-hut' and 'gliding poco a poco to misery'. She must have been dreadfully hurt at the time by the truth of his words. Gunther often reached for the wrong word when excited and maybe he meant 'sliding' rather than 'gliding', for he could see her 'sinking' to 'the bottom'. It was his duty as big brother to stop her sliding down that slippery slope before it was too late. She never thanked him for his concerned and timely intervention, or for rubbing her face in the truth, but the correspondence continued and she always seemed pleased to get his letters, if only for the dollar bills enclosed.

For most of the war and its aftermath, until they both

died in 1971, Gerda was Gunther's family, his only living connection with the past. And he was hers. Tatta had disappeared from her life in 1939, though it took him a further three years to make it a permanent absence. Kurt was distinguished by his absence, his subsequent reappearance in 1963 too brief to make much difference to his sister's life, and her diary is wordless on the subject, though that doesn't mean it meant nothing to her.

It was Gerda's good fortune (maybe misfortune) that the roles of father and eldest brother became vacant so early in her life, with Gunther more than willing to fill both. As her continuing connection with the family, he was more necessary to her than she cared to admit. Another cause of her apparent dislike was that he took the place of Tatta who once loomed so large in her life. A big space to fill. Gunther had the physical size, worrying about his weight (227 lbs) and Tatta-like girth and even once comparing himself to an elephant, though he had something else in mind then. 'The Elephant never forgets,' he wrote, reminding her of the family diamonds and their unexplained disappearance. Tatta died before he could blame her for the loss of the remaining family fortune, so Gunther continued where their father left off. The space he filled was more than physical. He turned into Tatta's portly proxy, criticising and controlling Gerda from afar. That was how he showed his love. 'In love', Gunther ended almost all his letters. 'In love and sweet kisses.' And still more touchingly: '1000 kisses, hu, hu, I get goose-pimples!' Even allowing for an ironical exaggeration of big brotherly affection (to cover his own embarrassment at such excess of feeling), it's a funny way for a brother to write to the sister he hadn't seen since 1938.

Aware of the gap growing between them, he tried to close it with a half-amused, half-meant profligacy of kisses. Such epistolary partings, widening rather than narrowing the Atlantic Ocean between them, are poignant reminders of how much family meant to him, and I wonder what she read into them. Gunther was desperate to get close to his distant sister – within epistolary kissing distance – not to cover her with amorous kisses, as his words suggest, but to recover a lost intimacy. His '1000 kisses', though unwelcome and undeserved, were not lost on her.

Gunther 'the bully' reproached and redirected his wayward sister when she went wrong. As her big brother and self-styled American success story ('*der reiche Onkel von Amerika*', as he referred to himself) Gunther understood his duty towards her. Actually (as his letters also suggest) he was the more vulnerable of the two – the sentimental one. Gunther liked to remind his sister of family holidays in the North Tyrol before the annexation of Austria, and their walks in the 'Sud Park' in Breslau when she was twelve. His enthusiastic plans to visit her in England were apparently not reciprocated and came to nothing, though as her letters are unavailable, I don't know if she simply avoided the subject whenever he raised it.

I didn't see you about thirty years. Quite some time, isn't it?

Far too long for Gunther, not long enough for Gerda.

By the time he died, he had not seen her for thirty-three years. As I now realise, Gunther held onto her for dear life, and the only circumstance in which he could have finally realised his plan to visit would have been to attend her funeral. It never came to that of course, as he died first, but had he survived her, I think he would have come, for we were also family and he would have liked to tell us more about her.

The measure of Gerda's evident dislike of the brother who always kept in touch can be gauged by her diary diatribe against me on 29 April 1968: 'He is getting more like Gunther every minute, and I can honestly say I do not like him at all.' As invidious comparisons go, that was the worst she could come up with. Yet if she so disliked her brother, why – following his unexpected death in the spring of 1971 – did she kill herself that same year? It can be no coincidence. Gunther was her last link.

If I 'did a Gerda' (she was always making lists) and listed the top ten reasons for her suicide, Gunther would head it. He died in April, she in December. Delaying her suicide by a week or two meant crossing the border to another year. That is in fact what happened, the life support machine being switched off on 2 January 1972, but she couldn't foresee being suspended between one state and another. 'Come Death. Do not be slow.' Unfortunately, it was.

Gunther heads the 'reasons for suicide' list because his death was a final disconnection. For all his faults he was family, and there was enough of Tatta in Gunther to remind her of the man who loved her all the more in her absence. With Gunther gone, and the family with him, it was her turn to feel abandoned, and I also wonder if his death brought home to her that she needed – even loved – him. It had been the same with Sandy. With Tatta too, perhaps. So maybe Gunther meant more to her than his money. You could never tell with her because, Sandy and

Joe apart, she expresses no love for anyone in three decades of intimate diaries, and even her praise for Jack at the end of the war was in recognition of how much he would do to make her happy. Gunther's unexpected death disturbed her because she hadn't realised until then how much he meant to her as a live connection with the past. It wasn't simply that he reminded her of Alpine holidays, walks in the park, and her year (1937- 38) at Victoria College. He had twice visited his then sixteen-year-old sister at her 'English Boarding School for Girls' during her 'beautiful Prague time'. The importance of such connections with her former life emerged with his death, though (like her) I am only just realising it. Gunther stirred up the past. She never sentimentalised it as he did – unless keeping paper piles of evidence of it in old brown suitcases was itself evidence that she did.

Gunther stirred up a darker past too, which couldn't be packed away. On 11 January 1958, when he first referred to the *Wiedergutmachung* (making good again), he deliberately brought Hitler and history back into her life. Only this time she welcomed the reminder and hoped to benefit from it.

'Making good again' required reparation payments by post-war Germany to compensate those wrongfully deprived of property and other assets during the Nazi era. There could be no 'atonement' for Nazi crimes or 'reconciliation' with the murderers of 'six million', but the programme's 'material approach' of limited financial compensation was enough for my mother to build her hopes of getting 'some money from Germany' (Gerda's Diary, 1 March 1958).

It gave her hope but raked up the past. By 2 September

that year, she worried that 'they don't really like foreigners at all in England' and 'I seem to make so many enemies and have people against me all the time because I am not like them'. These were the years (1958-61) when she cut out those Holocaust headlines and stories from *Oxford Mails*, *Daily Mirrors*, *Daily Heralds* and *Sunday Pictorials* and packed them away for me to find sixty years later. It was the time of the Eichmann abduction and trial, and it was when men like Mengele got another public opportunity to show what they were capable of.

No one would describe my mother's diaries before 1958 as easy reading. Anne Frank remained cheerful and optimistic in adversity; Gerda was the opposite. Though I have discovered more about her posthumously than she wanted anybody to know, and made the best of my inheritance, she would have been better advised not to bother with diaries. They brought out the worst in her. After 1958, it got worse. The 1960s did not begin well ('I live constantly in fear') and set the darkening tone for the decade.

It is easy to track back from her suicide and find the negatives. Her suicidal thoughts might not have started with the new decade, but it's when they first appear in her diaries. There are enough earlier instances of distance from other women, a sense of her difference, foreignness, Jewishness, to suggest there was nothing new about her fears. Gerda was afraid of women for most of her adult life, but the fear and distrust were initially offset by an awareness of her physical attractions and the interest of men. During the Eichmann trial in 1961, she turned forty. At seventy-two this seems enviably young to me but Gerda seemed to think that women aged irreversibly after twenty-one. By 1961, looking into the tarnished mirror of her diaries, she saw a 'very old' woman. By then she had (in her view) lost her looks. The loss left her feeling more exposed, and the ugliness of the world more apparent to her every day. She saw it as it really was: the Holocaust back again with a vengeance. Antisemitic slogans and slurs everywhere, the Holocaust revived in newspaper headlines and death camp accounts. And she saw it in the expressionless face of Eichmann behind bullet-proof glass.

My mother wasn't born to distrust herself and the world. She had Hitler and history to thank for that. Plus, the double misfortune of being German and Jewish in Britain during and after the war. For all the privations from 1945 and through the '50s, it was during the '60s that things really turned bad. It is then that the moths cluster in her diaries. They were always a fear, given her penchant for accumulating old clothes and stowing them away for the future. 'I am getting bulked up with clothes,' she complained, 'and letting the moths in.' It is no coincidence that moths came into her life and suitcases at a time when virulent antisemitism was on the rise and a second Holocaust coming. She envisaged them eating holes in everything that mattered.

She was going under. That was my inescapable conclusion a year ago. With her suicide ever in mind, I had read the diaries in reverse order, beginning with the last entry of 30 September 1969 and going back in time to the '50s, the war, the diaspora and beyond. I had soon gathered all the evidence I needed.

Considering her background and circumstances, it had taken my mother some time to sink, break up under cover of the diaries, but it was bound to happen sooner or later

– and when it finally did, she admitted that she was going to pieces and out of her mind. She did so privately, but that added weight to her words. Diarists have no reason to hide the truth from themselves, and I had no reason to question the veracity of her written words.

Suicide. Her life sloped down in that direction. There could be no other ending. She had wanted the diaries destroyed, and that in itself was evidence of advance planning. She had evidently given some thought to the matter of self-erasure. Housewife to the end, she was tidying things up after her death, leaving everything spick and span without her clutter, unwriting herself.

As a compilation of diary extracts and letters, *Remember Who You Used to Be*, published in 2023, disregarded my mother's single stated wish: not to be remembered. She could take comfort from the inattention she has received since publication. She remains largely unknown and forgotten. Anyway, I had done my duty by her. Having exhausted the available evidence, nothing remained for me to do. So, with more relief than regret, I packed Gerda and her first family back into their five old brown suitcases and looked forward to their uninterrupted absence.

What happened next is true. Just as I was putting the lid on them, I noticed a letter outside its airmail envelope. From Gunther. Having examined all his letters, this one from 2 July 1957 hadn't escaped my attention, but I read it again because 'Onkel Gunther' is lively and entertaining and seldom seemed to bear the weight of history as she did. It closed on a note somewhere between reproach and regret:

Peter Thornthwaite

I must state that while your former letters were always full of joy, now the content switched to bitterness. Never mind!

It was a revelation. Despite previous multiple readings of his correspondence, the extraordinary significance of this letter had escaped me. The 'bitterness' came as no surprise, but letters from my mother 'always full of joy'? That was news. A more rounded appraisal of the old family correspondence was limited by the absence of all her letters. They were unavailable simply because she had sent them and they were subsequently lost to history. Gunther, the main recipient of her letters, lived alone. There is no evidence of any more intimate relationship in his life. After he died, evidently nobody thought to go through his private papers, pick out old letters from a sister (joyful or otherwise) and forward them to my mother. So for her account of events I had only her diaries to go by, and they were getting darker by the day. The truth, as Gunther (intervening one last time in her behalf) revealed in that last line of his letter, was that I had already made up my mind about my mother before reading her diaries and expected nothing she wrote to be 'full of joy'.

Her diaries aren't easy bedtime reading at the best of times. Gerda had much more reason than Anne Frank to be cheerful, but her later diaries are repositories of darkness, not light, and that misled me. Maybe it was why she wanted them burned. She hated what she had become.

That last line of Gunther's letter, regretting the 'switch' from joy to bitterness in hers, led me back to Gerda. It suddenly lit up all the lighter moments in her diaries and draft letters, illuminating her at the darkest of times. One such luminous instance is her solitary record of a night in a

Not Drowning but Waving

London lit up by the Luftwaffe. In a rare sighting of Gerda during her time as a domestic during the Blackout and Blitz, she puts in a brief appearance in that fortuitously unsent letter (1 December 1940) describing another 'thrilling and exciting' night of aerial bombardment as the whole household cuddled up on the floor.

Not far into this present book (Chapter Two) I had a good look at that unsent letter from the London Blitz to her distant brother in Quito and considered it from a different angle: Gerda's concern for a Tatta still stuck in Nazi Germany and subject to its increasing persecutions while she meanwhile enjoyed night after thrilling night in the company of others on the floor. That chapter, as its title stated, concerned 'absences', and on 1 December 1940 during yet another visit from the Luftwaffe, absent Tatta was somewhere at the back of her mind. The draft letter she never posted revealed that she had never stopped worrying about her abandoned father, his isolation, and the worse dangers confronting him. That remains true. She hadn't forgotten him. The horror of his situation kept breaking through even as she thrilled to another nightly visit from the Luftwaffe. But what her unsent letter also revealed to me, when I returned to it after Gunther slyly at the last moment drew my attention to the 'joy' in her correspondence, was just how much Gerda loved excitement – even the excitement of German bombs, if that was what it took to shake things up.

She loved such reversals of normality, no matter the cause, for her life was too often 'boring and dull' and she looked forward to taking a break from it. That night in the London Blitz was one such interruption of normal life and a pleasantly prolonged one; she hadn't been 'in a real bed for nearly a year because of air raids'. And it wasn't the only break in her life at that time, the war having also interrupted correspondence with Gunther. The air raid letter of 1 December 1940 'is now already the third letter I write to you without getting a reply' and 'I hope very much that this letter will reach you'. It couldn't have done as it was unsent, yet I wonder if the accompanying frisson of fear at the widening rift in family correspondence was not altogether unwelcome.

In another unsent letter from the war (29 August 1941) Gerda reassured her brother that she was 'fine, couldn't be better, very happy, etc, etc'. Just at that moment she was out for a walk 'with the doggies' on 'a little mountain' called 'One-tree hill'. It was 'a lovely' day, with the Blitz now behind her, 'sitting here in my brown velvet slacks'. The 'doggies' were 'completely satisfied', having had 'liver for breakfast'. What she was doing so far from home, at 'One-tree hill' when it wasn't her day off and she worked in SE15, I don't know, but it's nice to see Gerda making the most of wartime sunshine in the open air, as replete as liver-fed 'doggies' and taking pleasure in simple things like her brown velvet slacks.

Seeing her there, enjoying sun and countryside two years into the war, she is a different woman from the mother I remember. Living in the moment. Making the most of every chance of uncomplicated happiness. It wouldn't surprise me if she missed the Blitz.

This fresh insight into Gerda returned me to earlier episodes in her life to see if I now viewed them differently. I felt I was onto something new.

That last year in Germany, for instance, as she planned to leave father, home, country and everything else, must have been frightening – terrifying. Yet that morning appointment with the Gestapo on 14 February 1939 left no trace in her diary. That might have been because a record of the meeting meant revisiting it, reliving the fear, but the absence of an entry also suggests that it went as well as could be expected – unpleasant enough, but there was no point dwelling on difficulties. She had things to do, actions to take, Gestapo to see.

Then there was the letter she drafted, in a rare emotional appeal for help, in which she admitted she was 'much afraid to be left here alone' and 'quite desperate about my future'. 'Afraid' and 'desperate', coming from a young Jewish woman trying to get away from Nazi Germany in 1939 – a woman who also happened to be my mother, albeit not for another twelve years – made quite an impression on me when I first read it. But re-examining it, in the light of my recent discovery thanks to Gunther, I realised that alongside desperation was unwavering determination. Yes she was afraid, but she could see her way to the other side of fear.

Gerda was living alone with her father. If he helped guide her through Nazi bureaucracy to obtain the necessary 'Permit' and a position in England, there is no record of it. Much as he doted on his daughter, he had problems of his own and saw no way past them. Perhaps, seeing how well she managed without him, Tatta let her get on with it. Gerda did exactly that. In his letter of 1 May from New York, Gunther praised her 'skilful proceed in your emigration matter' and wondered how Tatta, if he got out, would 'exist abroad when he is not trained to shine his shoes or to, for example, wash dishes'.

While 'emigration matters' occupied Gerda's last

months in Germany, the sudden dispossession of what had taken him years to accumulate preoccupied her father. As he contemplated his own shrinkage, she was growing up fast, changing from girl to an independent and resourceful young woman taking control of her life. Gerda would later (diary entry 25 September 1939) write of being 'strong and brave enough to take up the fight with destiny'. That stirring phrase related specifically to a later love affair in London, but her 'fight with destiny' is evident elsewhere. Long before she found her way out of Germany, the Reich had left her with no country, no citizenship, no rights. The 1939 diary lists no such losses. Lists were not yet a dominant feature of her diaries. But supposing she had made one, there was almost nothing it excluded. On the plus side, she was losing everything but her life, and any kind of future was better than none at all. It wasn't the future she could have expected as the daughter of a prosperous German businessman – but it was still a future, and having one as a domestic servant in England was preferable to having none as a Jew in Germany. By 20 May 1939, with confirmation of permit and visa, her first big 'fight with destiny' was over. She was getting away, and that was all that really mattered.

Gerda's situation before leaving recalls Anne Frank's, and I saw the connection after rereading Gunther's letter of 1 May 1939, thanking his sister for her 'delightful German written letter'. Destiny was coming for her, but like Anne she got on with things and stayed buoyant. There was the disgrace and discomfort of their new accommodation. Gunther was 'very sorry' that they 'have some trouble in settling the question of your apartment, your poor 2-rooms flat'. Presumably, 'the question' it posed was not that they had any choice in the matter, but how Tatta would cope with the shrinkage of living space. It reminds me of the Franks' situation in Amsterdam several years later (July 1942), when they leave home for hiding with other Jews in the reduced accommodation of the 'Secret Annexe'.

Under imminent threat of deportation, the Franks 'get out of there', 'get away' to the temporary refuge of a life in hiding. That wasn't Gerda's situation in 1939. Unlike the occupants of the 'Secret Annexe', she got away while they could only dream of doing so, as in that remarkable 3 February 1944 entry, in which Anne reports 'invasion news' in the newspapers, including a supposed Nazi plan to 'flood' Holland. I have mentioned this before – more than once, I'm sure – but it is worth mentioning yet again for its relevance to Gerda and my radically changing view of her. Anne's light-hearted diary entry, written six months before arrest and deportation, suggests a girl cheerful as usual in adversity. The ensuing discussion of opportunities arising from a potentially flooded Holland shows 'Secret Annexe' banter at its lightest as occupants consider how they might use the immersion of Amsterdam to their advantage and escape under cover of water. Rising water, far from threatening death by drowning, offers them an unexpected if unlikely chance to get away, and the irony of it is that the potential future flood released by the Nazis as a defence against the British could give hidden Jews an incredible opportunity to escape. For a few fanciful moments they are no longer victims trapped inside an old warehouse and waiting to be exposed, or for the war to turn against the Germans. The mere possibility of getting away, though imaginary, lifts their spirits as they plan what to do. After the option of wading through the flood is rejected because of their visibility as 'Jews', they consider putting on costumes and caps and swimming underwater.

In my earlier reading of this entry, I imagined my mother among them, but I just couldn't see her in that situation, discussing with the rest of them what to do for the best. It wasn't difficult imagining her in hiding. A 'Secret Annexe' would have suited her in some ways. It was the company of others in the same situation that she couldn't have borne. The real problem though, as I have now come to realise, is in me. I have never been able to see past my mother. She is the only 'Gerda' I have known, and not then at her best. She generally preferred her own company, and even at the best of times (and there were some) she wasn't known for her levity and 'light-hearted banter', either outside or inside the family. So, being trapped inside a warehouse with other Jews equally desperate to get out would have been her worst nightmare. Yet she had surely read the Diary (I recall a copy on her bookshelf) and with her own not dissimilar experience must have identified with Anne to some extent.

And now that I see her differently, I can imagine a young Gerda happily joining in the group discussion and adding to the banter that day, 3 February 1944, for my mother was sometimes light-hearted and also loved swimming, and if anybody could have swum out of an upper floor warehouse window in Amsterdam and got away under cover of floods, it was her.

As it happened, Gerda needed no great flood as a means of escape in 1939. It was still possible to leave by established transatlantic routes, such as that (Hamburg to

Not Drowning but Waving

New York) taken by the *SS President Harding* on 24 May. The official German policy of expulsion had not yet progressed to extermination, but with war closing in and doors closing everywhere, she had her doubts. She also had get-up-and-go and knew exactly where she wanted to go – away! Being Jewish didn't mean she had no right to a future. But she was well aware of the many women in similar situations. The Reich wanted them out, yet hindered emigration because they hated helping Jews even if it meant getting rid of them. For all her determination and drive, Gerda expected to fail and was pleasantly surprised when she didn't. Suddenly it was all happening, and she was cramming her life into a single suitcase, and leaving for Hamburg docks with Tatta, and waving back at him, and then she was aboard and elsewhere and beyond reach.

CHAPTER TWENTY-ONE:

LEAVING

My mother loved lists and was lost without them. When things got too much for her – and they were never less than that in later years – she looked to lists to show her the way. From the mid-1950s to the end, her diaries list identical new year resolutions, which she never kept, and principles for living. The straightforward linear order of lists marked out where to go and seemed easy to follow. What I mostly recall though, from her later diaries, are the lists of old clothes. It was in this burgeoning area of almost industrial activity that the two capitalised words she lived by – UTILISE and ORGANISE – came into their own. Big words for a big part of her life. During her last decade, the diaries functioned largely as a record and running total of the jumble sale and charity shop bargains required to meet the family's present and future clothing needs. The lists categorised and quantified them, so that she could check for gaps. When I opened her diaries three years ago, starting with 1969 (the last) and working my way in reverse through her intermittently diarised life, they were at first a big disappointment with their endless lists of clothes, as if she had nothing else on her mind. That was how she described me at the end of the 1960s – 'a big disappointment' – and it was exactly what I felt about her when I first dipped into her life. It wasn't what I expected from a dead mother's diaries. Surely a woman with her seismic history could do better. Anxieties, fears, hurt, pain, even explicitly suicidal thoughts, do surface, of course, in her last two decades, and I was grateful for such signs of disturbance and inner turmoil, because what I was after was the truth about her, however bad. The lists of clothing from jumble sales and charity shops seemed a waste of good diary space – until I realised what was really going on.

She couldn't stop herself. Couldn't stop accumulating old clothes, even after admitting she had more than enough and 'I can't take them with me'. It has taken me a while to realise that they reveal as much about my mother and what mattered to her as any of the more attention-seeking entries and sudden upwellings of ragged emotion. She regarded what she was doing, year after year, as 'degrading' and described the mounting heaps of clothes as 'junk', yet the lists persisted and in time she had packed over a hundred suitcases with old clothes, as per the grand 'Plan of Suitcases' inaugurated in January 1965. UTILISE and ORGANISE. With the help of her diaries, she amply demonstrated that these guiding words had shown her the way.

After initially disregarding the diarised lists of clothes, in time I radically revised my view of them as an interesting and even endearing eccentricity, not the sort of thing I was on the lookout for in her diaries but undoubtedly her and very much the mother I recalled as different; odd; a one-off. After all, they did no harm. They were simply lists of clothes set out in an orderly fashion as a daily record and means of identifying what she had and what she needed for the family. Later still, I saw they were riven with violent emotion and the latest and most convulsive phase of her quarrel with herself. Interrupting and breaking into the lists are repeated importunate imperatives, stressed with big capital letters and multiple exclamation marks. My mother believed people were against her (some were, I'm sure) but she was, too, and against herself she had fewer defences.

'I have to go bargain-hunting after all,' she insisted, 'otherwise life is too utterly boring.' There were variations on this: 'Must have a bit of fun, otherwise life is unbearably dull.' And I'm on her side. She deserved a break from boredom, and if her only sources of 'fun' in the 1950s and 60s were jumble sales and charity shops and spending money she should be saving, that says more about the time and place and limited opportunities available to a housewife and mother in her circumstances than it does about her. This is the woman who had not only missed the coming Holocaust, but had got away with diamonds. If jumbles and charity shops and 'junk' (her word, not mine) were her lot in life, she was making the best of it with the only materials to hand. In 1939 she had referred to her 'fight with destiny'. Two decades later, the 'fight' was with herself and all the deadlier for that:

WILLPOWER! BE STRONG! NO CHANGING MIND! FIGHT/RESIST/AVOID TEMPTATION! ONLY BUY WHAT I REALLY NEED STARTING NOW! GREED! GREED = DOWNFALL! MAKE DO AND MEND! STICK TO THE RULES! PACK IT IN NOW OR I MIGHT GET INTO TROUBLE! SACRIFICE! I HAVE TOO MUCH JUNK!

MUST STOP NOW! MAKE A NEW START! START AFRESH AGAIN! BREAK WITH CIRCUMSTANCES BEFORE THEY HAVE BROKEN YOU! PACK IT IN WHILE THE GOING IS GOOD!

Though the outcome was uncertain, it was the struggle that mattered. She might despise herself for gathering ever more 'junk' as the suitcases occupied every suitable and unsuitable space, but the satisfaction derived from categorising and quantifying her second-hand clothes in lists before marrying them up with suitable cases is evident in her later diaries. For a while my mother stopped complaining about her 'junk', and even the moths were in abeyance. Doing something eminently practical and decisive about her situation, which had been getting out of control, comforted and soothed the savage breast. At last, 'Utilise' and 'Organise' had shown her the way.

My mother knew where she was with lists. They meant that organisation and order could prevail even as everything was breaking down. They gave her a sense of direction when she most needed one and perhaps a sense of plenitude and prosperity at a time when (despite her father's once 'huge fortune'), all these years later she was reduced to counting the pennies. No diary entries note an insufficiency of any articles of clothing, only that she had far 'too much' of everything. As the lists (and the number of suitcases) grew, so her sense of security increased – or so I assume, as none of this can be known for sure.

At first, I didn't make the connection. It has only just occurred to me that the habit of making lists developed during the ATS years (1943-45) in the camp 'cookhouse'.

Peter Thornthwaite

From among her wartime diaries, a disintegrating black book of recipes for soups, broths, hotpots, stews, sponges, puddings, porridge, scones, buns, cakes, has just emerged. The numbered pages, many of them torn and flecked with yellow-brown spots of eighty-year-old food, have come away from their binding and are out of sequence, but the last surviving page is 72 – an odd coincidence as I'm also 72. More detailed inspection reveals the quantities of ingredients needed to feed a hundred men. This I know because she has written and underlined '100 men' against each recipe. 6 buckets of cocoa required 12 gallons of water, 6 pints of milk, 3 lbs of cocoa and 4 lbs of sugar. The black book of food-spattered wartime recipes falling apart in my hands is a salutary reminder that there is always something more to be found, and as I leaf through its lists (37 lbs meat, 10 lbs onions, 50 lbs potatoes for Meat Hot Pot, p. 66), I connect ATS Gerda with the mother I remember. For just as she gave two years of her life to filling up '100 men', so (two decades later) a hundred suitcases were waiting to be filled up with clothes. And if this seems a spurious connection, they fulfilled the same essential function and role. By feeding the army and fighting Hitler in the cookhouse, she had a chance at last 'to become a useful person of society and not just a useless being'. By stuffing a hundred suitcases with enough clothes to see the family through, she was finally doing something useful, fulfilling her duty as a mother.

So, the young woman of the ATS cookhouse from 1943 (the recipes listed are for June and July that year) isn't a complete stranger to me, and as I finger her much-used black-bound recipe and kitchen work schedule book, I feel the connection. Her birthday was around that time.

What (I wonder) was she doing on 26 June that year in the cookhouse when she turned twenty-two? The 'Daily Hint' that day was 'Too many cooks spoil the broth', which perhaps suited her as the list of duties involved no other women. Her birthday duties began at '06.00: RFD', which puzzled me until the explanation appeared some pages later: 'Report for Duty'. Her birthday moved on to lighting the oven (06.05), making tea, scrubbing tables, swilling floor, making breakfast, cleaning porridge basin, putting beef into boiler, cutting fat into pieces (11.15) and so on until 14.00: 'Dismissed'.

Had this food-spattered recipe book previously come to my attention, I'd have disregarded it as just that and dismissed it from further duty, much as 'M. Lyons, Sgt' dismissed Gerda at 14.00 on 26 June 1943. Knowing how much reassurance and comfort my mother got from lists, I now realise its significance. Four years as home help and maid in London SE15 had familiarised Gerda with domestic duties, but it must have felt very different and even satisfying in the ATS where she was serving her country. Also, she wasn't alone. As Private Gerda Lewinsohn, her name rather gave her away, but as just another woman in uniform she was less likely to stand out, which was all she wanted. Then the other aspects of ATS life – order, sequence, knowing what to do and when, not having to think for herself – they were all pluses. And the biggest plus of all was the availability of men in their hundreds, waiting to be fed, all hungry for what she cooked up for them.

Turning the loose pages of her cookhouse life, I see she has noted alongside the recipes every 'Daily Hint', such as 'Don't spoil the ship for a ha'p'orth of tar' (1 July 1943).

Peter Thornthwaite

That old English saying must have sounded strange to the German girl in her and, going by the large looping letters of her blue pen, she noted it with relish. The lists of daily duties run on, page after page - 'make Treacle pudding', 'wash up', 'scrub tables', 'peel beetroot', 'make sardine pasties' – but if a draft letter of 15 January 1944 to her brother is to be believed, Gerda was having the best of times. 'I am now in the English ATS,' she wrote to Gunther, 'and enjoy life very much. I am very happy here.' The letter remained unsent for reasons other than a disinclination to share her happiness with him.

Alongside the black book of recipes was another slim volume of recipes with a grubby orange cover and from her German past. It guided Gerda, not just through the cookhouse years, but from the start of her new life as a refugee. This foreign cookbook, *Wie koche ich in England* by Kitty Koberle, had been published in 'Wien' (Vienna) sometime in 1938, possibly following the 'Anschluss': the German annexation of Austria in March that year. The Foreword (in German) explained that this 'little book' was written for 'all those who work in an English household with limited language skills', and I quickly identified it as another major discovery. Just as Anne Frank found an intimate friend in the 'dearest Kitty' of her Diary, so Gerda found one in the equally helpful Kitty Koberle. The two Kittys functioned differently. For Anne Frank, Kitty was both alter-ego and uncritical friend, in whom she could confide without fear of reproach. 'Dearest Kitty' was always there and waiting for her, a constant companion throughout two difficult years, someone to whom Anne could turn and who survived the German death camps and endeared her to future readers. For

Gerda, the 'Kitty' cookbook was a practical guide to the layout, furnishings, kitchen equipment and culinary expectations of a middle-class English household, yet also a vital link with the past. Both Kittys helped them make the best of challenging new situations, and Anne and Gerda both had a friend when they most needed one.

Book Cover of Gerda's copy of Wie Koche ich in England *(1938, Wien), by Kitty Koberle*

Peter Thornthwaite

Gerda travelled light in May 1939, probably with just the one suitcase allowed, but the Kitty cookbook was slim enough (at 36 pages) to slip between the 'many nice clothes' she had 'to cram in'. She could no more leave her 'Kitty' behind than Anne (given the choice) could have left hers. Kitty was essential to Gerda's new position in London and what would be expected of a refugee domestic in a middle-class household. In her pre-emigration draft letters to the German Jewish Refugee Committee and International Au Pair Institute, Gerda highlighted her good 'cooking and baking skills'. Replies from interested English households offered refuge and 'a good home' for 'someone who can do housework and plain cooking'. That was something she could offer, something she could do in exchange for a future and a life. Before she left, her father appreciated this new practical side of a once spoilt daughter, praising Gerda for being 'so busy in the kitchen' and having such a 'great capacity for housework'.

When she finally left Tatta and her life as a girl, Gerda knew that the Kitty cookbook would come in handy, but she could not have foreseen that Kitty would later guide her through the ATS years. Britain and Germany were not yet at war when Gerda emigrated, and she hardly expected to enlist in the women's branch of the British Army. The 'Big Love', blackouts, Blitz, and other excitements awaiting a free young woman were all in the future.

Suddenly she had one again and could only look forward. As for me now, it's just the opposite. I can only look back. There is some advantage in this. Having read the diaries and letters, I know what happens next. Within a month of arriving in London, Gerda would record in her diary something she had never expected to write about her father. When she later hoped (28 September 1939) that the 'film' (as she then viewed it) of 'the story with Joe' would have 'a happy ending', I know it didn't and that before long she would be thinking of him as a 'stinking arsehole'. I know that by December 1939, she would be noting in her diary not only the approaching end of a memorable year, but the end of the 'Big Love' too, and that she would sit in her room and drink tea and face a Joe-less future and wait for him to call. There is much I know that she couldn't possibly know. Further still in her future (October 1941), her father would escape Hitler's Germany and the mass deportations of Jews imminently underway, only to find that a tumour 'of horrendous proportions' was all the time fattening inside his intestines and feeding on him. Aunt Bertha, deported to Kovno, would also be dead by the year end. The family diamonds would be lost or (more likely) sold by Gerda for next to nothing. The war would eventually end, and on 1 May 1945 (the day after Hitler's suicide) Gerda would write in her diary: 'Jack and I are married and I couldn't find a better husband anywhere.'

None of these things could be foreseen, including her suicide.

Safely aboard the *SS President Harding*, seventeen-year-old Gerda was more thrilled and excited than during the Luftwaffe air-raids still two years away in her diaries. It was not the first time she had left family and Germany to live away from home, but this time it was for good. She did not know then that leaving was already integral to her life. It may be 'better to travel hopefully than to arrive', but in her case it was the leaving that mattered. She knew where she was with leaving.

Another ship, the *St. Louis*, had left Hamburg docks ten days earlier (13 May) with 937 passengers, mostly Jewish refugees, bound for Cuba. Many refugees hoped to get to the United States by that route. Like Gerda, they relished all the food suddenly available to them aboard, including many items rationed in Germany, and they were also excited and relieved to escape persecution. They too could not foresee what lay ahead: that Cuba would refuse them permission to land, as would the US, then Canada, and that the *St. Louis* would turn back to Europe and an estimated quarter of them would die in Nazi death camps.

Among internet images of the ill-fated *St. Louis* and its passengers is a fifteen-year-old girl, Gisela Feldman. Because of their similar situations and the closeness of the departure times, she reminds me of Gerda. Facing the camera with the sun in her eyes (squinting against the glare) and the sea wind tousling her hair, the girl leans against the ship's rail. Though two years younger than Gerda, Gisela appears older than her years, in that liminal space between girl and womanhood. Her smart high-buttoned, double-breasted jacket, with its pale vertical stripe and pronounced shoulder pads, and the dark skirt reaching just below the knees, suggest maturity. There is no self-consciousness in her posture and pose, more self-possession. The future lies before her, but the half-closed eyes and slightly downturned mouth give her an inward, pensive appearance. Like Gerda, she would have fun aboard the luxury liner, spending her time wandering round the deck, chatting with boys, swimming in the ship's pool, and there was a dance band in the evenings and a cinema. Like Gerda, she might also have watched 'a cute film with Claudette Colbert'.

Compared to Gisela Feldman and other passengers aboard the *St. Louis*, Gerda's passage ten days later was unremarkable – except for meeting Joe and finding the 'Big Love' in transit. Only that pre-departure 'Journey Note' of 23 May 1939 marks her passage from one life to another, for her diary is blank between leaving Hamburg on the 24th and arriving on June 12th in 'London !!!' As personal intersections with history go, the short journey between past and future was uneventful. I have since learnt that the *President Harding* was owned by the United States Shipping Co and built (coincidentally) in 1921, Gerda's birth year. A virtual vintage postcard of the *SS President Harding* shows it passing the Statue of Liberty. Another depicts a rearing black prow, high as a cliff, parting the sea. Just before World War Two, the ship rescued fifty Viennese Jewish children and transported them to the US. It was the last passenger ship to fly the American flag in hostile waters when it sailed home from Southampton on 16 November 1939. Gerda left when the going was good.

Gisela was also fortunate. She also got away and survived. And something else links her with Gerda at a similarly liminal, in-between time. She is a girl escaping persecution, a refugee facing an uncertain future, yet in the photograph of her leaning against the ship's railing, she has such strength of presence. As it happened, the voyage of the *St. Louis* had a happier ending for Gisela and her mother and sister than for many others. They reached England, and at the age of ninety Gisela clearly recalled the fifteen-year-old girl boarding the *St. Louis* at Hamburg docks.

No such photograph survives (if one was taken) of Gerda aboard the *SS President Harding*, but she kept her 'Journey Note'. Rereading it (as I often do), I note the date and exact time – 'a quarter to midnight 23 Mai 1939' – as if it is new information. It moves me that she so precisely marked the moment of her freedom. Gerda was never happier than at that moment of getting away, and it was something she never forgot. My mother retained more written and photographic evidence of a previous life and history than many think or care to keep. That one brief euphoric 'Journey Note' might not count for much against future events, but it meant everything to her.

Lost and found:
the Stone Bench Photograph, Shotover, 1958

ACKNOWLEDGEMENTS

As before, my thanks and gratitude especially to Dr Sue Challis, who saw me disappear daily into the attic for another year or two, re-emerging at wine time for the usual distracted and confused explanation of what I had been getting up to all day. It is now January 2025 – four years since I started reading the diaries and letters packed into five old brown suitcases – and Sue's love and support have sustained me throughout this arduous and ardent search for missing persons.

I am also indebted to Dr Philip Dunham, whose interest and insights into the first book articulated what I was trying to do in the second and explained to me the meaning of absence. I wrote the pivotal third chapter of this present book following that seminal Zoom conversation.

I owe more than I can say to the many friends who took time not only to read the first book but to comment on it, often at length and in detail. Their appreciation and perceptive reflections on it encouraged me to write this second book. Of these friends I must mention in particular Alison Challis, Richard Green, Dr Julia Clarke, Anne McCay, Chloe Spiers, Cathy McGuire, Dr Guy Holmes and Dr Biza Kroese.

And of course I must mention my publisher, Katharine Smith of Heddon Publishing, who has done so much to edit the text, reduce unnecessary repetition, and above all express such a positive overview of the book. I wouldn't say that revisiting my mother in *Not Drowning but Waving* was easy for me, but it was a moving experience and something I had not seen in her before, or clearly identified, has finally emerged, and Katharine recognised this.

www.ingramcontent.com/pod-product-compliance
Lightning Source LLC
Chambersburg PA
CBHW030252100526
44590CB00012B/379